Play and
Early Literacy Development

SUNY Series, Children's Play in Society

Anthony D. Pellegrini, Editor

Play and
Early Literacy Development

Edited by

James F. Christie

State University of New York Press

Cover Photo: Ann Pacciano

Published by
State University of New York Press, Albany

For information, address State University of New York
Press, State University Plaza, Albany, N.Y., 12246

Production by M.R. Mulholland
Marketing by Fran Keneston

Library of Congress Cataloging in Publication Data

Play and early literacy development / edited by James F. Christie.
      p.   cm — (SUNY series, children's play in society)
    Includes bibliographical references and index.
    ISBN 0-7914-0675-X (alk. paper). — ISBN 0-7914-0676-8 (pbk.
alk. paper)
      1. Play.   2. Language arts (Preschool)   3. Language acquisition.
I. Christie, James F.   II. Series.
LB1140.35.P55P555   1991
372.6—dc20   90-42680
                                                                          CIP

10 9 8 7 6 5 4 3 2 1

Contents

Figure Captions

Preface

Children's play and early literacy development have been the subjects of intensive research during the past several decades. Psychological researchers have used quantitative methodology to study the nature of children's play behavior, how it changes with age and varies between individuals, and its impact on social and intellectual development. At the same time, sociolinguistically oriented investigators were using ethnographic and case-study procedures to study the development of written language in young children.

Although these two strands of research were initially conducted in isolation from one another, links between play and early literacy soon began to emerge. Play studies reported connections between play and literacy-related variables (e.g., use of literate language), and case studies of early literacy development contained vivid examples of how children often used play to explore the functions and structure of print. The result has been a rapid growth of research directly examining the connections between play and early literacy development.

This volume contains chapters from scholars who are on the cutting edge of play/literacy research. The role of children's play in early literacy is examined from a number of theoretical and research perspectives, including investigations of play's contributions to early reading and writing development and applied research on how teachers can promote literacy growth through play.

The book is divided into three parts. Part I, Research Foundations, is meant to serve as an overview of the major approaches to studying play and literacy. Hall's chapter presents a historical overview of play/literacy research, as well as a review of several landmark sociolinguistic studies of children's emergent literacy. Hall also describes his own pioneering research on direct connections between play and early reading and writing. The chapter by Christie reviews four major areas of psychological research on play, highlighting indirect and direct connections with early literacy. Two of these research areas—play settings and play training—form the foundation for much of the applied research reported in the third part of this book.

Part II, Play's Role in Early Literacy Development, contains basic research on the connections between play and literacy. The chapter by Pellegrini and Galda reports two longitudinal studies of the relationship between play, use of metalinguistic verbs, and emergent reading and writing. The pattern of relationships which emerge is complex and intriguing. Williamson and Silvern describe a series of studies on thematic-fantasy play's (guided story re-enactments) contributions to children's story comprehension. Again, a rather complex set of findings is reported, with the effectiveness of the play experiences being mediated by factors such as children's age and ability, level of adult involvement, and familiarity with the story being enacted. Finally, Branscombe's chapter details an ethnographic case study of two brothers' literacy experiences in and out of school. Her findings indicate that, when literacy activities are meaningful and child-centered, they are perceived by children as play and make important contributions to literacy growth. However, when reading and writing activities are adult-directed and isolated from real life, they are meaningless and ineffective. In the words of one of the brothers, such activities "ain't real."

Part III, Educational Applications, presents applied research on how literature activities, manipulation of play environments, and teacher involvement in play can encourage literacy to be incorporated into children's play. Martinez, Cheney, and Teale examined types of literature activities that encourage children to dramatically re-enact stories. Morrow and Rand also investigated connections between play and children's literature but with a focus on features of the classroom environment that encourage children to use library corners during free-play periods. In another study reported in the same chapter, Morrow and Rand examined the effects of adding literacy materials to dramatic play centers. Results indicated that, when coupled with subtle adult guidance, such materials resulted in a large increase in literacy-related play. Theme-related literacy materials and adult involvement in play are also the focus of research reported in several other chapters. The Neuman and Roskos chapter and the Schrader chapter describe how the addition of literacy props to play centers encouraged children to experiment with the functions of written language. Schrader also examined qualitative differences in how teachers interact with children during play, contrasting an effective, child-centered "extending" style with an ineffective, teacher-centered "redirecting" style. Finally, research reported by Vukelich paints a more complex picture of the effectiveness of theme-related literacy materials and adult involvement in play. Vukelich's study revealed that adding literacy materials to play centers had differential effects, depending on the amount of spon-taneous literacy activity the children were engaging in before the addition of the materials. She also found adult modeling was not very effective in promoting literacy-related play. The possibility exists, however, that Vukelich's adult modeling strategy was more "redirective" than the adult guidance used in the Morrow and Rand study, thereby reinforcing Schrader's finding that the type of adult involvement in play is a crucial variable.

By bringing together these diverse strands of research, this volume attempts to consolidate what has been learned about play's contributions to early reading and writing. It is hoped that, in so doing, this book will stimulate further research on play and literacy development. In addition, the applied research in Part III has direct implications for educational practice and should enable teachers to take better advantage of play's potential as a medium for literacy learning. Therefore, this book is intended for scholars, graduate students, and in-service teachers. The book can serve as a scholarly reference, an instructional resource, or a text for master's and doctoral level courses in early childhood language arts.

Part I

Research Foundations

1

Play and the Emergence of Literacy

Nigel Hall

Introduction

Both play and literacy have long been central concerns of educators, as is evident by the extensive literature that exists in both areas. The quantity of literature relating to literacy, however, far exceeds that relating to play, a difference that probably reflects the different stances toward each subject taken by both educators and the general public. On the whole, thinking about play has concentrated on its centrality to the life of the child. Play was considered an interesting phenomenon deserving of study simply because it was there. It was something exhibited by almost all children and therefore appeared to be a natural event in human development. Most thinking was concerned with *why* play existed, and researchers concluded that it was there to contribute in general ways to emotional, social, cognitive, and physical development. Despite that encouraging prognosis, play was viewed by society at large as a noneducational process: it was all right for very young children and all right outside of school. School, however, was for learning, and those who cared about the general educational value of play had to fight hard for its place in the school curriculum.

Learning in schools centered around literacy and, on the whole, thinking about literacy has concentrated on its economic utility: societies needed citizens who could read and write. Children were taught to read and write less because these skills were implicitly valuable as aids to personal development than because the ideological basis of Western societies saw literacy as vital to the economic future of those societies. Thus, the emphasis was on teaching children useful skills. These two stances reflect a critical difference in the way the two subject areas were conceived by educators: play came naturally, but literacy was something that had to be taught.

Curiously, although many educators were interested in both play and literacy, few were interested in them as critically related topics. How could play be related to literacy when play was something that started early, a seemingly naturally occurring event, and literacy, which had to be taught, did not begin until children were five or six?

During the last twenty years, changes in the way that literacy and play have been studied have resulted in the perception that—far from being distinct and discrete subjects—in print-oriented societies literacy and play (particularly sociodramatic play) are intimately related in quite fundamental ways. Unfortunately, even though this recent work has established more securely the educational value of play, there is evidence from some countries (including the United States) that play is being marginalized even further from the school curriculum (Partridge, 1988).

The view that literacy had to be taught had clear implications for where the responsibilities for literacy education lay. Those responsibilities belonged to teachers, who were supposed to plan, organize, structure, implement, monitor, assess, and generally control the learning of literacy. This is in complete contrast to the way play was usually viewed. Where play was concerned, children had the responsibility for managing activities. No one explicitly taught children how to play. Rather, it was seen as a process learned more appropriately through apprenticeship (Paley, 1986). This difference in the center of power between learning to play and learning literacy was another manifestation of literacy's perceived educational status. Unlike play, literacy was seen as too important to be left in the control of children.

Control by teachers has been a consistent feature of most literacy education this century (Hall, 1987). The influence of behaviorist psychology resulted in literacy being seen mainly as a visual/perceptual skill, and one which was highly individualized. This view resulted in learning experiences being structured in carefully controlled systematic sequences which atomized and segmented learning. It demanded the decontextualization of learning, the reading and writing of meaningless material, and the isolation of the learner. Ironically, above all, it required the de-skilling of learners: children had to ignore everything they knew about learning and submit to the ownership of their learning by teachers, publishers, and university academics. The consequence was that the process of learning literacy became very complex, ritualized, and, for the most part, utterly divorced from either pleasure or reality. Many children failed. Given the way school literacy learning was defined, it appeared somewhat bizarre to look for literacy learning prior to schooling. Those few children who did turn up on the first day of school able to read in a conventional manner were abnormal enough to be the subject of detailed study by psychologists (Torrey, 1979). Many teachers stuck to their sequences with such rigidity that the literacy abilities children did possess (sometimes very high levels of ability) were often ignored or remained unknown. Goodman (1980, p. 3) cites such an example. Jonathon, who had been writing stories at home that anyone could read, came home after his first week in kindergarten and refused to write anything other than his name. "His response to the question, 'Why don't you write a story?' was, 'I can't write till I'm in first grade' and he didn't." *use as example*

The failure of conventional-literacy educators to look for evidence of children's interest in and ability with print stems, of course, from their definition of what counted as knowledge of literacy. If one looks for the fully developed ability to act as a reader and writer in the conventional school sense, it is indeed unlikely that such ability will be found in very young children. In the past twenty years, perhaps the most significant issue in literacy education has been the change in notions about what counts as knowledge about literacy.

Previously, knowledge of literacy was conceived as an ability to perform in certain ways on tests administered by teachers. However, if one views literacy as an object of the world rather than one of schooling, and if one asks, "How do children come to have knowledge of 'significant' objects in the world?"—then it becomes possible to see the emergence of literacy as something truly developmental, something intellectually constructed and controlled by children, something beginning long before formal instruction occurs.

The key word here is *significant*. If children were to ignore print and view it as insignificant, then it might be necessary for teachers to draw their attention to this phenomenon. But do young children view print as irrelevant to their lives?

The present-day Western print environment is the most complex ever experienced by the human race. From birth, children are witnesses to both the existence of print and the relationships between print and people. Given the way that children involve themselves in all aspects of their world, it would seem somewhat strange to suggest that children were totally ignorant about one part of that world. Yet, as has already been pointed out, that is precisely what educationalists have done.

After searching the literature on literacy, Ferreiro and Teberosky (1982) stated:

We have searched unsuccessfully in this literature for reference
to children themselves, thinking children who seek knowledge,
children we have discovered through Piagetian theory. The
children we know are learners who actively try to understand
the world around them, to answer questions the world poses. . . .
It is absurd to imagine that four- or five-year-old children growing
up in an urban environment that displays print everywhere (on
toys, on billboards and road signs, on their clothes, on TV) do
not develop any ideas about this cultural object until they find
themselves sitting in front of a teacher (p. 12).

Recent evidence indicates that these thinking children are busy
making sense of the world of print. This sense is not, of course, the
same sense held by teachers. A multitude of studies reveal that children
are intensely interested in the object we call print. They are curious
about it, constantly puzzling out why it is there and what it does
(Baghban, 1984; Bissex, 1980; Cochran-Smith, 1984; Crago and Crago,
1983; Dyson, 1989; Ferreiro and Teberosky, 1983; Fletcher, 1987; Fox,
1985; Goodman, 1984; Harste, Woodward, and Burke, 1984; Heath,
1983; Hubbard, 1989; Kammler, 1984; Lass, 1982 and 1983; Newkirk,
1989; Sulzby, 1985; Taylor and Dorsey-Gaines, 1988).

When Ferreiro and Teberosky (1982) studied young Argentinian
children to discover what kind of sense children made of literacy, they
were not concerned with whether the children were right or wrong.
Rather, they were interested in the beliefs, constructs, and concepts
that the children actually held. For Ferreiro and Teberosky, print is
an object of knowledge like any other object or set of objects in the
world. Just as children develop knowledge hypotheses about how
things move, why some things fall to the ground, why some things
float, or why people get angry, they also generate ideas about how
print works. Ferreiro and Teberosky have carried out a series of
investigations into how children's ideas about the technical nature of
print develop as they get older. They suggest that children go through
a sequence of stages in their active construction of knowledge about
print. Central to their argument is the notion that, even though child-
generated hypotheses about language may be (in a conventional sense)
wrong, they are nevertheless intelligent and reflective behaviors.
Children's hypotheses lead to profound insights involving the nature
of how literacy works.

Whereas Ferreiro and Teberosky are interested in how young
children view literacy as an object of knowledge, Harste, Woodward,
and Burke (1984) are concerned with how children view literacy as

How children view literacy

a process. They focus on how children understand literacy in a social sense—not just on *how* print works, but on the *where, what, why,* and *when* of literacy in all its manifestations.

Harste, Woodward, and Burke argue that children are strategic in their approach to learning in general, and the learning of literacy in particular. They are strategic in the sense that they use knowledge from a variety of sources to orchestrate what seems to be an effective response to any problem. Even their notion of what constitutes a problem is strategic. Children analyze a situation using, again, a wide variety of knowledge sources, and it is the children who define or do not define a situation as problematic.

Whereas Ferreiro and Teberosky view children as progressing almost inevitably through various levels, Harste, Woodward, and Burke reject the idea that literacy development follows a fixed sequence of stages. They also argue that literacy development has nothing to do with IQ, class, color or race. Rather, it has to do with experience—in particular, experience of the freedom to negotiate, take risks, fine-tune, and have intentions where literacy is concerned. They would argue that utilizing those strategies is learning, and that if children are inhibited from using those strategies, then learning will slow down or cease.

The four strategies identified by Harste, Woodward, and Burke must always be considered in the context of the overall response of a young child. Being strategic, a child selects from a repertoire of choices. Thus, any analysis of young children's literacy behavior must involve looking at a whole range of events; the children's choices may be different for all of them. To a large degree, it is this ability to make choices which differentiates the effective user of literacy from the ineffective user. The child who cannot choose to vary strategies is stuck with a rigidity of responses that may often be inappropriate.

include when observe children

Despite their differences, these two teams of researchers are both concerned with analyzing the moves made by children and in recognizing that those moves represent powerful competencies that are present very early in a child's life. Both teams seem to share some important assumptions about the implications of their work for children in kindergarten and other levels of schooling. They agree that conventional practices relating to literacy instruction take no account of what we now know about how young children learn literacy most efficiently. Ferreiro (1986) states: "There are school practices that put the children outside the knowledge because they define the child as a passive expector or as a mechanical receptor. In these kinds of settings children learn that all their questions are irrelevant. They learn to answer without thinking and to accept without resistance" (p. 10). And Harste, Woodward, and Burke say: "The reading and writing curriculum should not be isolated from other curricular areas but rather be a natural and functional part of the opportunities selected by the class for exploring their world" (p. 204).

Both sets of researchers acknowledge that, under normal circumstances, children do not wait passively to be told what they should learn. Rather, they simply get on with learning by operating upon the world. They learn by having a go, by trying things out. Early childhood is a continual process of experimentation, risk-taking, and negotiation in purposeful, intentional ways. If children are growing up in a print-rich environment, these strategies will be applied to generating knowledge about literacy.

It is at precisely this point that the potentially crucial relationship between play and the emergence of literacy comes into sharp focus. That play is almost always a process of "experimentation, risk-taking, and negotiation in purposeful, intentional ways" has been well established. If play can operate in this way across a multitude of social and intellectual experiences, can it not operate in the same way for the emergence of literacy? Indeed, the question might better be: "*Does it operate like that?*" A small but steadily growing number of studies have explored dimensions of both questions, and the reports can be divided into four categories. The order in which these reports will be considered is related to the degree of specificity in the relationship between play and the emergence of literacy. All except the last category will be considered only briefly.

1. *Play as a fundamental cognitive activity is preparation for more complex cognitive activities such as literacy.* Reports in this category make a general case for the beneficial effects of play upon intellectual development and argue that play can facilitate the development of many complex abilities, including the ability to read and write. For example, Gentile and Hoot (1983) argue that, through painting, children become aware that "images on paper are meaningful and say someting" (p. 436). They claim that "movement activities also provide children with vocabulary and conceptual growth by allowing them to discuss body parts and positions" (p. 437). More specifically, a relationship is claimed with reading: "It is difficult to imagine how a youngster might possibly read and abstract meaning from a sentence 'John went into the box' if she had not had the concrete experience of crawling in and out of a real box" (p. 437). Thus, the relationship is a very general, albeit important, one. The connection between play

and literacy is to some extent incidental: precisely the same kinds of relationships could be established between play and many other cognitively demanding performances. The word *play* in this sense, is being used to denote a physical activity that provides a concrete experience. The relationship here is between play and the content of literacy rather than between play and the processes of literacy. A related example is provided by Resenbrick (1987) when she explores the notion of "writing as play." She claims that "the connection between play and writing is a rich one for children. It enables them to bring into the classroom their own compelling interests. . . . This abundant play material is transformed in various ways as children work with it in writing their own stories" (p. 602). Again, of concern is the general experience of play informing the content of literacy rather than the process of literacy itself.

   2. Symbolic behavior in play is related to the understanding of a representational system like written language. Bruner's work has been extensively directed toward examining the relationship between play and the acquisition of symbolic systems such as oral language. Bruner claims that "it is not so much instruction in either language or thinking that permits the child to develop his powerful combinatorial skills, but a decent opportunity to play around with his language and to play around with his thinking that does the trick" (1986, p. 81). Developing literacy means coming to grips with a second-symbol system. Isenberg and Jacob (1983) claim that "symbolic play, the process of transforming an object or oneself into another object, person, situation, or event through the use of motor and verbal actions in a make believe activity, provides an important source for literacy development" (p. 272). It does so because literacy means handling words in such a way as to represent objects, ideas, or actions. The work of both Piaget and Vygotsky suggests that this ability to handle symbolic systems has immense potential for facilitating literacy development. However, tracking this relationship at such a general level has proved difficult. Wolfgang (1974) sought to establish a relationship between levels of symbolic play and reading performance of seven-year-olds. He claimed that "the advanced readers have attained an equilibrium between assimilation (play) and accommodation that results in their advanced reading performance. The delayed readers, on the other hand, still are assimilating freely in fantasy play, which suggests an interference in their accommodation to reading 'signs' or that they could not use signifiers" (p. 342).

   Wolfgang and Saunders (1981) compared children's moves towards abstract, symbolic play with the shifts in understanding that children make when moving from scribbles representing writing to the use of particular signs to represent particular meanings. Unfortunately, they chose Clay's categories (1975) for their system of development in writing, even though Clay herself states that there is no sequence to her categories. They are merely categories, not stages, and children may switch between them or use combinations of them. Thus, the basis for Wolfgang and Saunders' comparison was invalid.

The examination of play by researchers usually entails giving children a random set of objects to be used as props for pretend play. For example, Wolfgang (1974) used wooden pieces and commercially manufactured miniature toys—people, dressers, TVs, sofas, and so on. Not a single one of these items was in any way directly literacy-related. Thus, the findings of these researchers is always simply that there is a general relationship between symbolic play and the development of literacy skills.

3. Language behavior in play is related to literate language. Studies in this category claim a relationship between certain types of disembedded language which can occur during play and the kinds of language children are going to experience when they become readers and writers. According to Galda and Pellegrini (1985): "The language used in play is similar to more formal, literate uses of language required of children in school" (p. vii). This argument seems to be a refinement of the more general claim by Scollon and Scollon (1981) that children in Western literate societies are inevitably encultured into ways of using literate language because the language structures in their communities derive from an 'essayist' culture rather than an oral culture. Thus, the Scollons were able to say that their daughter Rachel was effectively literate at two years of age.

Research in this area has closely examined children's ability to use complex linguistic and cognitive behaviors in sociodramatic play, particularly the way the children set out to structure play by making it fit certain patterns or *scripts*. Scripts are "schematic representations of events and include information about temporal and causal organization of a set of related acts, about which components of an event are obligatory, and which are optional, and about the props and roles associated with the events" (French et al., 1985, p. 1). The negotiation of scripts and the maintenance of play within a script involve the generation and sustaining of a "narrative line" (Sachs, Goldman, and Chaillé, 1985). While playing in this extended way, young children develop the ability to "treat their utterances, not as isolated comments, but as elements in a larger, integrated composition, largely set off from the surrounding contextual world" (Wolf and Pusch, 1985, p. 66). Thus, through symbolic play, children contextualize events by dissociating them from the immediate classroom context within which the play is actually occurring. Researchers hold that the cognitive and linguistic abilities to perform in this way are closely related to the abilities needed to become involved in written texts which essentially sustain a fictional context unrelated to the actual context within which the text is being read. Of the children they studied, Wolf and Pusch claim: "There is a remarkable similarity between these five-year-olds' oral narratives and the written texts they will soon work on reading and writing" (p. 75).

This relationship is certainly significant and potentially powerful. However, like the studies in the second category, these studies also examined children's behavior in play situations that involved general toys or objects as play items. Once again, therefore, the relationship can only be a general one.

4. *When children are offered play experience with literacy-related resources, they act in literate ways.* There seems to be a curious omission in all of the studies mentioned so far. Virtually none of these studies considered the relationship between play and literacy by giving children the opportunity to play with literacy-related objects in situations where using literacy would be an appropriate response. In these studies, one hardly ever sees children playing at literacy. Why not? It seems obvious that, is you want to study the relationship between play and literacy, then you should put children into situations where they are able to demonstrate what they do when they play with literacy. In other words, give children contextualized play situations where they can demonstrate what they know about the *what, why, when, where,* and *how* of literacy.

Play offers an opportunity to help children preserve this wider understanding of literacy by allowing them the chance to explore literacy in contextualized situations. This relationship between children's literacy-related play and their emergent literacy—a relationship which has rarely been examined—forms our fourth category.

Isenberg and Jacob (1985) observed two four-year-olds engaging in play in a literate environment. They found that "both girls engaged in playful literacy activities at home and in school." The authors offer extended reports of the girls engaged in veterinarian play. "Both four-year-old girls engaged in playful literacy activities in pretend and non-pretend play contexts, activities that seemed to involve two functions related to learning: the gradual incorporation of the new information into the children's behavior patterns with the formation of larger units of behavior and the elaboration and extension of known or familiar information to new contexts" (p. 20).

Literacy is a social skill and is invariably a means to some other end. The exception to this rule, of course, is literacy instruction. Literacy in school settings is frequently decontextualized and devoid of social, economic, personal, or political significance. When literacy occurs within play settings, those significances reappear. Jacob (1984) offers an example of literacy play overlaid with economic significance.

Marie: Make the shopping list, my friend . . . Now I'm done, I finally finished eating . . . (She puts doll on toy bicycle) . . . oh friend, I knocked you over . . .

Ivan: The list . . . take the list, Marie.

Marie: Well, give it to me.

Ivan: All this is the list, all that which is written.

Marie: Well give it to me; I'll take it. I'll carry it with me . . . the list was pretend, little boy.

Ivan: The list is right here. Look at it here, it's written.

Marie: I'm going to take the list, sir . . . Now I'll buy the food. Take, take the dollar, I have five left.

Ivan: The list. Did you bring the list?

Marie: No, they stayed with her . . . yes, I brought it, take it.

Ivan: Now, it says rice, lentils, soup . . .

Marie: That's why it cost me this much . . . well, they cost me five dollars.

Ivan: What?

Marie: Five dollars, things are expensive my friend, I don't know why. (Jacob, 1984, p. 81) [This extract has been shortened by the omission of the original Spanish and some of the action descriptions.]

In this out-of-school extract, the children are generating a sociodramatic play event in which reference to the world of literacy is a naturally occurring and embedded consequence. There is no distortion, no decontextualizing, no sequence of skills. The children select and use what seems appropriate in the context of the situation they have created, a situation instantly recognizable as possessing authenticity within human experience. These two children are demonstrating powerful connections between play, literacy, and learning. The origins of such conversations lie clearly in the observations by children of the shopping behavior of adults. A conversation between a mother and four-year-old child remarkably like the one above can be found in Tizard and Hughes (1984, p. 74).

Bessell-Browne (1985) examined the use of literacy in sociodramatic play areas in kindergartens and was able to identify ten types of literacy usage. The children used literacy as:

1. An oral language substitute (e.g., mark-making followed by an explanation of the message)
2. A source of information (e.g., using the cook book for ideas)
3. A tool for extending and exploring personal relationships (e.g., sharing feelings about animals while looking at a book on pets)
4. A tool for self-expression (e.g., to express sorrow at a death in the family)
5. A way to confirm identity (e.g., writing their names on everything and anything)
6. A means of presenting information (e.g., writing captions)
7. A tool for supporting memory (e.g., list-making)
8. A way to meet economic and business needs in their play (e.g., ordering from catalogs)
9. Models (e.g., copying names from labels)
10. A reflection of the official status of an activity (e.g., writing carefully because it was "important work")

Bessell-Browne reported that the literacy-related resources were used by almost all of the children and, for the most part, they were used in an appropriate and typical manner. Bessell-Browne comments: "Children used literacy in a variety of ways that were meaningful to them in the play setting. They also showed knowledge of many of the ways adults use literacy in the wider social context and incorporated this into their play indicating a developing understanding of the many uses of literacy in the real world. The children's spontaneous literacy play thus gave them an opportunity to extend their uses of literacy beyond those that may be generally encountered within a classroom" (p. 155). Thus, whatever kind of literacy instruction was present in the classroom, in their sociodramatic play the children had an opportunity to learn about and explore a valid and wide perspective on literacy.

Both Bessell-Browne (1985) and Schrader (1989) made some use of Halliday's (1977) categories of language functions. Bessell-Browne used them to guide her in choosing appropriate literacy-related resources, and Schrader used them to examine the written language functions of children's writing during play. Schrader found instances of the regulatory function (writing down appointments), the interactional function (writing letters and messages), the personal function (expressing ownership of drawings by writing of names), the informational function (writing values on pretend money or writing names and addresses), and the instrumental function (writing checks and shopping lists). The children in this study did not use written language for either imaginative or heuristic functions. Schrader commented that the children "demonstrated their developing knowledge of written language functions not only by writing for real-life purposes but by reading their writing and discussing the meaning of their written language with their classmates and teacher. The children's actions further verified the meaning intent of their writing" (p. 233).

Roskos (1988) studied reading and writing behaviors in the natural pretend play of four- and five-year-olds and "came away awed by the quantity of early literacy activities in the pretend play context" (p. 562). During her observation of eight children, she logged 450 reading or writing acts. "In putting literacy to work in their play," she claims, "these youngsters behaved like readers and writers. They assumed a literacy stance and in so doing exposed their theories-in-use about the functions and features of written language" (p. 563).

Hall and colleagues (1987) set up a play situation in which literacy was an embedded feature in order to see whether children made any use of the literacy-related objects. By adapting an existing "home corner" in a nursery classroom, we created a print environment that related in as many ways as possible to the real world of print outside school. Such an area was of interest for two principal reasons. First, such areas often contain a range of resources designed to encourage home-based play. And second, such areas are, on the whole, the province of children rather than teachers. Children are usually left to play in ways they decide are appropriate. Although adults may sometimes join in the play, such adult behavior is usually in the context of the "rules" generated by the children. The home area would therefore be an ideal place to create a print-rich area where children were free to use, in any way they wished, the materials provided.

For our investigation, we subjected the home corner to a "print-flood". Cookbooks, recipe pads, a recipe notebook, and writing utensils were placed by the stove. Throughout the home corner, a wide range of appropriate literacy materials was provided, including writing utensils. Harste, Woodward, and Burke (1984) reported that: "Children at three know that usually pens are used for writing and crayons for drawing. In fact, when Joan [a research assistant] asked one of her three-year-olds to write with a crayon, her young sophisticate said, quite matter-of-factly, 'No I need a pen.' " (p. 34).

The home corner also contained a desk area with paper, envelopes, and writing utensils. Newspapers and letters were pushed through the door before each session. Diaries, planners, telephone directories, books, catalogs and other print material were also placed in strategic locations. The children's play was videotaped unobtrusively, and children were free to come round the back and watch the monitor while recording was in progress. In addition, observers took notes while play was in progress.

With these resources added to the home corner, the children's behavior demonstrated a keen commitment to literacy. During the four days of observation, 290 events exhibiting literacy-related behavior were observed. These ranged from fleeting bits of engagement to highly organized and sustained play episodes in which literacy was a consistently embedded feature.

On certain occasions, the children seemed to be exploring the materials in very personal, nonplay ways. One young boy involved in some family play was told by one of the girls to read the newspaper. A five-minute solo engagement followed (the girl had gone away) in which the boy manipulated and maneuvered the paper to the correct orientation, then sat and scrutinized it intensely. It was as if he were not only exploring the orientation of the newspaper (which was a large and cumbersome object for him to handle) but also exploring the role of being a newspaper reader.

The nursery-school children demonstrated not simply a knowledge of some of the purposes of print, but also of the social contexts in which these purposes were embedded. Obviously, the range of understandings displayed was limited, but many functions are quite comprehensible to children. Children experience greetings cards, thank-you notes, letters, lists for Santa Claus, menus, advertisements for favorite products, familiar food packages, shopping lists, and—of course—stories.

The children displayed a very wide range of mark-making intended as writing. The experience of the children in using print was quite varied, and the results were often unconventional. Nevertheless, the children demonstrated how much they had learned already—a demonstration that would have been impossible without the appropriate resources and an opportunity for display.

The children in this nursery group were exploring the use of written language to establish ownership and identity, build relationships, remember or recall, request information, record information, fantasize or pretend, and declare. These children were not waiting for formal schooling to use literacy, but they had been waiting for the opportunity to display their use of it, and the play situation generated within the classroom allowed them such an opportunity.

In an attempt to see whether such behavior would manifest itself in other contexts, another literacy-related situation was set up in a nursery school. This time an office was created in a self-contained area within a classroom and amply supplied with all the relevant material. This area posed some problems for the children because an office is not part of the normal experience of young children. How would they make sense of the materials provided? Would they be able to contextualize them or would they simply play with them as discrete objects?

In order to answer that question, it is necessary to examine a piece of transcript from the first day of the play situation. The children in the following transcript are four years old.

9	Fiona:	Go and ask the man if we're allowed to stamp.
10	Laura:	Hey, this is. . . this is the. . . this is the calendar.
11	Rebecca:	Yes, I think we're allowed.
12	Fiona:	Well go on then.
13	Laura:	Look at. . .
14	Emily:	That's the day, that tells you what the day is.
15	Laura:	That tells you what today is.
16	Rebecca:	And the date, and the month.
17	Laura:	I'm gonna go here. I've got a book.
18	Fiona:	I've got a pen. Go and ask the man.
19	Rebecca:	No.
20	Fiona:	Go on, if you're allowed to stamp?
21	Emily:	And tell him are you allowed to draw?
22	Laura:	And go and tell the lady.
23	Rebecca:	Or shall we swap over places?
24	Voice:	Yes you're allowed to do anything you like in there — you can take the top of that pen as well.
25	Emily:	Are we allowed to draw?
26	Voice:	Yes.
27	Fiona:	You're allowed to do anything you want.
28	Rebecca:	You've got to. . .
29	Fiona:	Even smash the heads off.
30	Laura:	Beccy!
31	Fiona:	You're allowed to.

32 Emily: You're allowed to do anything you want.
33 Laura: Look, Fiona's done a stamp. Good stamp Fiona!
34 Rebecca: And Fiona.
35 Emily: You're allowed to do anything you want to.
36 Laura: I know that. Beccy, do one of them, right.
37 Rebecca: But we don't know what all these buttons are for, do
               we? I mean. . . all right.
38 Emily: Pretend you're one of the visitors.
39 Laura: Yeah.
40 Emily: Go on, go out there.
41 Laura: Pretend I'm a helper. Yeah.
42 Emily: Pretend you're the. . . pretend you're the person that
               comes to open the bank.
43 Laura: No, pretend, I er. . .
44 Emily: Was helping me, yeah.
45 Laura: No, let's pretend I'm a helper.
46 Emily: Yeah, you could help me. . . .
47 Laura: I know this could be where the aeroplanes come in,
               and. . . and. . .
48 Emily: This could be the office of the aeroplane.
49 Laura: Yeah, that's what I was going to say.
50 Fiona: It's open now, isn't it? You like a. . .
51 Laura: Here's a book. . .
52 Emily: Hello.
53 Laura: Look at this.
54 Fiona: That's going to be my pencil.
55 Rebecca: Look. This is what you write down. You write
               everything down in a big book.
56 Fiona: You can write. . .
57 Emily: Look at this. What's this for? Look, pins. Do this.
59 Laura: Staples, where's the staples?
60 Rebecca: Yeah, where's the staples? I don't know.

(Interruption)

61 Emily: I made a staple. Laura, Laura, Laura, I made in my book,
               a staple.
62 Fiona: Right, just a minute.
63 Emily: What madam?
64 Fiona: Staple? Madam?
65 Emily: Staple Madam.
66 Fiona: Staple madam.
67 Emily: Where are all the staples?

68 Rebecca: Guess what? My daddy goes to work and once he told
              me all about work, and guess what? People write
              everything and they do it in peace and quiet all the time
              and . . . in quiet.
69 Voice: I don't think we've got any . . . Why don't you write
              it down on your shopping list to get some now.
70 Laura: Write, write, write, that down, sopping, shopping list.
71 Emily: No, I work here.
72 Fiona: I work here.
73 Laura: But there's a shop. Can go, you can go shopping, with
              a shopping list.
74 Fiona: I know, let's all tell mummy all about it. We went in
              an office.

   This transcript reveals clearly the efforts of these four children
to locate a script for using the items in a way that made sense to them.
The children had simply been told that they could play in the office.
They were given no prior experience of, or discussion about, what
an office might be.

   At first, they are unsure about what they are allowed to do (lines
9, 20–22), but once they are reassured that they can do whatever they
like in there (something instantly logically extended by Fiona [line 29]),
their attention is focused on finding a way to operate. Emily starts it
off (line 38) by proposing that having visitors is an appropriate move.
This is instantly accepted by Laura and Emily, who (line 42) locates
a script by suggesting that the area is in a bank. A few lines later (47),
Laura proposes that the area is "where the aeroplanes come in." This
is not as obscure as it first seems. In another bay, the classroom had
a mock airport, plane, and desk. That area had been there for several
weeks and had been extensively used by all the children. Emily
confirms the identity of the area by actually using the word *office* (line
48), and Fiona suggests that it is now open. The children then talk about
some of the literacy items but are soon distracted by the discovery of
staples. Rebecca has nevertheless clearly gone on reflecting about the
problem, and she soon provides a description of an office, drawing
on her experience of what she has been told (line 68). In the final entry,
Fiona ofers an action which ties up the episode.

   In addition to generating a literacy-related script, the children
are using the vocabulary of literacy to talk about and use the items.
The terms *calendar, book, pen, draw, pencil, write,* and *shopping list*
are all used appropriately. At the same time, the children were using
the writing materials in ways that clearly indicated that writing-type
marks were intended.

There are a number of important features to note. There was high level of cooperation going on during this episode. The effort to negotiate a script that would allow the play to incorporate all the literacy-related resources was a group effort. Within this negotiation, the children introduced each other to new ideas and new knowledge. A child's offering may or may not be taken up by the others, but such offerings are constantly being made in children's play. For example, the event with the calendar (lines 10–16) is one of continual extension. Once Rebecca has identified it, there is practically a competition to make explicit what a calendar can demonstrate. Isenberg and Jacob (1985) identified the potential for such exchanges. Once such knowledge has been made explicit, it can be incorporated into the wider scripts of the play and can lead to the generation of new scripts. In the context of these children's play, such discussion is part of their exploration of the materials in order to produce a context sufficiently clear to allow extended play to continue.

This episode seems to operate at all four levels of specificity discussed in this chapter. At one level, there is the physical exploration of resources: the children push buttons, hit keys, bang staples, and use the stamp. On the next level, the children use their sophisticated abilities to engage in symbolic play in association with a particular type of symbolic behavior—that of literacy. The entire time the children were talking, they were mark-making—writing on the pads, the cards, the calendar, and the notice board. Such behavior is impossible to capture in a transcript. On the third level, the children are engaged in play that demands a certain explicitness of language. By using language in this way, they are able to generate a script. French and colleagues (1985) comment that such scripts "constitute one of the young child's earliest, most stable, and richly represented forms of knowledge. In addition to allowing young children to organize and interpret their experience, that is, to predict 'when', 'what', and 'who' in familiar situations, scripts appear to provide an essential basis for further cognitive development" (p. 2). The language is syntactically, semantically, and pragmatically more advanced when the children's discourse is knowledge-based, or *scripted.* On the final level, the children are being literate people. When faced with certain kinds of resources—in this case, mostly related to literacy—they do not ignore them or use them for fighting, dressing up, or playing house. Rather, they seek to incorporate these resources in a structure that enables them to be used in an appropriate and meaningful way. To borrow the term of Harste, Woodward, and Burke (1984), the children are being *strategic* in organizing and selecting their literacy experiences.

Most of the examples given so far rely on children using their general literacy knowledge and embedding it within their play. Of course, the relationship can often be more specific, and much sociodramatic play derives from literature-based experiences. When two-and-a-half-year-old Scott climbed on his mother's bed and replied to his mother's greeting of "Good morning Scott", with "Oh me not Scott. Me Dorothy", he was drawing on a recent viewing and reading of *The Wizard of Oz* (Spreadbury, 1989). His mother comments, "Since then we have often played various scenes from *The Wizard of Oz*. Scott's favourite is when he (Dorothy) throws a bucket of water over the wicked witch (me) who then melts into a mere hat on the floor. Different visitors at our home are cast into the roles of Scott's favourites—Auntie Em, Uncle Henry, Scarecrow, Tinman, the Cowardly Lion, the Great Oz, the Wicked Witch and her monkeys, and, of course, Toto, Dorothy's little dog" (p. 14). One wonders what the local hairdresser made of Scott's reply to his greeting, "Oh, me not Scott. Me Toto. Me come to have me hair cut. Hair very long, very hot. Woof Woof" (p. 13). Equally, two-and-a-half-year-old Joseph (Robinson, 1989) must have caused some confusion when—borrowing from the repertoire of his favorite characters in *Thomas the Tank Engine*—he told an aunt, "You are a danger to the public" (p. 17).

The children's own stories frequently form a basis for socio-dramatic play, as is evidenced by the work of Paley (1981, 1988). The stories developed by her children owed a lot to both traditional tales and the more modern tales of superheroes that formed much of the children's TV viewing.

(Conclusion)

Linking play and literacy in this way can be mutually supportive. Play provides a context within which the emergence of literacy can be manifested and explored. The literacy in turn enriches the play, helping the development and processing of scripts. For those who work with young children, such settings (as suggested by Schickedanz, 1977 and 1986; Dukes, 1982; Schrader, 1990; Christie, 1990; Hall, 1988; and Hall and Abbot, in press) have the potential to inform and enrich the literacy learning experiences of children and to help educators gain insight into the literacy development of the children. Teachers who provide literacy-rich play opportunities:

— Have access to a better view of what children actually know about literacy.

— Allow themselves to observe literacy behavior in the widest possible contexts.
— Give children opportunities to demonstrate what they know.
— Allow children the chance to help each other through the cooperative work in play.
— Through the diversity of play situations offer children maximum opportunity to explore new ways of representing meanings and using literacy.
— Offer children a purposeful rationale for engaging in literacy and literacy-related behaviors.
— Acknowledge that children can control aspects of their own learning.
— Facilitate the "natural" emergence of literacy.

It is important, however, to sound a cautionary note. When structured in this way, play is essentially an open-entry and open-ended activity. Children can come into the play at many different levels, use it in many different ways, and end it at points which seem to them to be appropriate. It would be unhelpful, and probably extremely counterproductive to try to force the play to be anything other than what it needs to be according to the children. There is no advantage to the children's learning to make play an instructional context for literacy. To offer literacy-related resources within sociodramatic play is one thing; to insist that these resources be used in particular ways would destroy all the powerful learning potential of play. It is powerful precisely because it offers children a chance to contextualize literacy in their own way. Play should never be made a slave to a teacher's instructional desires. If play ceases to be a pleasure, it ceases to be play.

Although play has become marginalized as an educational activity in some countries, in England the relationship between play and literacy has recently been enshrined in law. The New National Curriculum (which began in September 1989 and is mandatory upon all state schools in Great Britain) states clearly that all children at Key Stage One (five to seven years) should: "Read in the context of role-play and dramatic play—e.g., in the home play corner, class shop, or other dramatic play setting such as a cafe, hospital or post office. Such reading might include a menu, a sign on a door, a label on a packet, or a sign above a counter." And that: "Pupils should write in a wider range of activities. Early 'play' writing—e.g., in a play house, class shop, office, hospital—should be encouraged and respected" (Her Majesty's Stationery Office, 1989).

If literacy-related resources are offered sensitively to children within sociodramatic play, then the relationship between the emergence of literacy and play is not a general one. Play offers a chance to be literate. The presence of literacy-related resources is in no way threatening or inhibitory. On the contrary, such resources seem to open up new ways of using literacy and make legitimate, in school contexts, the knowledge that children already possess about literacy. The evidence appears to demonstrate that, when given the opportunity in appropriate play situations to reveal literacy behavior, children demonstrate a commitment to literacy, a knowledge about literacy, and an inquisitiveness about literacy. Play can allow both learning about literacy and the demonstration of what has already been learned about literacy. This potentially powerful relationship between play and literacy ought to ensure that young children's classrooms are never without such opportunities.

References

Baghban, M. (1984). *Our daughter learns to read and write.* Newark, DE: International Reading Association.

Bessell-Browne, T. (1985). *Literacy play in kindergarten.* Ph.D. dissertation, University of Oregon.

Bissex, G. (1980). *Gnys at wrk: A child learns to read and write.* Cambridge, MA: Harvard University Press.

Bruner, J. (1986). Play, thought, and language. *Prospects, 16*(1), 77–83.

Christie, J. (1990). Dramatic play: A context for meaningful engagements. *The Reading Teacher, 43,* 542–545.

Clay, M. (1975). *What did I write?* London: Heinemann Educational Books.

Cochran-Smith, M. (1984). *The making of a reader.* Norwood, NJ: Ablex Publishing Corporation.

Crago, H., and M. Crago (1983). *Prelude to literacy: A pre-school child's encounter with print and story.* Carbondale, IL: Southern Illinois University Press.

Dukes, L. (1982). Dramatic play + symbolic props = reading. *Day Care And Early Education, 9,* 11–12.

Dyson, A. H. (1989). *Multiple worlds of child writers: Friends learning to write.* New York: Teacher's College Press.

Ferreiro, E., and A. Teberosky (1982). *Literacy before schooling.* Exeter, NH: Heinemann Educational Books.

Ferreiro, E. (1986). *Literacy development: Psychogenesis.* Paper given at World Congress on Reading, London.

Fletcher, L. (1987). *Ben's story: A deaf child's right to sign.* Washington, DC: Gallaudet University Press.

Fox, C. (1985). The book that talks. *Language Arts, 62,* 364–84.

French, L., et al. (1985). The influence of discourse content and context on preschoolers' use of language. In: L. Galda and A. Pellegrini (Eds.), *Play, language and stories.* Norwood, NJ: Ablex Publishing Corporation.

Galda, L., and A. Pellegrini (Eds.). (1985). *Play, language and stories.* Norwood, NJ: Ablex Publishing Corporation.

Gentile, L., and J. Hoot (1983). Kindergarten play: The foundation of reading. *The Reading Teacher, 36,* 436–439.

Goodman, Y. (1980). The roots of literacy. In: M. P. Douglass (Ed.), *44th Yearbook of the Claremont Reading Conference.* Claremont, CA: Claremont Graduate School.

——— (1984). The development of initial literacy. In: H. Goelman, G. Oberg, and F. Smith (Eds.), *Awakening to literacy.* Exeter, NH: Heinemann Educational Books.

Hall, N. (1987). *The emergence of literacy: Young children's developing understanding of reading and writing.* Exeter, NH: Heinemann Educational Books.

——— (1988). Write from the start: A curriculum for emergent writing in the nursery school. *Child Education, 65,* 16–18.

Hall, N., et al. (1987). The literate home corner. In: P. Smith (Ed.), *Parents and teachers together* (pp. 134–144). London: Macmillan.

Hall, N., and L. Abbot (In press). *Play in the primary curriculum.* London: Hodder and Stoughton.

Halliday, M. A. K. (1977). *Learning how to mean: Exploration in the development of language.* New York: Elsevier-North Holland.

Harste, J., V. Woodward, and C. Burke (1984). *Language stories and literacy lessons.* Exeter, NH: Heinemann Educational Books.

Heath, S. B. (1983). *Ways with words.* Cambridge: Cambridge University Press.

Her Majesty's Stationery Office. (1989). *The National Curriculum (English).* London: HMSO.

Hubbard, R. (1989). *Authors of pictures, draughtsmen of words.* Exeter, NH: Heinemann Educational Books.

Isenberg, J., and E. Jacob (1983). Literacy and symbolic play: A review of the literature. *Childhood Education, 59*(4), 272–276.

———— (1985). Playful literacy activities and learning: Preliminary observations. In: J. Frost and S. Sunderlin (Eds.), *When children play.* Wheaton, MD: Association for Childhood Education International.

Jacob, E. (1984). Learning literacy through play: Puerto Rican kindergarten children. In: H. Goelman, A. Oberg, and F. Smith (Eds.), *Awakening to literacy.* Exeter, NH: Heinemann Educational Books.

Kammler, B. (1984). Ponch writes again: A child at play. *Australian Journal of Reading, 7*(2), 61–70.

Lass, B. (1982). Portrait of my son as an early reader (1). *The Reading Teacher, 36*(1), 20–28.

———— (1983). Portrait of my son as an early reader (2). *The Reading Teacher, 36*(6), 505–515.

Newkirk, T. (1989) *More than stories: The range of children's writing.* Exeter, NH: Heinemann Educational Books.

Paley, V. (1981). *Walley's stories.* Cambridge, MA: Harvard University Press.

———— (1986). *Mollie is three: Growing up in school.* Chicago: University of Chicago Press.

———— (1988). *Bad guys don't have birthdays.* Chicago: University of Chicago Press.

Partridge, S. (1988). *Children's free play: What has happened to it?* (ERIC Document ED294665.) Washington, DC: Educational Resources Information Center.

Pellegrini, A. (1985). Relations between preschool children's symbolic play and literate behavior. In: L. Galda and A. Pellegrini (Eds.), *Play, language and stories.* Norwood, NJ: Ablex.

Rensenbrick, C. (1987). Writing as play. *Language Arts, 64,* 598–602.

Robinson, M. (1989). Bookspeak. In: N. Hall (Ed.), *Writing with reason: The emergence of authorship in young children.* Exeter, NH: Heinemann Educational Books.

Roskos, K. (1988). Literacy at work and play. *The Reading Teacher, 41,* 562–566.

Sachs, J., J. Goldman, and C. Chaillé (1985). Narratives in precshoolers' sociodramatic play: The role of knowledge and communicative competence. In: L. Galda and A. Pellegrini (Eds.), *Play, language and stories.* Norwood, NJ: Ablex Publishing Corporation.

Schickedanz, J. (1977). *Using symbolic props in play: A curriculum guide and discusson for pre-school teachers.* (ERIC document ED142292). Washington, DC: Educational Resources Information Center.

————— (1986). *More than the ABCs.* Washington, DC: National Association for the Education of Young Children.

Schrader, C. (1989). Written language use within the context of young children's symbolic play. *Early Childhood Research Quarterly 4,* 225–244.

————— (1990). Symbolic play as a curricular tool for early literacy development. *Early Childhood Research Quarterly, 5,* 79–103.

Scollon, R., and B. Scollon (1981). *Narrative, literacy and face in interethnic communication.* Norwood, NJ: Ablex Publishing Corporation.

Spreadbury, J. (1989). The day Toto had a haircut: Roleplay at home and school. *Wordsworth: Journal of the English Teachers Association of Queensland. 22*(2), 12–16.

Sulzby, E. (1985). Kindergarteners as readers and writers. In: M. Farr, (Ed.), *Children's early writing development.* Norwood, NJ: Ablex Publishing Corporation.

Taylor, D., and C. Dorsey-Gaines (1988). *Growing up literate.* Exeter, NH: Heinemann Educational Books.

Tizard, B., and M. Hughes (1984). *Young children learning.* London: Fontana Books.

Torrey, J. (1979). Reading that comes naturally. In: T. Waller and G. Mackginnon (Eds.), *Reading research: Advances in theory and practice.* New York: Academic Press.

Wolf, D., and J. Pusch (1985). The origins of autonomous texts in play boundaries. In L. Galda and A. Pellegrini (Eds.), *Play, language and stories.* Norwood, NJ: Ablex Publishing Corporation.

Wolfgang, C. (1974). An exploration of the relationship between the cognitive area of reading and selected developmental aspects of children's play. *Psychology in the Schools, 11*(3), 338–343.

Wolfgang, C., and T. Saunders (1981). Defending young children's play as the ladder to literacy. *Theory into Practice, 20*(2), 116–120.

2

Psychological Research on Play: Connections with Early Literacy Development

James F. Christie

Play is one of the most common forms of behavior during childhood, making it an object of keen interest to researchers in the areas of developmental and educational psychology. As a result, children's play has been the focus of hundreds of psychologically oriented investigations, some dating back to the early 1930s (Rubin, Fein, and Vandenberg, 1983). Recently, the pace of play research has increased, with more than two hundred books and journal articles being published during the 1970s (Sutton-Smith, 1985) and undoubtedly even more during the past decade.

Most of this psychological play research has focused on dramatic play (also known as sociodramatic, symbolic, pretend, fantasy, and make-believe play). This is the type of play in which children use make-believe transformations and role-playing to act out scripts and stories. For example, a child may use a box as an imaginary car and pretend to drive it, or several children may take on the roles of family members and act out a story with a domestic theme. Dramatic play has been of particular interest to psychologists because of its prevalence during the preschool years, its cognitive complexity, and its important role in the developmental theories of Piaget (1962) and Vygotsky (1976).

Relevant to the topic of this book, dramatic play is the form of play that has been most commonly linked with early literacy development. It is not surprising, therefore, that virtually every chapter in this volume focuses on dramatic play. Several chapters examine the ways in which dramatic play can contribute to children's literacy growth, and others investigate how this type of play can provide children with opportunities to have meaningful engagements with literacy in school settings.

Psychological play research has generated a wealth of information about play in general and dramatic play in particular, some of which has a direct bearing on the play/literacy connection. For example, research on the definition of play has resulted in the identification of factors which characterize play and make an activity seem play-like to children. Knowledge of these characteristics can help guide educators in devising playful literacy experiences for their students. A second strand of research has provided information about how the quantity and quality of dramatic play changes with age. This information can help teachers understand the relative maturity of individual children's play patterns and to decide when intervention or enrichment is appropriate. A third group of investigations has focused on how different types of play materials and room arrangements can increase the amount and quality of children's dramatic play. The findings of this research can help teachers create a classroom environment conducive to rich, literacy-related play. A final group of studies has investigated the effects of play training on children's play and social-intellectual development. This research has shed light on the importance of adult involvement in play and has identified several strategies which teachers can use to encourage children to incorporate literacy behaviors into their dramatic play.

Most of this research has been published in psychology journals such as *Child Development* and *Developmental Psychology*, thereby limiting its accessibility to reading and language arts specialists. The purpose of this chapter is to review these four areas of psychological play research—characteristics of play, age trends in play behavior, play settings, and play training—focusing on findings which have implications for using play to facilitate early literacy development. These play 'basics' will place the research reported in subsequent chapters of this book within the context of the total body of play research and should help educators to take better advantage of dramatic play's potential to promote early reading and writing.

The Characteristics of Play

In a book on play and literacy, it is important to define exactly what play is. Unfortunately, finding a precise definition for play has proven to be an extraordinarily difficult task (Vandenberg, 1982). This is due to play's inherent diversity and complexity and to the many ways in which the term *play* is used. For example, the second edition of *Webster's New Universal Unabridged Dictionary* lists more than 60 meanings for the word *play*.

While à precise definition of play has eluded researchers, progress has been made in identifying traits or dispositional factors that set play apart from other behaviors (Garvey, 1977; King, 1979; Rubin, et al., 1983; Smith and Vollstedt, 1985). These characteristics include:

1. *Nonliterality.* Play events are characterized by a play frame within which internal reality takes precedence over external reality. The usual meanings of objects are ignored, new meanings are substituted, and actions are performed differently from when they occur in nonplay settings.

2. *Means over ends.* When children play, their attention is focused on an activity itself rather than on the goals of the activity. In other words, means are more important than ends.

3. *Positive Affect.* Play is usually marked by signs of pleasure and enjoyment. Smiles, laughter, and joking are some of the most obvious signs that play is occurring.

4. *Flexibility.* Children are more apt to try novel combinations of ideas and behaviors while playing than while engaged in goal-directed activity.

5. *Voluntary.* Play is spontaneous and freely selected. King (1979) found that kindergartners considered an activity such as block building to be play if they chose to do it. They considered the same activity to be work if it were assigned by the teacher.

6. *Internal Control.* In play, the players are in control and determine the course of events. King's (1979) research revealed that, when a teacher took over control of an ongoing play episode (e.g., by telling children what to build with blocks), the children perceived the activity as work rather than play.

The last two characteristics of play have important implications for using dramatic play as a means to foster literacy development. As will be described in several subsequent chapters of this book, there are occasions when teachers may wish to intervene in children's play by changing room arrangements, introducing material, making suggestions, or even by taking part in an ongoing dramatization and modeling play behaviors. Such interventions can often be successful in encouraging richer, more complex dramatizations and in getting children to incorporate reading and writing into their play. But teachers must be careful not to take over too much control of the activity. As soon as dramatic play becomes adult-mandated and externally controlled, it ceases to be play and becomes work from children's perspective.

Age Trends

A number of investigations have observed children during indoor free-play periods in order to determine how the frequencies of different types of play change with age. Many of these studies used Smilansky's (1968) adaption of Piaget's (1962) play classifications to categorize different types of play:

1. Functional play — involving repetitive muscle movements with or without objects. Examples include: (a) running and jumping, (b) stacking and knocking down blocks, (c) digging in a sand pit, and (d) bouncing a ball against a wall.
2. Constructive play — involving using objects (blocks, Lego, Tinkertoys) or materials (sand, Playdough, clay) to build something.
3. Dramatic play — involving role-playing and/or make-believe transformations. Examples include: (a) make-believe activities: pretending to drive a car (arm movments), sound a horn (vocalization), or make a phone call with a block of wood (object use); (b) role-playing: pretending to be a parent, baby, fire fighter, shark, or monster.
4. Games with rules — involving recognizing, accepting, and conforming to preestablished rules.

Rubin and colleagues (1983), summarizing the results of this research, identified several major age trends with respect to these cognitive play categories. In accordance with Piaget's theory, functional play is the most prevalent form of play during the first three years of life. Starting at approximately eighteen months, both constructive and dramatic play appear and begin to increase. Between the ages of four and six years, constructive play is the modal form of play activity, accounting for almost half of the play observed in preschool and kindergarten classrooms (due, in part, to the abundance of construction materials in school settings). During this same period, dramatic play continues to increase at the expense of functional play, rising to approximately 20 to 30 percent of all play by age six. As children enter the primary grades, dramatic play declines in frequency. Dramatic play thus appears to follow an inverted U developmental progression, first appearing between the ages of eighteen months to two years, increasing during the preschool years, peaking at about age six, and then declining during middle childhood.

Several aspects of dramatic play change during the preschool period. Fenson (1984) has identified three of these major developmental trends:

(1) Decentration — Dramatic play becomes increasingly social with age. Whereas initial attempts at dramatic play are solitary and are centered on the self (e.g., a single child pretends to comb her own hair), later episodes involve other people and inanimate objects (e.g., several children take on the roles of parents and pretend to give a doll a bath).

(2) Decontextualization — There is decreasing reliance on physical similarity between symbols and referents in make-believe transformations. Early object transformations involve symbols which are similar in size and shape to the object being symbolized (e.g., a small rectangular piece of wood is used as if it were a comb). Later, nonprototypical objects (e.g., a rubber ball) or invisible objects (e.g., holding one's hand as if it contained a comb) can be used for the same purpose. These changes mark the growing maturity of children's representational abilities.

(3) Integration — There is increasing ability to combine separate actions into coordinated sequences. As a result, the story lines children enact in their pretend play become more complex with age, changing from isolated events (e.g., feeding a doll) to complex, interrelated episodes (e.g., cooking a make-believe meal, serving it to guests, and then eating the meal while conducting polite conversation).

In addition, the roles and themes children enact change with age, becoming more creative and unusual (Garvey, 1977; Rubin et al., 1983). Initially, children adopt highly familiar roles (those of family members, for example) and act out very routine domestic activities such as preparing dinner or going shopping. As children mature, they begin taking on less familiar roles, such as occupations (e.g., firefighter) and fictional characters (e.g., Batman). They also begin to introduce unusual elements into their dramatizations (e.g., an earthquake may occur during a shopping trip).

As a result of this research, we now have a clearer picture of how both the quantity and quality of dramatic play changes with age. Children's initial make-believe play begins at around age two and is marked by solitary dramatizations, prototypical object transformations, isolated actions, and familiar roles. By the time dramatic play reaches its peak—at approximately six—it has evolved into a complex undertaking that typically involves groups of children, nonprototypical and imaginary object transformations, interrelated action sequences, and highly imaginative roles and themes.

An important implication of this research is that teachers need to take children's ages into consideration when observing and interpreting their free-play behaviors. Although the beginnings of dramatic play begin to appear by two years of age, most children do not engage in fully elaborated group dramatic play until age four or later (Rubin, et al., 1983). Therefore, teachers should not worry if two- and three- year-olds' dramatizations consist of isolated actions and prototypical object transformations and are conducted in a solitary, nonsocial fashion. However, if these characteristics persist at ages 4 or 5, teachers may want to take steps to facilitate children's play development. Possible interventions include manipulating the classroom play environment and using play training, the topics of the last two sections of this chapter.

Play Settings

During the 1930s, a number of studies investigated the effects of indoor and outdoor play settings on children's play patterns. Much of this early research was motivated by practical concerns about how best to design and equip classrooms and playgrounds (Herron and Sutton-Smith, 1971). Following several decades of inactivity, there was a resurgence of ecologically oriented play research during the 1970s, due in part to renewed interest in preschool education and child development and to the growing influence of Bateson's (1955) theory, which emphasizes that play texts (specific play behaviors) and contexts (the settings in which play behaviors occur) are interconnected and should not be considered in isolation from one another.

Research on indoor play settings has focused on a number of variables, including space, materials, and the time frame in which play takes place. The findings of these investigations have important implications for creating classroom play areas that encourage rich, literacy-related dramatic play.

Space

The space available for play and the way this space is arranged have a considerable influence on children's play behavior. Important spatial features of classroom settings include: (a) the types of play areas in the room, (b) the amount of space in these areas, and (c) whether these areas are open or partitioned.

Preschool and kindergarten classrooms are typically divided into several distinct activity centers, including housekeeping, block, library, table toy, and art areas. Not surprisingly, research has shown that children's play patterns vary in these different classroom locations. For example, sand and water areas tend to evoke functional play, block areas encourage constructive play, and housekeeping centers elicit dramatic play (Pellegrini and Perlmutter, 1989; Rubin and Seibel, 1979). The social level of preschoolers' play has also been found to vary according to location, with solitary play being observed most often in the game or "table toy" area, parallel play (children play along side each other but do not interact) in the art and book areas, and group play in the block and housekeeping areas (Shure, 1963). The block and housekeeping areas have also been found to elicit the use of more imaginative and multifunctional language than other activity areas (Pellegrini, 1984).

Taken together, these findings point out the importance of housekeeping and block areas, both of which encourage large amounts of social interaction and the use of more mature, complex language. Housekeeping centers have the additional advantage of eliciting large amounts of dramatic play.

High levels of dramatic play can also be evoked with theme centers — areas that contain props which suggest specific settings that are familiar to children. For example, an area of the classroom might be set up with props and furniture relating to a grocery store, a doctor's clinic, a business office, or a restaurant. Theme centers have been found to be effective in stimulating dramatic play, particularly in boys (Dodge and Frost, 1986; Woodard, 1984). They also have the advantage of broadening the scope of the scripts that children enact during their dramatizations.

Other ecological research studies have revealed that chidlren's play is affected not only by the types of play areas available but also by certain characteristics of those areas, including spatial density and partitioning.

Spatial density refers to the amount of space per child in a play setting and is an index of crowding. Smith and Connolly (1980) conducted a carefully controlled study of this variable, systematically varying the amount of space, number of children, and amount of equipment in preschool classrooms. Spatial densities of 75, 50, 25, and 15 square feet per child were examined. The authors found that 25 square feet per child appeared to be optimal. When the space per child was above this 25-square-foot level, children engaged in large amounts of gross motor activity such as running and jumping. When the space per child went below this level, the increased crowding resulted in more aggression and reduced amounts of group play. This implies that play areas should be spacious but not huge.

Other studies have investigated different room arrangements, comparing play occurring in large, open rooms with play in rooms divided into well-defined, partitioned areas (Field, 1980; Sheehan and Day, 1975). Results suggest that children engage in higher social levels of play and more dramatic play in rooms with smaller, well-defined play areas. Rooms with large open areas (referred to as "dead spaces") tend to encourage more running, chasing, and rough-and-tumble play — behaviors which teachers usually try to discourage in indoor settings.

Although it appears advantageous to partition off classroom areas, Kinsman and Berk (1979) suggest that openings should be left between complementary areas such as the block and housekeeping centers. They found that removing a partition between these two areas resulted in more boy/girl play and an increase in play episodes integrating blocks and housekeeping materials.

Later chapters in this volume will illustrate that housekeeping centers and theme areas can encourage children to engage in a variety of valuable literacy activities. The research findings regarding play space discussed here have several important implications as to how these dramatic play centers should be set up and arranged. First, housekeeping and theme areas should be large enough so that four or five children can fit in them without being crowded. If space limitations dictate that dramatic play centers be smaller in size, teachers can avoid crowding by setting limits on the number of children who can use the area at one time. Second, these dramatic play centers should be well-defined and partitioned off from the rest of the classroom. 'Encapsulated' areas have a home- or building-like atmosphere that encourages theme-related role-playing. Partitions also shield players from distractions in other parts of the classroom, leading to more sustained dramatizations. Third, placing the housekeeping and theme areas near each other encourages children to combine play in the two areas. For example, a 'family' in the housekeeping center could make a trip to the grocery store theme center. This would not only encourage more sustained and complex dramatizations, but it would also create opportunities for additional types of literacy activities (e.g., writing a shopping list, reading product labels, and so on).

Materials

Early childhood educators have long been aware that children's play is affected by available play materials. Research has shown that both the social and cognitive aspects of play are affected by the types of materials located in classroom play areas and by the realism of these materials.

Housekeeping props, dress-up clothes, dolls, and cars and other vehicles encourage high levels of group play, whereas art construction materials (scissors, paints, crayons), instructional materials (beads, puzzles), small blocks (Lego), and clay tend to encourage nonsocial, solitary, or parallel play activities (Hendrickson, et al., 1981; Parten, 1933; Rubin, 1977; Van Alstyne, 1932). Unit blocks and large hollow blocks, among the most popular classroom play materials, appear to encourage equal amounts of group play and nonsocial play.

Researchers have also found that different materials encourage different cognitive levels of play:

1. Dramatic play — housekeeping props, theme-related props, dress-up clothes, dolls, vehicles, unit blocks, and large hollow blocks;
2. Constructive play — all types of blocks, paints, crayons, and scissors;
3. Functional play — playdough, clay, sand, and water (Rubin, 1977; Rubin and Seibel, 1979).

Preschool and kindergarten classrooms tend to be abundantly stocked with materials that encourage constructive play—which may explain why construction is the most frequently observed type of play in school settings (Rubin, et al., 1983).

Rather than comparing broad categories of play materials, other researchers have investigated differences between materials of the same type (e.g., dolls). Most of this research has focused on two closely related stimulus characteristics: realism and structure. Realism is the degree to which a toy resembles its real-life counterpart. A detailed replica of a fire engine is highly realistic, whereas Creative Playthings vehicles — which look like blocks of wood with wheels — are very low in terms of realism. Structure refers to the extent to which a toy's uses are restricted by its construction and appearance. High-realism toys tend to be high in structure. For example, a realistic replica of a fire engine has high structure, lending itself to only one use — being a fire truck. Creative Playthings vehicles, on the other hand, are low in structure and can be easily used to represent any kind of wheeled vehicle.

Results of toy realism research, on the whole, go along with developmental trends in children's representational abilities. Younger (two- and three-year-old) preschoolers need very realistic props to start engaging in dramatic play (Elder and Pederson, 1978; Fein, 1975; Jeffree and McConkey, 1976). Four- and five-year-olds, on the other hand, can engage in dramatic play using low-realism materials and may actually play more creatively with these low-structure props (Johnson, 1983; McLoyd, 1983; Pulaski, 1973). However, older preschoolers *prefer* high realism materials (McGhee, Ethridge, and Benz, 1981), and realistic, theme-related props have been found to elicit more dramatic play in four- and five-year-olds than low-structure materials (Dodge and Frost, 1986).

The findings of this play materials research has several important implications for promoting literacy-related dramatic play. First, housekeeping and theme areas should be well-stocked with theme-related props that encourage dramatic play. The realism and structure of these materials should correspond to the developmental level of children's representational abilities and to their play preferences. Dramatic play areas used by younger preschoolers should be almost exclusively stocked with high-realism play materials such as miniature replicas of household objects. Play areas for older preschoolers and kindergartners should also contain collections of theme-related, realistic props. These are the types of materials that children of this age prefer to play with, and research has shown that such materials result in higher amounts of dramatic play than low-realism materials. However, teachers may also want to include some low-structure props—featureless dolls, clay, hollow blocks, and empty cardboard boxes—in older children's dramatic play areas in order to stimulate creative make-believe transformations and scripts.

The second implication of play materials research is that dramatic play centers should contain theme-related literacy materials. Given the considerable influence of materials on play behavior, it stands to reason that children will be more likely to incorporate literacy activities into their dramatizations if props are available which suggest reading and writing activities. As Hall points out in Chapter 1 of this volume, it is unfortunate that literacy materials have traditionally been omitted from classroom dramatic play areas. Hall's informal study, in which a housekeeping area was subjected to a "print flood" of home-related literacy materials, indicated that adding such materials can lead to a substantial increase in literacy activities during play (Hall, et al., 1987). This pioneering investigation has stimulated a number of more extensive, carefully controlled studies of theme-related literacy materials, four of which are reported in this book (see Chapter 7, 8, 9, and 10). Results of these studies confirmed Hall's initial finding that, when play areas are stocked with theme-related reading and writing materials, children engage in a variety of literacy behaviors during dramatic play. These literacy-related play activities allow children to refine their growing conceptions of the functions of written language and provide valuable, highly meaningful practice with emergent reading and writing.

Time

One other important aspect of play settings is the time frame in which play occurs. Observational research has revealed that children require a considerable amount of time to plan and initiate group-dramatic play (Giffin, 1984). Before beginning such play, children must: (a) recruit other players, (b) assign roles, (c) designate the make-believe identities of objects, and (d) agree on the story line to be dramatized. Given young children's limited social skills, such preparations often take a long time. If play periods are short, children have to end their dramatizations right after they have started. When this happens frequently, children tend to switch to less advanced forms of play, such as functional play or simple construction activity, which can be completed in brief sessions.

The issue of the duration of time allocated for play has taken on special significance in recent years because of the 'back-to-basics' movement and the accompanying pressures to devote more time in early childhood programs to structured academic activities and less to free play (Glickman, 1984). At one time, it was traditional for indoor free-play periods to be quite long, lasting an hour or more. Today, however, it is quite common to find preschool and kindergarten programs that have very brief play periods, some as short as ten minutes.

Christie, Johnsen, and Peckover (1988) compared preschoolers' play patterns during 15- and 30-minute play periods, and found that children engaged in significantly more group-dramatic play during longer play periods. During shorter periods, children were more likely to wander about unoccupied or to engage in low-level functional play. These findings suggest that indoor free-play periods should be at least 30 minutes long—which gives children adequate time to plan, initiate, extend, and bring their dramatizations to a satisfactory conclusion. If a school's daily schedule currently has two short play periods, combining them into one longer play period would be more conducive to the occurrence of the type of rich, sustained dramatic play that is likely to have an impact on children's literacy development. In schools where academic curriculum demands prohibit daily play periods of this length, it may be preferable to have several long play periods per week than short ones every day. With such a schedule, children will at least be able to experience the benefits of extended dramatic play on a regular basis. The ideal solution in such situations, of course, would be to adjust the school curriculum so that there is time for 30-minute free-play periods on a daily basis.

Play Training

Before 1970, most early childhood educators were schooled in the psychoanalytic theory of play, which maintained that play's main function was to enable children to work out their inner conflicts (Spodek, 1974). According to this theory, teachers have a very limited role in classroom play: they should merely set the stage and not become directly involved in children's play activities (Johnson, Christie, and Yawkey, 1987). It was believed that adult intervention would disrupt play, inhibit children from revealing their true feelings, and reduce play's therapeutic benefits.

This hands-off attitude toward play has changed recently as a result of two factors. First, psychoanalytic theory's influence in early childhood education has declined, being replaced by the cognitively oriented theories of Piaget (1962) and Vygotsky (1976). Second, a series of play training studies (stemming back to Smilansky's [1968] study in Israel) have shown that classroom play can be greatly enriched by teacher participation, with positive effects not only on children's play, but also on their social and cognitive development.

Two basic types of play training have been used by researchers: sociodramatic play training and thematic fantasy play. Sociodramatic play training, originally developed by Smilansky (1968), attempts to help children incorporate into their play elements such as role-playing, object transformations, and social interaction. Teachers do this by supplying theme-related props, by suggesting play themes and activities, and by joining in the play from time to time, modeling desired play behaviors. Thematic fantasy play, first used by Saltz and Johnson (1974), involves helping children enact fairy tales or stories (e.g., "The Three Billy Goats Gruff"). The teacher reads a story, assigns roles to the children, and helps them enact the story by prompting and at times by taking a role in the dramatization. Stories enacted in this type of training tend to have a higher degree of fantasy then the themes used in sociodramatic play training. Thematic fantasy training is very structured, with the teacher supplying children with ready-made roles and plots. In contrast, sociodramatic play training encourages children to work together to create their own roles and to plan their own story lines.

The results of play training research have been, on the whole, quite positive. Findings indicate that both types of play training not only lead to more frequent and higher quality dramatic play but also result in gains in creativity, IQ, perspective taking, conservation attainment, and social competence. (For reviews of this research, see: Christie and Johnsen, 1985; Johnson, et al., 1987.) Results have also shown that play training promotes growth in literacy-related variables, including oral language development and vocabulary (Christie, 1983; Levy, Schaefer, and Phelps, 1986; Smith, Dalgleish, and Herzmark, 1981), story production (Saltz, Dixon, and Johnson, 1977; Saltz and Johnson, 1974), and story comprehension (see Chapter 4 in this volume).

Unfortunately, in many play training studies, differences in social interaction with adults and peers were confounded with play, thereby making it difficult to establish that play per se caused the gains on the social-cognitive measures. Some researchers believe that the adult tuition and peer conflict that accompany play training are primarily responsible for its effects on cognitive performance and social competence (Rubin, 1980; Smith, et al., 1981). Although this question does limit the usefulness of training research in establishing causal links between play and development, it in no way diminishes the value of play training as a means of fostering children's social and intellectual growth.

An important implication of this play training research is that, in order for dramatic play to have a positive effect on children's emergent literacy, teachers may have to do more than set the stage for play. Indeed, this is exactly what Morrow and Rand report in Chapter 7 of this book. They discovered that simply providing children with enriched play settings stocked with lots of theme-related literacy materials did not insure that children would use these materials in their play. Rather, they found that children were much more likely to engage in literacy-rich play when teachers used sociodramatic play training procedures— for example, by suggesting how reading and writing materials could be used in conjunction with ongoing play themes.

Play training must be used cautiously because excessive or ill-timed adult involvement can disrupt children's play. To prevent this possibility, teachers should base their involvement on careful observation of ongoing play activities, try to leave as much control of the activity as possible with the children, and phase out play training as soon as children begin exhibiting the desired play behaviors (Christie, 1982; Griffing, 1983; Johnson, et al., 1987; Woodard, 1984). When used in an appropriate manner, adult involvement in play can be enjoyable and beneficial for both children and their teachers.

Conclusion

The psychological research on play reviewed in this chapter has several important implications for early childhood language arts programs. Investigations of the characteristics of play have identified factors such as self-selection and child-centered control that can make classroom literacy activities more play-like and enjoyable for children. The results of studies on age trends in play behavior allow teachers to interpret children's play patterns in terms of developmental expectations. Ecologically oriented play research has produced valuable information about arranging and equipping classroom areas that encourage rich, literacy-related dramatic play. And finally, play training studies have revealed the importance of adult involvement in children's dramatic play and have shown that teachers can, by suggesting and modeling theme-appropriate literacy activities, encourage children to incorporate reading and writing into their dramatizations. Taken together, these research findings can help educators maximize play's contributions to children's early literacy development.

References

Bateson, G. (1955). A theory of play and fantasy. *Psychiatric Research Reports, 2*, 39–51.

Christie, J. J. (1982). Sociodramatic play training. *Young Children, 37*(4), 25–32.

——— (1983). The effects of play tutoring on young children's cognitive performance. *Journal of Educational Research, 76,* 326-330.

Christie, J. F., and Johnsen, E. P. (1985). Questioning the results of play training research. *Educational Psychologist, 20,* 7-11.

Christie, J. F., E. P. Johnsen, and R. B. Peckover (1988). The effects of play period duration on children's play patterns. *Journal of Research in Childhood Education, 3,* 123-131.

Dodge, M. K., and J. L. Frost (1986). Children's dramatic play: Influence of thematic and nonthematic settings. *Childhood Education, 62,* 166-170.

Elder, J. L., and D. R. Pederson (1978). Preschool children's use of objects in symbolic play. *Child Development, 49,* 500-504.

Fein, G. G. (1975). A transformational analysis of pretending. *Developmental Psychology, 11,* 291-296.

Fenson, L. (1984). Developmental trends for action and speech in pretend play. In: I. Bretherton (Ed.), *Symbolic play: The development of social understanding* (pp. 249-270). Orlando, FL: Academic Press.

Field, T. M. (1980). Preschool play: Effects of teacher/child ratios and organization of classroom space. *Child Study Journal, 10,* 191-205.

Garvey, C. (1977). *Play.* Cambridge, MA: Harvard University Press.

Giffin, H. (1984). The coordination of meaning in the creation of a shared make-believe reality. In: I. Bretherton (Ed.), *Symbolic play: The development of social understanding* (pp. 73-100). Orlando, FL: Academic Press.

Glickman, C. D. (1984). Play in public school settings: A philosophical question. In: T. D. Yawkey and A. D. Pellegrini (Eds.), *Child's play: Developmental and applied* (pp. 255-271). Hillsdale, NJ: Erlbaum.

Griffing, P. (1983). Encouraging dramatic play in early childhood. *Young Children, 38*(4), 13-22.

Hall, N., et al. (1987). The literate home-corner. In: P. Smith (Ed.), *Parents and teachers together* (pp. 134-144). London: Macmillan.

Hendrickson, J. M. et al. (1981). Relationship between toy and material use and the occurrence of social interactive behaviors by normally developing preschool children. *Psychology in the Schools, 18,* 500-504.

Herron, R. E., and B. Sutton-Smith (1971). *Child's play.* New York: Wiley.

Jeffree, D. M., and R. McConkey (1976). An observation scheme for recording children's imaginative doll play. *Journal of Child Psychology and Psychiatry, 17,* 189-197.

Johnson, J. E. (1983). Context effects on preschool children's symbolic behavior. *Journal of Genetic Psychology, 143*, 259–268.

Johnson, J. E., J. F. Christie and T. D. Yawkey (1987). *Play and early childhood development.* Glenview, IL: Scott, Foresman.

King, N. R. (1979). Play: The kindergartners' perspective. *Elementary School Journal, 80,* 81–87.

Kinsman, C. A., and L. E. Berk (1979). Joining the block and housekeeping areas: Changes in play and social behavior. *Young Children, 35*(1), 66–75.

Levy, A. K., L. Schaefer, and P. C. Phelps (1986). Increasing preschool effectiveness: Enhancing the language abilities of 3- and 4-year-old children through planned sociodramatic play. *Early Childhood Research Quarterly, 1,* 133–140.

McGhee, P. E., O. L. Ethridge and N. A. Benz (1981). *Effect of level of toy structure on preschool children's pretend play.* Paper presented at the meeting of The Association for the Anthropological Study of Play, Fort Worth, TX (April).

McLoyd, V. C. (1983). The effects of the structure of play objects on the pretend play of low-income preschool children. *Child Development, 54,* 626–635.

Parten, M. B. (1933). Social play among preschool children. *Journal of Abnormal and Social Psychology, 28,* 136–147.

Pellegrini, A. D. (1984). The effects of classroom ecology on preschoolers' functional uses of language. In: A. D. Pellegrini and T. D. Yawkey (Eds.), *The development of oral and written language in social contexts* (pp. 129–141). Norwood, NJ: Ablex Publishing Corporation.

Pellegrini, A. D., and J. C. Perlmutter (1989). Classroom contextual effects on children's play. *Child Development, 25,* 289–296.

Piaget, J. (1962). *Play, dreams and imitation in childhood.* New York: Norton.

Rubin, K. H. (1977). The social and cognitive value of preschool toys and activities. *Canadian Journal of Behavioral Science, 9,* 382–385.

——— (1980). Fantasy play: Its role in the development of social skills and social cognition. In: K. H. Rubin (Ed.), *Children's play* (pp. 69–84). San Francisco: Jossey-Bass.

Rubin, K. H., G. G. Rein and B. Vandenberg (1983). Play. In: P. H. Mussen (Ed.), *Handbook of child psychology,* Vol. 4. *Socialization, personality, and social development,* 4th ed. (pp. 693–774). New York: Wiley.

Rubin, K. H., and C. G. Seibel (1979). *The effects of ecological setting on the cognitive and social play behaviors of preschoolers.* Paper presented at the meeting of the American Educational Research Association, San Francisco (April).

Saltz, E., D. Dixon, and J. Johnson (1977). Training disadvantaged preschoolers on various fantasy activities: Effects on cognitive functioning and impulse control. *Child Development, 48,* 367–380.

Saltz, E., and J. Johnson (1974). Training for thematic-fantasy play in culturally disadvantaged children: Preliminary results. *Journal of Educational Psychology, 66,* 623–630.

Sheehan, R., and D. Day (1975). Is open space just empty space? *Day Care and Early Education, 3* (December), 10–13,47.

Shure, M. B. (1963). Psychological ecology of a nursery school. *Child Development, 34,* 979–992.

Smilansky, S. (1968). *The effects of sociodramatic play on disadvantaged preschool children.* New York: Wiley.

Smith, P. K., and K. J. Connolly (1980). *The ecology of preschool behavior.* Cambridge, England: Cambridge University Press.

Smith P. K., M. Dalgleish, and G. Herzmark (1981). A comparison of the effects of fantasy play tutoring and skills tutoring in nursery classes. *International Journal of Behavioral Development, 4,* 421–441.

Smith, P. K., and R. Vollstedt (1985). On defining play: An empirical study of the relationship between play and various play criteria. *Child Development, 56,* 1042–1050.

Spodek, B. (1974). The problem of play: Educational or recreational? In: D. Sponseller (Ed.), *Play as a learning medium* (pp. 7–27). Washington, DC: National Association for the Education of Young Children.

Sutton-Smith, B. (1985). Play research: State of the art. In: J. L. Frost & S. Sunderlin (Eds.), *When children play* (pp. 9–16). Wheaton, MD: Association for Childhood Education International.

Van Alstyne, D. (1932). *Play behavior and choice of play materials of preschool children.* Chicago: University of Chicago Press.

Vandenberg, B. (1982). Play: A concept in need of a definition? In: D. J. Pepler and K. H. Rubin (Eds.). *The play of children: Current theory and research* (pp. 15–20). Basel, Switzerland: Karger.

Vygotsky, L. S. (1976). Play and its role in the mental development of the child. In: J. S. Bruner, A. Jolly, and K. Sylva (Eds.), *Play: Its role in development and evolution* (pp. 537–554). New York: Basic Books.

Woodard, C. Y. (1984). Guidelines for facilitating sociodramatic play. *Childhood Education, 60,* 172–177.

Part II

Play's Role in
Early Literacy Development

3

Longitudinal Relations among Preschoolers' Symbolic Play, Metalinguistic Verbs, and Emergent Literacy*

A. D. Pellegrini and Lee Galda

This chapter addresses the ways in which specific dimensions of preschool children's symbolic play develops into specific dimensions of early literacy. The theoretical links between symbolic play and dimensions of language and literacy are explicit in the seminal theories of Vygotsky (1967, 1978) and Piaget (1962, 1970). Both of these theorists examined the role of symbolic play in preschool children's cognitive and linguistic development. In symbolic play, preschoolers develop the semiotic, or representational, function by practicing the representation of objects, roles, and events with signifiers. With age, preschool children's choice of signifiers becomes more abstract. By three to four years old, children are capable of ideational play transformations, or transformations which are not dependent upon props (McLoyd, 1980; Pellegrini, 1987). These structural theories posit that the representational competence gained through this form of play generalizes to other representational domains—language comprehension (Fein, 1979), language production (McCune-Nicolich, 1977), metalinguistic awareness (Cazden, 1974; Pellegrini, 1985a, 1985b), and emergent reading and writing (Galda, 1984; Galda, Pellegrini and Cox, 1989).

Vygotsky's theory specifically suggests that the representational competence gained in symbolic play becomes transformed into facility with a specific set of socially defined symbols—written words. Indeed, for Vygotsky, symbolic play is part of the continuum leading to the ability to write individual words. The symbolic competence of using arbitrary play signifiers is seen as similar to the use of written words. With both systems children are using abstract, but socially defined, signifiers to convey meaning. Further, Vygotsky's theory suggests that, in symbolic play, children begin to understand the representational process per se. They come to realize that language is used to execute abstract transformations. Without verbal explication of abstract transformations, play is typically not sustained between children (Pellegrini, 1982). As part of this meaning explication process, children come to reflect on the linguistic processes necessary to make these transformations. As such, metalinguistic awareness should develop in these situations where meaning is conveyed about symbolic play transformations. Cross-sectional (Pellegrini, 1985a) and short-term longitudinal work (Galda, Pellegrini, and Cox, 1989) has found that ideational transformations co-occur with the use of metalinguistic verbs for 3½-year-old children.

The use of metalinguistic verbs indicates that children are reflecting on the language they use (Olson, 1983). For example, in saying, "That's not a word. You can't write that," a child is both reflecting on what a word is and also using the lexicon through which literacy events are conducted. Literacy instruction, particularly reading lessons, are typified by metalinguistic terms such as *word, sentence, read* and *write* (Olson, 1983). As such, use of metalinguistic verbs should be related to children's comprehension of the lexicon of literacy events. The comprehension of the lexicon of literacy events, however, may be more accurately labeled 'metaliteracy' (Watson and Shapiro, 1988).

Use of metalinguistic verbs should also predict early reading status. This hypothesis is based on Olson's work with emergent literacy in school-age children. Olson (1983) suggests that, as children encounter print in schools, they are forced to explicate meaning linguistically. The use of metalinguistic verbs characterizes this process. We differ from Olson to the extent that we see metalinguistic awareness as developing in symbolic play before it appears in primary school literacy lessons. In symbolic play, as in later encounters with print, children must consciously reflect on the verbal explication of meaning. As such, the use of metalinguistic verbs should occur in symbolic play situations as part of the meaning explication process.

To summarize, we predict (following Vygotsky's theory) that the level of abstraction in symbolic play should predict preschoolers' emergent writing status. Furthermore, the metalinguistic verbs that characterize preschoolers' symbolic play should predict their subsequent knowledge of the lexicon of literacy events and their emergent reader status.

Despite these well-established theoretical arguments, there is a paucity of longitudinal data addressing the relationship between symbolic play and emergent literacy. The extant research tends to be cross-sectional, wherein correlations are calculated between measures of symbolic play and measures of literacy. Longitudinal studies are necessary if we are to understand the ways in which symbolic play *develops*, or transforms, into emergent literacy. That is, *development* should—indeed, can only be—studied longitudinally (McCall, 1977). Cross-sectional studies, though initially important, only address *age differences*, not development. The other benefit of longitudinal work, of course, is that the antecedent-consequent relations allow us to begin to make causal statements about the *effect* of symbolic play on literacy. These necessary (but insufficient) relationships constitute an important step in the study of the function of play at this time. In short, we have good theories and good correlational evidence for expected relations between symbolic play and literacy. It is now time to proceed with the important longitudinal work.

This chapter summarizes our longitudinal research work examining the ways in which two dimensions of symbolic play— abstract transformations and use of metalinguistic verbs—predicted emergent literacy. We will discuss two related longitudinal studies—a short study (with a three-month lag) and a longer one (with a one-year lag).

The Short-Term Longitudinal Study

In this study (Galda, Pellegrini, and Cox, 1989), we examined the extent to which symbolic play and use of metalinguistic verbs differentially predicted children's emergent literacy. The measures of literacy used were our adaptations of Sulzby's (1985a, 1985b) emergent writing and emergent reading measures and Clay's (1972) Concept of Print Test. Sulzby's system of emergent writing status was used because of its congruence with Vygotsky's (1967) theory. We should note, however, that—unlike Sulzby—we used this measure as a developmental continuum. Sulzby's emergent reading model was used because it is based on the notion that reading involves the processing of decontextualized, literate text. Furthermore, Clay's instrument measures children's knowledge of the language surrounding book reading—the words *word, sentence,* and *period,* for example. The first and second objectives of the study were to examine the predictive relationships between children's use of metalinguistic verbs and symbolic play and their emergent writing and reading status, respectively. The third objective was to examine the predictive relationship between metalinguistic verbs and performance on the Concepts of Print measure.

Method

Participants. The children in this study all attended a university preschool and were in three separate classrooms with a similar curriculum. Based on a median-split procedure, children were placed in two age groups for data analyses. The older group (n = 26) had a mean age of 55.00 months (SD = 3.75) and the younger group (n = 24) had a mean age of 43.56 months (SD = 3.83).

Procedure. The curriculum in the class we observed was such that children were given two free-play periods each day. During these free-play periods, teachers encouraged children to play in a variety of play centers in the classrooms. This policy of encouraging play in different areas minimized children's consistent self-selection into a limited number of play contexts (Pellegrini and Perlmutter, 1989). Thus, differences in children's play and language use due to self-selection into limited play areas were minimized. Furthermore, because the children were being observed in a number of different situations, we did not anticipate sex differences due to self-selection (Cole and LeVoie, 1985; Harper and Sanders, 1976; Mathews, 1978).

Observations of Play and Language. During the fall and winter terms, children's free play was audiotaped (with wireless microphones) for nine 15-minute sessions. Observational data for these quarter-hours were analyzed for this study. Observers noted children's actions and location during the observed play periods using running time behavioral recordings. Children's symbolic play transformations and metalinguistic verb use were derived from these free-play observations notes and audiorecordings.

Assessment Sessions. Children's IQ and literate behavior were also assessed. Children were given the Peabody Picture Vocabulary Test (Dunn and Dunn, 1981) at the midpoint of this study. Children's emergent literacy status, assessed during spring term, will be analyzed here. By emergent literacy, we mean the language and actions the children used when they encountered print in the reading and writing tasks.

The Writing Task. In this procedure, children were first shown three thematically related pictures for each of two sessions. They were asked to tell, dictate, and write a story about the pictures to an experimenter. The picture sequences came from A. Hines' books, *Maybe a Bandaid Will Help* and *Daddy Makes the Best Spaghetti.* The three pictures from the first book were of a child sewing a doll, the same child pricking her finger, and the child's mother putting on a Bandaid. The three pictures from the second were of a father picking up a child from school, grocery shopping, and cooking dinner.

The children were told to tell a story about the set of thematically related pictures. In the telling condition, they were told: "Tell me a story so that I can understand (the content of pictures)." For the dictation procedure, they were told: "Now let's try dictating. You tell the story to me, and I'll write down what you say." These sessions were audiotaped. The telling and dictation procedures served the purpose of maximizing children's writing task performance. That is, because these procedures preceded the writing task, children had a story in mind before writing; consequently, they should have had more cognitive resources to allocate to the writing processes (Shatz, 1983). We did not want the generation of a story to inhibit the children's production of written stories.

For the writing task, the children were told: "Try to write a story about these pictures. Write the same story you just told me. Show me how you can best write it down." After writing their stories, the children were asked to read them aloud: "Show me how you can read what you wrote." All sessions were audiotaped while the experimenter took notes on the children's gestures. Children's writing samples were coded according to an adaptation of Sulzby's (1985b) emergent writing system. The unit of analysis was the highest level children reached on this measure. Unlike Sulzby, we treat this measure as a hierarchy.

The Reading Task. In two separate sessions, children were observed reading two age-appropriate books after they were read the books by an experimenter. They were read and then asked to read F. Brandenberg's *Aunt Nina and Her Nieces and Nephews* and V. Jensen's *Sara and the Door.* Children's behavior in these sessions was categorized according to Sulzby's (1985a) model of emergent reading. The unit of analysis here was the highest level the children reached on the scale.

Measures

Symbolic Play. Children's symbolic play scores were derived from the audiotapes and the running behavior notes during the observational sessions. Individual fantasy utterances were coded as object or ideational transformations (McLoyd, 1980; Pellegrini, 1987). Object transformations included the sum of subcategories 1–4:

1. *Animation:* Giving inanimate objects living attributes. For example, a child feeding a make-believe dog says, "Now eat, puppy."
2. *Reification:* Reifying an imaginary object which is functionally related to an existing object. For example, a child pretending to drink from an empty cup says, "Umm, good."
3. *Attribute of object property:* An object property is attributed to an existent or imaginary object which is functionally related to a real object. For example, a child makes a motor sound ("Brummm") while pushing a toy truck.
4. *Substitution:* An existing object is given a new identity. For example, a child using a block to represent a truck says, " 'Like my truck?"

Ideational transformations were the sum of subcategories 5–8:

5. *Object realism:* Pretends an imaginary object exists. The imaginary object, however, bears no relation to the play object. For example, a child says, "I'm using this brush to cut the grass."
6. *Attribution of nonexistent object property:* A make-believe or substutue object is given a nonexistent object property. For example, a child pretending to take a nonexistent vitamin says, "This is my vitamin."
7. *Situation attribution:* Pretends that a make-believe situation exists. For example, a child says, "This can be the doctor's office."
8. *Role attribution:* Portrays a fantasy role. For example, a child says, "I'll be the daddy."

Children's scores were the frequencies of object and ideational transformations aggregated across the nine observations.

Metalinguistic verbs. The children's use of metalinguistic verbs generated during free play were coded along three dimensions.

1. *Idiomatic uses:* Metalinguistic verbs used idiomatically but not referring to linguistic process. For example, a child says, "You can *say* that again."

2. *Linguistic processes:* These verbs refer to interlocutors' actual uses of language. For example, a child says, "What did the doll *say?*"

3. *Contrastives:* Both idiomatic and linguistic process verbs were examined for their contrastive properties. Coders determined the extent to which children used verbs to note discrepancies between the different linguistic processes. For example, a child says, "But doctors *don't say* poo poo."

Writing. Children's writing was coded according to our adaptation of Sulzby's (1985b) scale. Children's mean scores (for two sessions) on the highest level reached on this scale from the spring writing sessions were analyzed. More specifically, children's individual writing samples were scored according to their highest level as measured by the writing scale. For example, if a child exhibited both drawing and scribbling in one writing session, a score of 2 (for scribbling) would be assigned. The measure has six levels:

1. *Drawing:* Children drew pictures of the story they were asked to write.
2. *Scribbling:* Children used curved lines which did not resemble words.
3. *Letter-like units:* Children made graphs that resembled letters but were not letters.
4. *Well-learned units:* Children used different letters to form different word combinations—e.g., AAA BBB JJJ.
5. *Invented spelling:* Children used invented spelling where they had a symbol for each phoneme/word.
6. *Conventional orthography:* Children used the conventional letter forms and spellings for individual words.

Again, Sulzby does not use these categories hierarchically, but we do.

Reading. Children's book reading was assessed according to Sulzby's (1985a) emergent reading model. The mean highest score from the two spring reading sessions was analyzed. Again, the highest level of performance exhibited was scored. For example, if a child exhibited strategy-dependent attempts and aspectual attempts in a single reading session, a score of 2 (for strategy-dependent reading) would be assigned. The 11-category system is:

A. *Attempts Governed by Pictures*

1. *Labeling:* The child merely labels (rather than describes) individual pictures.

2. *Action-governed attempts:* The child describes individual pictures without using past tense, temporal markers, and endophora.

3. *Disconnected oral dialogue:* The child does not use exclusively pictures to tell a story. One or many partial stories are given. The child uses past tense and temporal markers.

4. *Stories told for audience:* The child tells connected stories by pointing to or attending to the pictures, not the print. These stories are characterized by endophora and a temporal ordering of the different pictures into a story—that is, they use the pictures to form a cohesive story.

5. *Created story:* The child's story uses the same characters as are in the text but a different sequence of events.

6. *Similar to written text:* The child creates a story that resembles the original but is not a verbatim account.

7. *Verbatim-like attempts:* The child points to the pictures, not the print, and tells a memorized story.

B. *Attempts Governed by Print*

8. *Print-governed refusal:* The child refuses to try to read the print because he/she cannot read print.

9. *Aspectual attemtps:* The child focuses on one or more of the following aspects of reading at the expense of the whole:
   a. *Letter/sound* (trys to sound out words)
   b. *Known words* (reads only known words)
   c. *Comprehension* (tries to recite the text from memory)

10. *Strategy-dependent:* The child reads, but he/she over-emphasizes one or more strategies (for example, explicitly sounding out words). Children can use these strategies but they are not used to integrate words or used flexibly.

11. *Independent reading:* The child is actually reading print.

Concepts of Print Test. Clay's (1972) measure of children's knowledge of the lexicon of books and print was administered to children individually.

Results/Discussion

The first two objectives were to examine the predictive relationships between preschool children's symbolic play and their use of metalinguistic verbs and emergent literacy. The relationships tested in this study were predictive. That is, we analyzed language and play behaviors at Time 1 and literacy at Time 2. These relationships are necessary, but not sufficient, to make causal statements. Furthermore, in all analyses, children's IQ was used as a co-variate so that the variance due to IQ in the criterion measures was removed before measures of play or metalanguage were entered. This procedure allowed us to make predictive statements about our predictor variables per se—not intelligence, symbolic play, and metalanguage.

First, we will briefly discuss how our data analysis strategies fit into extant development theory. Our strategy involved analyzing separate predictive relations for each of two age groups. As developmentalists, we believe that the function of specific behaviors co-varies with age. More specifically, our speculation was that younger children's and older children's use of play transformations and metalinguistic verbs would differ. Developmental theory (e.g., Piaget, 1962) and recent empirical studies (reviewed in Pellegrini, 1985b) suggest that symbolic play may be a more effective learning/practice medium for younger children than for older children. In symbolic play, preoperational children learn and practice skills which are useful in later life. For example, young children's symbolic play is characterized by literate language (Pellegrini, 1986). A variant of this formal register is subsequently used in school-based literacy events. Data from the present study corroborate these findings. There were positive, significant relationships between younger children's symbolic play and their use of metalinguistic verbs, but no such relationships were found for older children. These data (see table 3.1) are consistent with

Short-term Data

Table 3.1

Correlation Coefficients Between Metalinguistic Verbs and Play by Age

	Process	Idiomatic	Contrast
Object			
Older	.28	.44*	.18
Younger Age	.79**	.72**	.47*
Ideation			
Older	.13	.003	.15
Younger	.82**	.71**	.58**

$n = 24$
*$p = < .05$
**$p = .01$

Vygotsky's (1967) theory in suggesting that, for younger children, the representational nature of symbolic play necessitated their use of metalanguage. They often used metalinguistic verbs to clarify players' roles (e.g., "Now you can say 'hooray.' "). Older children's use of metalinguistic verbs was not limited to symbolic play episodes, where they earlier may have learned how to use them. In short, correlations suggest that symbolic play is an important area in which children learn to use and practice matalinguistic verbs. With age, their use of these terms is expanded and generalized to other contexts. These results support Vygotsky's (1967) theory that symbolic play is the context in which children come to understand other representational media such as language. This finding further suggests that children's metalinguistic awareness develops before they encounter written texts in primary school.

More specific to our results for Objectives 1 and 2, we had very different regression models for older and younger children. Only IQ predicted younger children's writing. Older children's symbolic play and idiomatic verbs (a negative predictor), in addition to IQ, predicted writing. This finding is consistent with Vygotsky's (1978) theory of first-order symbolism. That is, at one point in their development as writers, young children's early writing consists of marks which are "written symbols which denote objects, people, or actions rather than words" (Dyson, 1983, p. 20). Early writing, like symbolic trans-formations, has signifiers. For example, the written word *ball* represents the object, not the oral word. One child, pointing to his letter-like forms, explained: "This is the Daddy. This is the boy. And this is the spaghetti."

Short-term Data

Table 3.2

Significant* Predictors of Children's Highest Level of Writing Status by Age

Variable	Step Entered	df	B-value	R²	F
Older					
IQ	Forced 1	1,14	.03	.26	4.65
Play Objects Trans	2	2,14	.08	.43	3.47
Idiomatic Meta-Verbs	3	3,14	-.65	.55	4.56
Younger					
IQ	Forced 1	1,14	.13	.25	3.99

*$p = < .05$

Although this relationship between symbolic play and writing is consistent with Vygotsky's theory of early writing, we would have expected to observe it in younger rather than older children. That our results for the older children support Dyson's (1983) results with kindergartners, does, however, suggest that early writing may be a first-order symbolization process.

In the second objective, we tried to predict children's emergent reading status. (See Table 3.3.) We found that symbolic play was not a significant predictor. Older children's use of metalinguistic process verbs was a positive predictor, and younger children's use of idiomatic verbs was a negative predictor. These findings have a number of important implications. First, children's use of metalinguistic verbs fits nicely into the extant early reading literature, which suggests that facility with metalinguistic terms (e.g., knowledge and facility with letter names) is associated with young children's reading (Walsh, Price, and Gillingham, 1988). Second, the different B-values for process and idiomatic verbs is an important methodological finding to the extent that researchers should, in the future, differentiate between those two types of verbs. Indeed, it may clarify some of the inconsistent findings between metalanguage and literacy in the literature (e.g., Watson and Shapiro, 1988).

Short-term Data

Table 3.3

Significant* Predictors of Children's Highest Level of Reading Status by Age

Variable	Step Entered	df	B-value	R^2	F
Older					
IQ	Forced 1	1,14	.006	.009	.12
Process Meta-Verbs	2	2,14	.07	.19	2.69
Younger					
IQ	Forced 1	1,13	.0005	.01	.00
Idiomatic Meta-Verbs	2	2,14	– 1.07	.44	8.77

*p = < .05

A third important finding in the Objective 2 analyses concerns children's use of metalinguistic verbs. These verbs indicate children's reflection on linguistic processes. Older children seem more able to do this than younger children. Indeed, there was a significant age difference between the older and younger groups for the proportional use of metalinguistic verbs (M = .76 and M = .38, respectively). These results, like those of Shatz and colleagues (1983) and our previous work (Pellegrini, 1986), suggest that children have conscious awareness of a specific cognitive process—language—at an earlier age than previously described in the literature. Thus, metalinguistic awareness seems to develop in contexts, other than writing, that require children to lexicalize meaning, such as symbolic play. Play seems to be an arena in which children exhibit high levels of competence (Galda, 1984). That metalinguistic verbs co-occurred with fantasy transformations for younger children supports this claim.

A fourth important implication for the Objective 2 results relates to the paucity of significant play predictors. This result may be due to the emergent reading measure used: It is a measure of children's facility with decontextualized text. Had we used Sulzby's (1988) revised reading model, our results may have been different. As Olson (1983) and others (e.g., Goelman and Pence, 1988; Reeder, Wakefield, and Shapiro, 1988) noted, this facility is related to metalinguistic awareness and develops during the school years. Thus, the emergent reading measure seems to tap older children's metalinguistic awareness; the emergent writing measure (as we use it) seems to tap representational competence.

A comparison of the reading and writing measures is interesting in its own regard. When IQ was controlled, the measures were not significantly intercorrelated for either the younger (r = .12, p < .60) or older (r = .10, p < .62) groups. Contrary to the structural theories of the development of representational competence (e.g., Piaget 1970), these data suggest that literacy is not a unitary construct.

To conclude the discussion of the data from Objectives 1 and 2, we have found interesting relationships between measures of play, language, literacy, and age. The predictive relationship between measures of play and language and literacy should, however, be interpreted very cautiously to the extent that a small (though significant) amount of the variance in the criterion measures was explained. Thus, we should not be overly optimistic about the contribution of play to early literacy. It seems to play a role, but a very limited role.

Objective 3 results present a different picture from the Objectives 1 and 2 results to the extent that our model (see Table 3.4) accounted for 88 percent of the variance in the Concepts of Print instrument. As previously noted, this instrument measures children's knowledge of the language of book reading. Our predictor variables were metalinguistic verbs. As with Objective 1 and 2 results, process verbs were positive predictors and idiomatic verbs were negative predictors.

Short-term Data

Table 3.4

Significant* Predictors of Concepts of Print for Older Children

Variable	Step Entered	df	B-value	R^2	F
IQ	Forced 1	1,12	.05	.50	10.82
Idiomatic Meta-Verbs	2	2,12	-.92	.65	4.29
Process Meta-Verbs	3	3,12	.04	.88	15.29

*p = < .05

This model held only for older children. In short, and not surprisingly, older children's use of process verbs is an excellent predictor of their knowledge of the language of book reading; in both cases, meta-language was being assessed. These results suggest that, as teachers and researchers, we can make accurate predictions about school-related competence by observing children's discourse during free play. Preschool children seem to exhibit high levels of competence in this context (Galda, 1984; Vygotsky, 1967).

The Objective 3 results are also instructive for future research. As noted, we need better models of early literacy to the extent that the present models do not predict most of the variance in our criterion measures. Sulzby's (1988) recent efforts are notable in this regard. Results from Objective 3 suggest that criterion measures should be 'near transfers' to our predictors. That is, our measures should be conceptually close. Examinations of specific aspects of literacy (both in terms of predictors and criterion measures) should provide further needed insight into the multidimensional nature of literacy.

The Long-Term Longitudinal Study

In Study 2, we examined the relationships among the same variables but with a longer longitudinal lag. The results from this study should provide information on the replicability of the results from the short-term study. The children who took part in this phase of the study had also participated in the first study. There were twelve children (seven boys and five girls) whose mean age was 42.75 months at the beginning of the year and 63.75 months at the end of the study. The measures of play, metalinguistic verbs, and early literacy were the same as in the short-term study. In year two, as in year one, children's free play was observed nine times during the first two quarters of the second year.

Results/Discussion

Each of the results from the short-term study was replicated in the long-term study. First, metalinguistic process and process-contrast verbs predicted Concepts of Print. The three types of metalinguistic verbs (see Table 3.5) tended to co-occur within each of the two years of study. However, only the process and process-contrast verbs seemed to indicate metalinguistic awareness. (See Table 3.6.) Future research should examine the predictive relationships between use of metalinguistic verbs and other domains of metalinguistic awareness such as phonological, semantic, syntactic, and pragmatic awareness. That is, what exactly are the domains of metalinguistic awareness that are tapped by the use of metalinguistic verbs? Or it may be that the use of metalinguistic verbs is a reflection of children's perspective-taking status to the extent that, by using such verbs, children are reflecting on the making of meaning (Flavell, Green, and Flavell, 1989).

Second, play transformations predicted writing status. Thus, both symbolic play and single-word writing are similar representational activities. These results are also displayed in Table 3.6. This relationship, however, would probably change with different measures of writing. For example, measuring writing as the ability to verbally explicate meaning probably requires other, more metalinguistic skills. Following Olson (1983), writing processes which require meaning to be conveyed at the text level (not the individual word level, as in the present studies) probably require and facilitate the reflection on the meaning explication process. Thus, our results are developmentally complementary to Olson's. We have found that early writing is initially a representational act, and competence for this has some roots in make-believe play. Later, school-based writing is potentially more linguistic to the extent that language is used to convey meaning. Reading, too, is more of a linguistic phenomenon than a representational one. In reading, children must decode language to construct meaning. As such, use of metalinguistic verbs, not measures of play, are important predictors.

Third, process and process-contrast verbs predicted emergent reading status. These results (see Table 3.6) suggest that early reading is related to children's ability to explicate meaning linguistically in the form of metalinguistic verbs. These findings are consistent with the short-term study and Olson's theory suggesting that reading involves the processing of decontextualized text—that is, text in which meaning is lexically, not contextually, explicated. Unlike Olson, however, we suggest that there are contexts other than encounters with the written

Table 3.5

Significant Coefficients Between Metalinguistic Verbs and
Fantasy Transformations by Year

	Within Year 1				Within Year 2		Year 1 to 2				
	1	2	3	4	1	2	1	2	3	4	5
Metaling: Idiom (1)	.54*						.50*				
Metaling: Process (2)		.68**									
Metaling: Contrast (3)					.50*	.77**			.55*		
Object (4)	.91***	.63**			.80***					.84***	
Idea (5)	.94***	.62**		.95***	.90***					.83***	

N = 12
* p = < .10
** p = < .05
***p = < .01

Longitudinal Early Literacy

Table 3.6

Partial[a] Correlations For Play Transformations and
Metalinguistic Verbs Predicting Literacy

	Year 2: Concepts of Print	High Reading	High Writing
Year I			
Metalingusitic: Idiomatic	.45	.23	-.20
Metalinguistic: Process	.67**	.61**	.62**
Metalinguistic: Contrast	.51*	.65**	.51*
Transformations			
Object	.45**	.39	.63**
Ideational	.44*	.38	.62**

$N = 12$
[a]Partialled-out of the relations are children's PPVT scores and Year 1 levels
of criterion measures noted for Year 2.
*$p = <.10$
**$p = .05$

word which facilitate this explication. One such context for 3½-year
olds seems to be symbolic play. By 4½-years (in both the long- and
short-term studies), children's use of these verbs did not co-occur with
fantasy; it occurred in other, more realistic, peer discourse contexts.
It may be that children learn to practice using metalinguistic verbs in
fantasy peer discourse and then, with development, generalize their
use of metalinguistic verbs to more realistic peer discourse and literacy
contexts. Symbolic play, then, seems to serve specific functions at
specific periods. To generalize these effects to other periods of
development is inappropriate.

Finally, we again found (in both studies) that measures of
emergent writing and reading were not interrelated when IQ was
controlled. There are a number of possible explanations. First, the
theory of multiple intelligences (Malkus, Feldman, and Gardner, 1988)
states that there are multiple forms of literacy (Wolf, et al., 1988); thus,
it should not be surprising that these two forms are independent.

The second explanation is a transitional knowledge theory, which
is related to the first- and second-order symbolism issues discussed
earlier. It may be that, at specific periods, reading and writing are not
related, even though the two processes are later interrelated. The extant
research suggests that reading and writing are independent throughout
the preschool period (the present study; Galda, et al., 1989) and

through kindergarten and first grade (Kamberlis and Sulzby, 1987). Longitudinal research across the primary grade years will provide insight into this issue. It may be that writing and reading are interrelated only when our measures of writing assess children's ability to produce meaning textually, rather than with individual words. Text-level writing and reading may both be related to the extent that they require explication and comprehension, respectively, of text-based meaning.

The third explanation, of course, is that the measures of literacy do not measure what they purport to measure. The strong theoretical bases for these models is an obvious, and necessary, first step in this type of research. Now we need to know the degree to which these measures are related, contemporaneously and longitudinally, to other measures of writing and reading. In short, we need concurrent, construct, and predictive validity data to rule out the last explanation for the nonrelationship between writing and reading.

Fourth, it may be that we used the writing measure inappropriately—i.e., as a scale—and this resulted in the low correlation. Clearly, more research on the hierarchic properties of this measure is needed. Scalogram analyses appear promising in this regard.

In conclusion, a word of caution is in order. Except for the relationship between metalanguage and Concepts of Print, the relations presented here were of low, though statistically significant, magnitude. As such, the problem of equifinality exists in this work, as in most studies positing a functional role for play (Martin and Caro, 1985; Smith, in press). The problem of equifinality suggests that there are alternate routes—that is, routes other than via play—to competence in certain areas, including literacy. That children spend relatively little time and expend relative little energy in play suggests that the benefits may be minimal. (For an extended discussion of this issue, see: Martin and Caro, 1985.) Educators and developmental psychologists have willingly participated in the 'play ethos'—i.e., proclaiming that play is all good to all children (Smith, 1988)—despite definitional problems with play and equivocal findings. Although play appears to be one route to literacy, it seems time to chart alternate routes that children may be taking.

What Next?

Like most research, this project has raised many new questions. We will address two interrelated questions here, both of which relate to metalinguistic verbs.

The first question is, Where do metalinguistic verbs come from? We found that children use them, first in symbolic play and then later, in diverse peer discourse. Following Vygotsky, we can posit that children may be exposed to this class of verbs "interpsychologically" while interacting with a more competent other. For example, when mothers and their preschool children interact around storybooks, mothers use metalinguistic verbs (Pellegrini, et al., 1990; Watson and Shapiro, 1988). It may be that children then 'take' these verbs into a play context and use them in various ways in order to master them. This phase of use is akin to Vygotsky's phase of thought wherein children's overt language reflects previous social interaction with a more competent tutor. Later in development, this metalinguistic awareness goes underground (becomes intrapsychological) and becomes part of the children's cognitive make-up.

The next question, also related to metalinguistic verbs, is: What is the psychological mechanism responsible for the predictive power of metalinguistic verbs? Like other 'metas,' it probably involves a degree of perspective-taking (Flavell, et al., 1989). That is, children must first realize that external phenomena and their corresponding mental representations are different. This, in turn, involves the ability to understand that phenomena are perceived differently by others. In make-believe play, children seem to develop these perspective-taking abilities (Burns and Brainerd, 1979). It may be that the process of communicating an abstract transformation to a peer facilitates this process.

Note

* A version of this chapter was presented to the University of British Columbia's Literacy Research Group. The authors acknowledge the comments of that group: V. Froese, H. Goelman, K. Reeder, J. Shapiro, and R. Watson. This work was partially funded by a grant from the National Council for Research in English.

References

Burns, S., and C. Brainerd (1979). Effects of constructive and dramatic play as perspective taking in very young children. *Developmental Psychology, 15*, 512–521.

Cazden, C. (1974). Play with language and metalinguistic awareness: One dimension of language experience. *Urban Review, 1*, 23–39.

Clay, M. (1972). *Concepts of print.* Auckland, New Zealand: Heinemann Educational Books.

Cole, D., and J. LeVoie (1985). Fantasy play and related cognitive development in 2- to 6-year-olds. *Developmental Psychology, 21,* 233–240.

Dunn, L., and L. Dunn (1981). *Peabody Picture Vocabulary Test: Revised.* Circle Pines, MN: American Guidance Services, Inc.

Dyson, A. (1983). The role of oral language in early writing processes. *Research in the Teaching of English, 17,* 1–30.

Fein, G. (1979). Play and the acquisition of symbols. In: L. Katz (Ed.), *Current topics in early childhood education.* (pp. 195–225). Norwood, NJ: Ablex Publishing Corporation.

Flavell, J., F. Green, and E. Flavell (1989). Young children's ability to differentiate appearance-reality and Level 2 perspectives in the tactile modality. *Child Development, 60,* 201–213.

Galda, L. (1984). Narrative competence: Play, storytelling and story comprehension. In: A. Pellegrini and T. Yawkey (Eds.), *The development of oral and written language in social context* (pp. 105–119). Norwood, NJ: Ablex Publishing Corporation.

Galda, L., A. D. Pellegrini, and S. Cox (1989). Preschoolers' emergent literacy: A short term longitudinal study. *Research in the Teaching of English, 23,* 292–310.

Goelman, H. and A. Pence (1987). Some aspects of the relationship between family structure and child language development in three types of care. In: D. Peters and S. Kontos (Eds.), *Annual advances in applied developmental psychology, Vol. II: Continuity and discontinuity of experience in child care.* Norwood, NJ: Ablex Publishing Corporation.

Harper, L., and K. Sanders (1975). Preschool children's use of space: Sex differences in outdoor play. *Developmental Psychology, 11,* 119.

Kamberelis, G., and E. Sulzby (1987). *Transitional knowledge in emergent literacy.* Paper presented at the National Reading Conference, St. Petersburg, FL (December).

Malkus, U., D. Feldman, and H. Gardner (1988). Dimensions of mind in early childhood. In: A. D. Pellegrini (Ed.), *Psychological bases of early education.* (pp. 25–38). Chichester, U.K.: Wiley.

Martin, P., and T. Caro (1985). On the functions of play and its role in behavioral development. In: J. Rosenblatt, et al. (Eds.), *Advances in the study of behavior, Vol. 15* (pp. 59–103). New York: Academic Press.

Mathews, W. (1978). Sex and familiarity effects upon the proportion of time young children spend in spontaneous-fantasy play. *Journal of Genetic Psychology, 133,* 9–12.

McCall, R. B. (1977). Challenges to a science of developmental psychology. *Child Development, 48,* 333–344.

McCune-Nicolich, L. (1981). Towards symbolic functioning: Structure of early pretend games and potential parallels with language. *Child Development, 52,* 785–797.

McLoyd, V. (1980). Verbally expressed modes of transformation in the fantasy and play of Black preschool children. *Child Development, 51,* 1133–1139.

Olson, D. (1983). "See! Jumping!" Some oral language antecedents of literacy. In: H. Goelman, A. Oberg, and F. Smith (Eds.), *Awakening to literacy* (pp. 185–192). Exeter, NH: Heinemann Educational Books.

Pellegrini, A. D. (1982). Explorations in preschoolers' construction of cohesive text in two play contexts. *Discourse Processes, 5,* 101–108.

———— (1985a). Relations between symbolic play and literate behavior. In: L. Galda and A. Pellegrini (Eds.), *Play, language and story: The development of children's literate behavior* (pp. 79–97). Norwood, NJ: Ablex Publishing Corporation.

———— (1985b). The relations between symbolic play and literate behavior: A review and critique of the empirical literature. *Review of Educational Research, 55,* 207–221.

———— (1986). Play centers and the production of imaginative language. *Discourse Processes, 9,* 115–125.

———— (1987). The effects of play contexts on the development of children's verbalized fantasy. *Semiotica, 65,* 285–293.

Pellegrini, A. D., and J. Perlmutter (1989). Classroom contextual effects on children's play. *Developmental Psychology, 25,* 289–296.

Pellegrini, A. D., et al. (1990). Joint book reading between Black Head Start children and their mothers. *Child Development, 61,* 443–453.

Piaget. J. (1962). *Play, dreams, and imitations.* New York: Norton.

———— (1970). *Structuralism.* New York: Basic Books.

Reeder, K., J. Wakefield, and J. Shapiro (1988). Children's speech act comprehension strategies and early literacy experiences. *First Language, 8,* 29–48.

Shatz, M. (1983). Communication. In: J. Flavell and E. Markman (Eds.), *Handbook of child psychology: Cognitive development* (pp. 841–890). New York: Wiley.

Shatz, M., H. Wellman, and S. Silber (1983). The acquisition of mental verbs: A systematic investigation of the first reference to mental state. *Cognition, 14,* 301–231.

Smith, P. K. (1988). Children's play and its role in early development: A re-evaluation of the "play ethos." In: A. D. Pellegrini (Ed.), *Psychological bases for early education* (pp. 207–226). Chichester, U.K.: Wiley.

————— (In press). The role of rough-and-tumble play in the development of social competence: Theoretical perspectives and empirical evidence. In: B. Schneider (Ed.), *Social competence in developmental perspective.*

Sulzby, E. (1985a). Children's emergent reading of favorite storybooks: A developmental study. *Reading Research Quarterly, 20,* 458–481.

————— (1985b). Kindergartners as writers and readers. In: M. Farr (Ed.), *Advances in early writing research, Vol. 1: Children's early writing development.* Norwood, NJ: Ablex Publishing Corporation.

————— (1988). A study of children's early reading development. In: A. Pellegrini (Ed.), *Psychological bases of early education* (pp. 39–75). Chichester, U.K.: Wiley.

Torrance, D., and D. Olson (1984). Oral language and the acquisition of literacy. In: A. D. Pellegrini and T. D. Yawkey (Eds.), *The development of oral and written language in social context* (pp. 167–182). Norwood, NJ: Ablex Publishing Corporation.

Vygotsky, L. (1967). Play and its role in the mental development of the child. *Soviet Psychology, 12,* 62–76.

————— (1978). *Mind in society.* Cambridge: Harvard University Press.

Walsh, D., G. Price, and M. Gillingham (1988). The critical but transitory importance of letter naming. *Reading Research Quarterly, 23,* 108–122.

Watson, R., and J. Shapiro (1988). Discourse from home to school. *Applied Psychology: An International Review, 37,* 395–409.

Wolf, D., et al. (1988). Beyond A, B, and C: A broader and deeper view of literacy. In: A. Pellegrini (Ed.), *Psychological bases of early education* (pp. 122–151). Chichester, U.K.: Wiley.

4

Thematic-Fantasy Play
and Story Comprehension

Peter A. Williamson
and Steven B. Silvern

Sara Smilansky (1968) conducted the seminal empirical study of the effects of play training on low-socioeconomic status (SES) Israeli children. Her study was grounded on the observation that these children were less able to engage in appropriate pretend play than middle-class children. Smilansky trained the children in sociodramatic play, during which they re-enacted situations drawn from real life experiences such as visits to a medical clinic or grocery store. The children in this study were explicitly "taught how to engage in and sustain sociodramatic play" (Smilansky, 1968, p. 100). Adults engaged in two types of intervention during the play episodes. One was 'inside' intervention, which consisted of the adult actually assuming a role in the play. This allowed for modeling and demonstrating appropriate behaviors. In 'outside' intervention, the adult did not assume a role but addressed the children within the frame of reference of the make-believe theme. From this vantage point, the adult made suggestions, gave directions, clarified behavior, and asked questions. It is important to note that, although the adult's role in both types of intervention was quite intrusive, the sociodramatic play episodes were spontaneous. That is, children were free to come to the play area when they chose, no standardized story line was scripted, and the adult was free to vary the type of intervention from moment to moment. Results of this study suggested that sociodramtic play training improves both the quality and amount of low-SES children's play.

As a result of the positive findings of Smilansky's study a virtual avalanche of studies ensued which examined the effects of play on creativity (Dansky, 1980; Dansky and Silverman, 1973, 1975; Feitelson and Ross, 1973; Johnson, 1976; Singer and Rummo, 1973; Smith and Syddall, 1978); language development (Collier, 1979; Lovinger, 1974; Pellegrini, 1984; Pellegrini and Galda, 1982; Silvern, 1980; Silvern, Taylor, et al., 1986; Silvern, Williamson, and Waters, 1983; Smith and Syddal, 1978); logical skills (Fink, 1976; Golomb and Cornelius, 1977; Guthrie and Hudson, 1979, Saltz, Dixon, and Johnson, 1977; Saltz and Johnson, 1974); problem solving (Simon and Smith, 1983; Smith and Dutton, 1979; Vandenberg, 1981); and social knowledge (Burns and Brainerd, 1979; Connolly, Doyle, and Reznik, 1983; Fink, 1976; Iannotti, 1978; Rosen, 1974; Rubin and Maioni, 1975; Saltz, Dixon and Johnson, 1977; Saltz and Johnson, 1974; Taylor and Asher, 1984).

This body of research is anything but unified; it encompasses observational as well as experimental research. The operational definitions for play range from Parten's (1932) classifications to Smilansky's (1968) sociodramatic categories, from thematic-fantasy play (Saltz and Johnson, 1974) to make-believe (Dansky, 1980). Drawing upon the conclusion that fantasy play is most facilitative for cognitive outcome measures, especially comprehension (Saltz et al., 1977), recent researchers have focused on the thematic-fantasy paradigm as the most appropriate vehicle for examining the effects of play on story comprehension. It is important to note that there are several differences between the thematic-fantasy paradigm and Smilansky's sociodramatic design. Whereas Smilansky's sociodramatic training was informal, thematic-fantasy training is very tightly structured. Typically, children are grouped in teams of four (two boys and two girls) and read a fantasy story, often a fairy tale such as "Goldilocks and the Three Bears," which has four characters. After the story is read, the researcher leads a discussion to elicit the characters and events in the story. Finally, the children assume the roles of the characters and re-enact the story. Typically, children are pre-tested on certain aspects of story comprehension, they undergo a series of play or control experiences, and then they are post-tested.

The rationale for using structured thematic-fantasy stories rests on two assumptions about comprehension—mental reconstruction and the development of story schemes. Mental reconstruction is thought to occur as children physically re-enact stories they have heard. That is, in order to accurately act out a story, children must be able to re-create the characters and events, and this should lead to increased understanding (Pellegrini and Galda, 1982). Additionally, as children re-enact several stories, it is assumed that they develop schemes for stories, such as (a) that all stories have characters, (b) that all stories have a beginning and an ending, and (c) that things happen in predictable ways. Developed over time, these schemes enable children to increasingly understand the broader concept of story and lead to comprehension of stories more generally (Silvern, et al., 1986).

As indicated by Christie (1987), studies that examined the effects of play training on story comprehension have increasingly employed the thematic-fantasy paradigm. Research by Saltz and Johnson (1974), Pellegrini and Galda (1982), and Silvern, Williamson, and Waters (1983) documented the positive effects of this type of training on story comprehension. It should be noted that these three studies included a very directive role for the adult, a component of play training research which had not been questioned to that time. Smith and Sydall (1978), however, argued that this entire line of research might be confounded by an intrusive adult role. They contended that adult tuition rather than play could well be the variable that accounts for positive outcome measures. In response to this concern, Pellegrini (1984) designed a study that attempted to address this issue by including both adult-directed and peer-directed play groups, and he found positive effects for each. Christie (1987) critiqued the play training literature more broadly and raised several crucial issues which, at that time, had not been exhaustively addressed—(a) adult intervention, (b) familiar versus unfamiliar stories, (c) age of subjects, and (d) context of the play situation. This chapter reviews three studies carried out by the authors during the past few years which address these issues raised by Christie and the additional question of whether or not thematic-fantasy training facilitates comprehension of stories not acted out.

The first study, which consisted of two experiments, addressed the issues of adult intervention, comprehension of stories not acted, children's ages, and familiar and unfamiliar stories within the thematic-fantasy play paradigm. The second study is more narrowly focused and is a re-analysis of the first study. It was constructed to more closely examine the issue of age. The third study is an exploratory investigation of the components of thematic-fantasy play episodes to determine exactly what accounts for the facilitation of aural story comprehension.

Study 1
Silvern, Taylor, Williamson, Surbeck, and Kelley (1986)

In their definitions of play, Neumann (1971) and Garvey (1977) noted that play is a voluntary activity. Using this conceptualization,

Sutton-Smith (1883a, 1983b) and Christie and Johnsen (1983) have criticized empirical studies which have directed children to play. They argue that, when researchers direct children to play, they are removing the voluntary nature of play and the resulting behavior, therefore, cannot be considered play per se. But the question *must* be asked: What aspect of playing is necessarily voluntary? If telling children that they can or must play removes the voluntary nature of play, then children who are playing because their parents told them to are not really playing. This, of course, is the absurd extension of the criticism that children playing in empirical studies are not really playing. The position taken here is that the voluntary nature of play can come about—not in choosing whether or not to play, nor in selecting what to play— but in the choice of how to manipulate the play situation. Children are playing if they are the manipulators of play—that is, if they are free to choose the materials with which and the manner in which they will play.

Although significant effects have been found for story memory and storytelling (Saltz and Johnson, 1974), story interpretation among intellectually more mature preschool children (Saltz, Dixon, and Johnson, 1977), and story recall (Pellegrini and Galda, 1982), it is difficult to determine if the effects were due to play or to the tutoring that went along with the thematic-fantasy play situation (Smith, 1977; Smith and Syddal, 1978). In each of these studies, the experimenter acted as leader of the play situation by assigning children roles to play, initiating the play activity, and helping the children sustain the play situation. The research reports do not indicate if the experimenter made sure that all parts of the story were played, but with the heavy involvement of the experimenter, it seems clear that the children were not always the primary manipulators of the material and manner of their play.

The first purpose of Experiment 1 was to examine the effects of thematic-fantasy play when the experimenter served a less directive role and the children chose their respective roles and designed the play experience. The role of the experimenter in the study was to read the children a story and help them should they request it, but to otherwise be unobtrusive in the play situation.

From a Piagetian perspective, symbolic play and imitation both serve important functions in the child's construction of representational thought (Piaget, 1962). Symbolic play is viewed as a form of mental assimilation where thought is constructed through the free application of external reality to the ego. Thus, symbolic play is highly personalized and individual. Imitation, on the other hand, is viewed as a form of mental accommodation where thought is constructed through adjusting to reality. Internal representations, then, are viewed as imitations or copies of external models. Working in concert, both symbolic play and imitation contribute to the child's cognitive development and ability to use and understand language.

Thematic-fantasy play seems to incorporate elements of both play and imitation in that it allows for symbolic play through the use of make-believe, and at the same time it involves imitation through role enactment of familiar models—e.g., Mother Bear cooking porridge. Piaget (1962) suggests that this type of activity becomes adapted representation, a special case of creative play which is part symbolic and part constructive activity.

Pellegrini and Galda (1982), examining only immediate story reconstruction, did not consider the cognitive constructive characteristics of thematic-fantasy play. If thematic-fantasy play is a constructive activity, then children are learning more than the details of a particular story when they engage in such play. As a constructive activity, children could be developing metalinguistic knowledge about stories. Thus, play experiences should allow children to perform better on story recall in general, rather than simply on a story with which they have had direct play experience. Accordingly, the second purpose of Experiment 1 was to examine the effects of thematic-fantasy play on children's recall of a story they have not acted out. It was expected that children who received a thematic-fantasy play treatment would have better recall of a story that had not been acted out than would the control children.

The third purpose of Experiment 1 was to investigate whether the effectiveness of thematic-fantasy play varies with age. Piagetian theory suggests that younger children, whose thinking is still preoperational in nature, need direct active experience with phenomena in order to construct schemes for dealing with such phenomena. Older children, whose thinking is more operational in nature, are better able to relate new phenomena to schemes already present in their schematic repertoire. Because thematic-fantasy play allows for direct active experience with stories, it may provide opportunities for younger children to construct schemes about stories in general. Given that schemes are related to experience and indirectly to age, these metalinguistic story schemes may already be present to some degree in older children. Therefore, it was hypothesized that if thematic-fantasy play is a constructive activity, there would be an interaction between the story treatments and age. It was predicted that the younger children in the thematic-fantasy play group would recall more of the post-test story than would the younger children in the control group and that older children's recall of the post-test story would not differ significantly across the two treatment conditions.

Experiment 1

Method

Subjects. The subjects were 505 children, whose ages ranged from 5 to 9 years, with a mean age of 6.5 years. There were 257 subjects in the treatment classes and 248 in the control classes; 266 subjects were male, and 239 female. The economic status of the subjects ranged from low- to middle-income brackets.

Experimenters. Thirteen female primary grade teachers within a 70-mile radius of Auburn, Alabama served as the experimenters. Each teacher used her class and one other class of the same grade level at the same school for the treatment and control classes.

Materials and procedures. Two forms of a story recall test were developed to assess recall ability before and after treatment. Each included a simple story consisting of 12 propositions (see: Stein, 1978) and ten multiple choice questions, one for each of the first ten propositions in the story. The two tests were similar in that the structure of the story and questions remained intact, but the content was altered.

Story recall pre-tests were administered on the first week of the experiment, and post-tests were administered on the eighth week. No thematic-fantasy play was associated with either the pre- or post-test. The subjects in both the treatment and control groups simply listened to the stimulus story and then immediately responded to the test questions.

Stories selected by the investigators for story reading during the implementation phase were reviewed by the teachers to ensure that the stories would be understandable and interesting at all grade levels. Stories were selected that would provide an opportunity for a large number of subjects to be involved in the reenactment. Unfamiliar stories were selected so that the children's actions would be based on conscious attention to the story rather than on past experience with it. The stories were typed onto 8½ " × 11" pages with no illustrations.

Treatment and control conditions were conducted during a 30-minute period after the subjects' lunch period. To limit adult intervention so that the effects of play could be tested, no formal teacher-directed discussion followed the story reading for either the treatment or control group. There was informal discussion between participants in the play group, but it centered on selecting roles and props and not on the recall of the story line. These discussions may be viewed as the metacognitive remarks associated with the act of playing identified by Piaget (1962) as the mechanism in play associated with adaptive representation.

Thematic-fantasy play is described first. Because the public school had large numbers of children enrolled in the classes, each treatment class was arbitrarily divided in half. Every week, each group (one half of the class) listened to one story read by the teacher, selected roles and props, and then acted the story out while the remainder of the class observed. The same story was read to both groups on alternating days, so that both groups were exposed to each story twice—once through thematic-fantasy play, and once through observing the play of the other group. The mode of first exposure to each new story—listening or observing—was random throughout each session. The same procedures were followed throughout. The teachers were instructed to be facilitative but nondirective. Their primary role was to prompt, "What happened next?"

Classes serving as control groups listened to each story twice on alternating days to ensure exposure to the content equal to that of the treatment group. After completing each story, control classes engaged in regular classroom activities for the remainder of the 30-minute period. Teachers were instructed to be enthusiastic in their reading, with their primary role being to share an interesting story.

Results

Data were analyzed using a multiple regression analysis of variance. Results indicated that story recall increased with age, and children in the play treatment condition (M = 7.65, SD = 2.27) performed significantly better (F, [4,500] = 81.79, p < .001) on story recall than did children in the control condition (M = 7.18, SD = 2.70). A significant interaction suggested differential effects of the play treatment for differing age groups, and subsequent analysis examined the nature of that interaction. Regression equations were used to predict story recall at six-month age intervals, and contrasts between treatment groups were calculated at each age level. Significant contrasts were found for age groups through 80 months, indicating a 95% probability that children up to the age of 6.7 years benefit from the play treatment. For the remainder of the population sampled, there was no significant difference between treatments.

Children exposed to thematic-fantasy play performed better on an unfamiliar story recall task that was not acted out than did those in control classes. This finding supports the notion that thematic-fantasy play is a constructive activity as described by Piaget (1962). Piagetian theory is further supported by the disordinal interaction which indicates that younger children benefit more from the treatment than do older children. There was no significant difference between older children in treatment and control conditions, but there was between younger children.

Experiment 2

In Experiment 1, there were problems with the conceptualization of play as voluntary. Although experimenters were instructed to be unobtrusive in the thematic-fantasy play, logs kept by the experimenters indicated that attempts were made to make sure that all parts of the stories were acted out by the children. This type of intervention negates the voluntary aspect of play. Active intervention by the experimenters made it impossible to determine if the effects were due to play or adult intervention. Experiment 2 was carried out to control for the amount of adult intervention. Experimenters were divided into directive and facilitative groups. Directive experimenters were told to make sure that the children acted out the story faithfully. Facilitative experimenters were trained in techniques to encourage the children to control their environment and not rely on the presence of an adult. If, as Smith (1977) suggests, amount of tutoring is the cause of treatment effects, then children in the directive condition should perform better on a story recall task than children in the facilitative condition.

We were also concerned that previous studies had used familiar stories, whereas Experiment 1 had used stories judged to be unfamiliar to the children. To control for possible story effects, subjects were assigned to either a familiar story treatment or an unfamiliar story treatment.

Method

Subjects. The subjects were 340 children whose ages ranged from 4.7 to 13 years, with a mean age of 7.28 years. There were 79 subjects in the facilitative play condition, 106 in the directive play condition, and 155 in the control condition; 162 subjects were female and 178 male. The sample was representative of the same population cited in Experiment 1.

Experimenters. Ten female primary grade teachers within a 70-mile radius of Auburn served as experimenters.

The five teachers in the directive group were encouraged to take personal responsibility to make sure that the reenactment of the story was accurate. Although they were not told to take roles, they were instructed to narrate, prompt, and direct the action. The five teachers in the facilitative group were instructed to establish the situation so that the children themselves controlled the reenactment. Emphasis was placed on strategies the teachers could use to shift control from themselves to the children.

Materials and testing procedures. The two forms of the story recall test used in Experiment 1 were again used in this study.

Two sets of stories were used. The set labeled unfamiliar was the same set used in Experiment 1. The set labeled familiar contained six fairy tales identified by the teachers as well-known to the children.

Six teachers presented familiar stories to both their particular treatment condition (i.e., facilitative or directive) and to their story-discussion control group. Four teachers presented unfamilar stories to these groups.

Results and Discussion

Data were analyzed using a two-way analysis of covariance (Treatment by Story Type). A significant main effect on story recall was found for treatment condition (F [2,333] = 7.58, $p <$ .001), with post hoc analysis indicating significant differences favoring facilitative play (M = 7.78) and directive play (M = 7.67) over control (M = 6.95). No significant difference was found between the two play conditions.

There was no main effect for story type, but there was a significant interaction between story type and treatment condition. Sheffe post hoc analysis indicated that children who heard familiar stories performed better in the facilitative condition than in the directive condition, whereas children who heard unfamiliar stories performed better in the directive condition than in the facilitative condition.

In both Experiments 1 and 2, children in the play condition performed better on story recall than did children in the control condition (F [2,333] = 8.16, $p <$ .001). In essense, Experiment 2 replicated the findings of Experiment 1. Children who are given the experience of acting out a story (thematic-fantasy play) recall a story that is not acted out better than does a control group. Because the criterion was not a simple reconstruction of a story, the thematic-fantasy experience would seem to provide children with information about stories in general (metalinguistic knowledge) rather than just the reconstruction of story facts. This seems especially true given the disordinal Age × Treatment interaction. Older children (6.5 years to 9 years), who would be expected to have metalinguistic knowledge about stories, showed no differences between treatment groups. Younger children, who would likely lack story knowledge, performed better in the play condition than did children in the control condition.

In Experiment 1, there was no attempt to control for adult intervention. In Experiment 2, different degrees of adult intervention were allowed. If effects were due to adult intervention rather than play (Smith, 1977; Smith and Syddall, 1978), then it would be expected that children in the directive condition would perform better than would children in the facilitative condition or the discussion condition. This was not the case. Children in both play conditions performed better on story recall than did children in the discussion condition, with no differences between the play conditions. Because experimenters in the facilitative condition encouraged the children to control the play, the results appear to be due to play and not adult intervention.

Although the issue of play control (Christie and Johnsen, 1983; Sutton-Smith, 1983a, 1983b) was not resolved by this study, the lack of difference in results between facilitative and directive conditions seems to indicate that control of play, as defined in this study, is not an important factor. Yet, an interesting interaction indicates that educators should be aware of play conditions and necessary adult roles. Children's story recall was highest in the facilitative condition when the story was familiar and in the directive condition when the story was unfamiliar—findings which indicate that children need adult assistance when they are required to accommodate new information. Thus, the need for children to control their play must be tempered with the realization that, at certain times, adult intervention can add to the outcomes of play.

Study 2
Williamson and Silvern (1990)

The results of Study 1 support the position of others (e.g., Dansky, 1980; Saltz and Johnson, 1974; Saltz, Dixon, and Johnson, 1977; Smilansky, 1968) that sociodramatic play and thematic-fantasy play are most facilitative for cognitive growth in the preschool or kindergarten years. None of these studies used subjects older than kindergarten age. More recently, age has been entered as an independent variable and results to this point would seem to confirm that the positive effect of play is inversely related to age.

Specifically, Pellegrini and Galda (1982) found that the ability to answer specific story recall questions was not facilitated by play for second graders relative to drawing or discussion conditions. Study 1 found that kindergarten and first grade children in a play condition outperformed a discussion-only control group in the comprehension of a post-test story which was heard but not acted out. Second and third graders, however, performed just as well in the control as in the play condition. As noted earlier, young children—whose thinking is still preoperational in nature—need direct active experience with phenomena in order to construct schemes for dealing with such phenomena. Older children—whose thinking is more operational in nature—are better able to relate new phenomena to schemes already present in their schematic repertoire. Because thematic-fantasy play allows for direct active experience with stories, it may provide opportunities for younger children to construct schemes about stories. Given that schemes are related directly to experience, and indirectly to age, these metalinguistic story schemes already may be present to some degree in older children.

According to this explanation, and according to Christie (1987), it is plausible that there are a minority of older subjects who have not constructed metalinguistic story schemes. If thematic-fantasy play is facilitative for these children, the effect might well be masked by the majority of children who have already constructed metalinguistic story schemes. To the extent that this is accurate, a new question arises: Is thematic-fantasy play facilitative for older primary children who have not developed story schemes through such metalinguistic experiences? That is, are there subgroups of older primary children who do not have well-developed story schemes for whom play might be facilitative? To investigate this possibility, Study 2 reanalyzed selected data from Study 1 in an attempt to determine if thematic-fantasy play is a viable treatment for selected older children.

Method

Subjects. The original sample of Study 1 consisted of 845 children in kindergarten through third grade. Findings suggested that play treatments were facilitative for children 80 months or younger. For the reanalysis, therefore, only subjects older than 80 months were used, resulting in an initial subject pool of 436 (with a mean age of 92.92 months and a standard deviation of 14.08 months).

As reported earlier, a pre-test was used to assess recall ability before treatment. The mean score on the pre-test was then calculated for these 436 children and was determined to be 7.31 (out of 10), with a standard deviation of 1.86. To identify the subjects most likely to have the least metalinguistic ability and experiences, children who scored at least one standard deviation below the mean were selected (a pre-test score of 5 or lower).

This procedure reduced the subject pool to 75 children, with a mean age of 87.23 months and a standard deviation of 6.03 months. Of these subjects, 37 were in the original control group and 38 were in the experimental play training group.

Results and Discussion

A one-tailed t-test was calculated on post-test mean scores and yielded a value of 1.69 ($df = 73, p < .05$). Mean and standard deviations for the play training group were $M = 6.92, SD = 2.42$; for control, $M = 5.95, SD = 2.57$. Results of this reanalysis suggest that the re-enactment of story schema for subgroups of older primary children is facilitative in a manner similar to that found in previous studies for younger children. This finding supports the constructivist explanation of the facilitative nature of play espoused in Study 1. Furthermore, it seems reasonable to suggest that, in the few studies that have considered age differences, a 'masking' effect might have occurred. That is, when all of the older primary subjects are included in an analysis, the average and above average subjects mask the possible beneficial effects of play for the least able. When only children who are poor comprehenders are identified, however, thematic-fantasy play appears to make a significant difference in their ability to understand stories. Surely, future research must examine the variables of age and ability much more closely.

Two strands of research would be of interest. One strand would consist of a determination of when play training is no longer facilitative, even for less competent older children. One way to investigate this would be to employ the same criterion measure used in this study, continue to isolate the least able children at progressively higher age levels, and document the age at which play training is no longer valuable for this subgroup.

On the other hand, in order to determine if play will ever again be helpful to more able children, another strand of investigation would consist of employing different dependent variables. Study 2 has suggested that average and above average comprehenders do not need to play to facilitate understanding of age-appropriate stories. It is surely possible that, as the difficulty or novelty of the dependent variable increases (causing disequilibration), play might again serve as a mediating process for these more able children.

Study 3
Williamson and Silvern (1989)

The purpose of Study 3 was to examine a theoretical paradox: If play is largely assimilative (as stated by Piaget), then thematic-fantasy play should not facilitate comprehension—which it clearly does. In a re-examination of Piaget's theoretical perspective, Rubin (1980) provided an explanation for what may be transpiring in the play episodes. Rubin contended that Piaget viewed the play episode—but *not* play per se—as contributing to cognitive and social growth. It is the social interaction and peer conflict that take place during frame breaks in the play episode (e.g., arguments that occur when the children are not in role) that create disequilibrium and serve an accommodative function. For instance, a child playing Red Riding Hood might step out of character to tell another child, "Wolves don't do that!" Rubin would argue that this is an instance above and beyond simple re-enactment. For the play to continue, both children must be satisfied with the outcome of the exchange. This 'metaplay'—meta-communication about play (Fein, 1981) and conflict resolution within the play context—serves as the causal variable for increased social-intellectual competence.

Whereas Rubin's hypothesis was primarily concerned with metaplay's contribution to the development of social cognition, Pellegrini (1984) empirically examined the value of metaplay in story comprehension. He attempted to operationalize Rubin's hypothesis by creating an "Accommodation Questioning Condition" and found that this condition was facilitative for comprehension on a delayed assessment when compared to a control condition. The Accommodation Questioning Condition involved an adult experimenter in a central role, asking questions and directing children's attention to discrepancies between responses. In the play conditions, adults assigned roles to children, thus eliminating one (but not all) highly sensitive opportunity for conflict among chidren and conflict resolution by children (e.g., "I want to be the wood chopper!" and "You can't, you're a girl!"). Although Pellegrini found that the Accommodation Questioning Condition was superior to a control group, there was no difference between this condition and play conditions. Thus, it is plausible that the naturally occurring metaplay in the play conditions was equivalent to adult-directed conflict resolution in the Accommodation Questioning Condition. Pellegrini's design, however, does not permit this conclusion. That is, we do not know what aspects of play contributed to comprehension. Furthermore, the central role of adults in Pellegrini's study leaves unanswered the question of whether the effect was due to opportunity to resolve conflict or adult tuition.

Research has clearly documented that children who re-enact stories (especially with thematic-fantasy play) will over time increase their quality of play and their ability to comprehend. That is, involvement in the general construct of play facilitates story comprehension relative to other conditions such as discussion or drawing (see: Pellegrini, 1985). As discussed earlier, this would seem to contradict Piagetian theory, which views play as primarily assimilative and nonadaptive. From a Piagetian perspective, therefore, something else must be transpiring during the play episode that places children in a state of disequilibrium and allows accommodation to occur. The purpose of the study, then, was not to redocument the contribution of play to comprehension, but rather to closely examine the play episode to determine which aspects of the re-enactment are most crucial for adaptation to occur.

The study's first objective was to examine the contribution of naturally occurring metaplay within thematic-fantasy play to the facilitation of story comprehension—that is, to extend Pellegrini's operationalization of Rubin's hypothesis. It was hypothesized that, because metaplay is accommodative, it would contribute more to comprehension than play would. Moreover, the finding that play or metaplay contributes to the understanding of a played story might seem rather mundane. However, to the extent that the play episode (including the peer conflict and negotiation implicit in our conception of metaplay) is adaptive, then children might well be learning more than the details of a particular story and instead be developing a more general metalinguistic knowledge about stories. Play experiences, then, might enable children to perform better on story recall in general, rather than simply on a story with which they have had direct play experience. In the present study, if these experiences also contribute to the comprehension of an unfamiliar story that was heard, *but not played,* the impact of re-enactment as a contributor to comprehension becomes far-reaching.

Method

Subjects

The 120 kindergarten children included in the study were selected to provide an equal number of boys (60) and girls (60). The children's ages ranged from 67 to 87 months, with a mean of 73.08 months. Children in each classsroom were randomly assigned to five play groups per classroom. Two boys and two girls were in each play group.

Procedure

The procedure consisted of five separate sessions—two play sessions, one play/test session, one story/test session, and one delayed test session. For all sessions, play groups were taken by an experimenter to a play area separate from their classroom.

Play sessions. The experimenter told the children that they would be read a story and that they should listen to the story because they would be playing the story after it was read.

In the first session, the experimenter read "Goldilocks and the Three Bears." In the second session, the experimenter read "The Three Billy Goats Gruff." Both stories were read so that the children could see the pictures and the text.

The experimenter then told the children that they should decide who was going to play which part and how they were going to play the story. The children were told to let the experimenter know when they were ready to begin acting out the story. The experimenter did not interfere in the planning sessions and did not answer children's questions directly.

Play/test session. In this session, children were read the story, "Little Red Riding Hood." The session followed the format of the two previous play sessions. When the children completed the play, they were individually tested on (a) a Criterion Referenced Test (CRT) of "Little Red Riding Hood," (b) a retelling task, and (c) a sequencing task.

Story/test session. The play groups were brought to the playroom and read the story "The Man and the Wife in the Vinegar Jug." This story was chosen because it contained story grammar similar to the other fairy tales and because, according to the children's teachers, it was unfamiliar to the children in the study. After hearing the story, the children did *not* play the story. They were then tested individually on (a) a CRT of the story, (b) a retelling task, and (c) a sequencing task. In addition, the children were given a language production task.

Delayed test session. On the fifth school day (6 intervening days) after the story/test session, the children were retested on the CRTs for both stories and were given retelling and sequencing tasks for both stories.

Data Analysis

The videotapes of the three play sessions were coded for play and metaplay and for verbal and nonverbal behavior. Categories for both play and metaplay were derived from the work of Christie (1982) and Smilansky (1968). The primary distinction between play and metaplay is that metaplay consists of language or actions external to the play itself. The play categories were:

1. Nonverbal Transformation of Action—Pretending to have or use an object. For example, miming picking flowers or chopping wood.
2. Nonverbal Inrole Pretense—Acting in the manner of the character being played. For example, crawling on all fours as a billy goat or pretending to sleep while the bears went through the "someone's been sleeping" routine.
3. Verbal Inrole Pretense—Saying exactly what the character said or providing words in the sense of the character. For example, "Someone's been sleeping in my bed" or "Where does your grandma live?"

Categories for metaplay were:

1. Nonverbal directions—Attempting to get another child to do something using nonverbal methods. For example, waving a hand as in "go on" or pushing another child to a certain spot. The remaining metaplay categories were verbal.
2. Object—Communication indicating that the other players should accept a prop or mimed prop. For example "Pretend this is an ax" or "Pretend I have some flowers."
3. Action—Communication indicating that the other players should accept a particular action. "Pretend I'm on the bed" or "Let's pretend we're going to cross the bridge."
4. Story line—Communication about what is supposed to be happening in the story. For example, "You're supposed to stop her" or "Don't you run away now?"

5. Assign roles—Communication regarding who will play each role in the story. "I want to be the chopper," "You be the troll," or "You can't be grandma—you're a boy."
6. Directing or rebuking—Telling a child to perform a specific act or criticizing an action. "No, you have to wait!" or "Go into the house!"
Coding began when the children started planning and continued through the entire play episode. The maximum length for planning and play was 10 minutes.

Results and Discussion

The data were analyzed with both simple correlation and multiple regression techniques and are too bulky to report in detail here. However, results indicate that play is not related to comprehension ($r = .18$), metaplay ($r = .17$), or language production ($r = .04$). Furthermore, metaplay and language production are unrelated ($r = .09$), indicating that coding of play, metaplay, and language production produced independent measures. However, both metaplay and language production are significantly related to and contribute to total comprehension ($r = .46$ and $r = .32$, respectively). Children who engage in more metaplay and who already possess language production competence comprehend stories better than children who engage in less metaplay and do not demonstrate as much language production competence.

After a broad multiple regression indicated that metaplay contributed to comprehension, a specific model was designed to examine the components of metaplay. It was found that only the directing component of metaplay contributed significantly to story comprehension.

The objective of this study was to determine the relative contributions of play, metaplay, and language production competence (within thematic-fantasy play) to the facilitation of comprehension of a familiar re-enacted story and an unfamiliar story that was not re-enacted. The most striking finding of this study lay in the contribution of both metaplay and language production competence to the comprehension measures and the lack of contribution of play. As far as the relationship between play and metaplay is concerned, the results both support and extend the work of Rubin (1980) and Pellegrini (1984). In a design in which adult tuition could not be a contributing factor, metaplay correlated significantly with all measures of comprehension, whereas play failed to approach significance. This finding has two important implications.

First, data from this investigation provide evidence that there are at least two aspects in a play situation—pretend play (at which time the children are 'in role') and metaplay (at which time the children are 'out of role' but communicating about play). Based upon outcome measures, it may be concluded that the play itself is primarily assimilative. In play, children pay attention to personal motives and not external events. Thus, play is not related to story comprehension. On the other hand, certain dimensions of metaplay serve an accommodating function. In metaplay, children must coordinate points of view and attend to external story events such as plot, characters, and directing. Therefore, metaplay is related to comprehension. This finding supports the theory that it is the play episode and not play itself serving an accommodative function.

Second, metaplay cannot take place outside of the context of the overall play situation. We think this is an important point for caregivers of young children who might decide as a result of this study that play is not so important after all. This study suggests just the opposite—that is, that creating play situations is extremely important. Otherwise, there is no context in which metaplay can naturally occur.

It is interesting to note that only the combined metaplay component of directing contributed significantly to comprehension. A qualitative examination of the videotapes revealed that children who scored high in directing tended to be in charge of their group. That is, they seemed to take leadership in helping to coordinate points of view and making sure the others attended to external story events. Rubin (1980) suggested that peer interaction (i.e., metaplay) is the causal variable for aspects of social and cognitive growth. Implicit in this argument is the idea that not only the director but also the person directed should benefit by the interaction. Results of the present study do not support this hypothesis. That is, nonmetaplayers rarely rose to the level necessary to engage in conflict. They simply did what the director told them and, thus, were never in a state of disequilibrium. To more fully examine Rubin's hypothesis will require much longer treatment conditions. If it is true that metaplay is partly a social phenomenon, then two experimental conditions must be carefully controlled—the ratio of metaplayers and nonmetaplayers in each group and presage personality traits of the subjects.

Of importance is the contribution of metaplay to comprehension of the story that was not played out, implying that comprehension was not simply a result of rehearsal. Rather, it seems that good metaplayers develop a structure that is related to understanding and directing stories.

The study supported Rubin's (1980) hypothesis, and thus Piaget's theory (1962), that talk outside of play advances cognitive functioning and extended Pellegini's (1984) study to show that talk during play (whether conflicting or not) is related to story comprehension. Special pains were taken to ensure that the children were in control of discussing and enacting their play. Thus, comprehension is related to child actions and not adult tuition, findings that partially replicated those of Pellegrini (1984).

Summary

The three studies reviewed in this chapter have provided some insight into the effect of adult intervention, the relationship between age and the effectiveness of thematic-fantasy play, the effect of familiar versus unfamiliar stories, the ability to generalize to stories not acted out, and the crucial element of metaplay in the play episode. To us, the conceptualization of metaplay is especially intriguing because it truly explains the seeming paradox in Piagetian theory regarding play. Future research regarding metaplay might explore several questions. For example, what is the relationship between metaplay and perspective taking? Are metaplayers the children who can take others' points of view or are they simply the children who have a good grasp of the story? Are comprehension and perspective taking related? That is, are the comprehenders children who have decentered enough to take into account the interrelated story schemes? And finally, is metaplay a mediator of perspective taking or simply reflective of perspective taking?

Note

* Portions of this research were partially funded by an Auburn University grant-in-aid and by a College of Education, Auburn University Research Assistance Grant. The authors are deeply grateful to Michael Kelley, Elaine Surbeck and Janet Taylor who collaborated on portions of the research reported.

References

Burns, S. M., and C. J. Brainerd (1979). Effects of constructive and dramatic play on perspective taking in very young children. *Developmental Psychology, 15,* 512–521.

Christie, J. F. (1982). Sociodramatic play training. *Young Children, 37,* 25–32.

———— (1987). Play and story comprehension: A critique of recent training research. *Journal of Research and Development in Education, 21,* 36–43.

Christie, J. F., and E. P. Johnsen (1983). The role of play in social-intellectual development. *Review of Educational Research, 53,* 93–115.

Collier, R. G. (1979). Developing language through play. *Elementary School Journal, 80,* 89–92.

Connolly, S. A., A. Doyle, and E. Reznik (1983). *Social fantasy play: Its effects on peer social relations.* Paper presented at the biennial meeting of the Society for Research in Child Development, Detroit (March).

Dansky, J. L. (1980). Make-believe: A mediator of the relationship between play and associative fluency. *Child Development, 51,* 576–579.

Dansky, J. L., and I. W. Silverman (1973). Effects of play on associative fluency in preschool-age children. *Developmental Psychology, 9,* 38–43.

———— (1975). Play: A general facilitator of associative fluency. *Developmental Psychology, 11,* 104.

Fein, G. G. (1981). Pretend play in childhood: An integrative review. *Child Development, 52,* 1095–1118.

Feitelson, D., and G. S. Ross (1973). The neglected factor—play. *Human Development, 16,* 202–223.

Fink, R. S. (1976). Role of imaginative play in cognitive development. *Psychological Reports, 39,* 895–906.

Garvey, C. (1977). *Play.* Cambridge: Harvard University Press.

Golomb, C., and C. B. Cornelius (1977). Symbolic play and its cognitive significance. *Developmental Psychology, 13,* 246–252.

Guthrie, K., and L. M. Hudson (1979). Training conservation through symbolic play: A second look. *Child Development, 50,* 1269–1271.

Iannotti, R. (1978). Effect of role-taking experiences on role taking, empathy, altruism, and aggression. *Developmental Psychology, 14,* 119–124.

Johnson, J. E. (1976). Relations of divergent thinking and intelligence test scores with social and nonsocial make-believe play of preschool children. *Child Development, 47,* 1200–1203.

Lovinger, S. L. (1974). Socio-dramatic play and language development in preschool disadvantaged children. *Psychology in the Schools, 11,* 313–320.

Neumann, E. A. (1971). *The elements of play.* New York: MSS Information.

Parten, M. B. (1932). Social participation among preschool children. *Journal of Abnormal Psychology, 27,* 243-269.

Pellegrini, A. D. (1984). Identifying causal elements in the thematic-fantasy play paradigm. *American Educational Research Journal, 21,* 691-701.

———— (1985). The relations between symbolic play and literate behavior: A review and critique of the empirical literature. *Review of Educational Research, 55,* 107-121.

Pellegrini, A. D., and L. Galda (1982). The effects of thematic-fantasy play training on the development of children's story comprehension. *American Educational Research Journal, 19,* 443-452.

Piaget, J. (1962). *Play, dreams, and imitation in childhood.* New York: Norton.

Rosen, C. E. (1974). The effects of sociodramatic play on problem solving behavior among culturally disadvantaged preschool children. *Child Development, 45,* 920-927.

Rubin, K. H. (1980). Fantasy play: Its role in the development of social skills and social cognition. In: K. H. Rubin (Ed.), *Children's play* (pp. 69-84). San Francisco: Jossey-Bass.

Rubin, K. H., and T. Maioni (1975). Play preference and its relationship to egocentrism, popularity and classification skills in preschoolers. *Merrill-Palmer Quarterly, 21,* 171-179.

Saltz, E., D. Dixon, and J. Johnson (1977). Training disadvantaged preschoolers on various fantasy activities: Effects on cognitive functioning and impulse control. *Child Development, 48,* 367-380.

Saltz, E., and J. Johnson (1974). Training for thematic fantasy play in culturally disadvantaged children: Preliminary results. *Journal of Educational Psychology, 66,* 623-630.

Silvern, S. B. (1980). Play, pictures, and repetition: Mediators in aural prose learning. *Education Communication and Technology Journal, 28,* 134-139.

Silvern, S. B., et al. (1986). Young children's story recall as a product of play, story familiarity, and adult intervention. *Merrill-Palmer Quarterly, 32,* 73-86.

Silvern, S. B., P. A. Williamson, and B. Waters (1983). Play as a mediator of comprehension: An alternative to play training. *Educational Research Quarterly, 7,* 16-21.

Simon, T., and P. K. Smith (1983). *The study of play and problem solving in pre-school children: Methodological problems and new directions.*

Paper presented at the International Conference on Play and Play Environments, Austin, TX (June).

Singer, D. L., and J. Rummo (1973). Ideational creativity and behavioral style in kindergarten-age children. *Developmental Psychology, 8,* 154–161.

Smilansky, S. (1968). *The effects of sociodramatic play on disadvantaged preschool children.* New York: Wiley.

Smith, P. K. (1977). Social fantasy and play in young children. In: B. Tizard and D. Harvey (Eds.), *Biology of play* (pp. 123–145). Philadelphia: Lippincott.

Smith, P. K., and S. Dutton (1979). Play and training in direct and innovative problem solving. *Child Development, 50,* 830–836.

Smith, P. K., and S. Syddall (1978). Play and non-play tutoring in preschool children: Is it play or tutoring which matters? *British Journal of Educational Psychology, 48,* 315–325.

Stein, N. L. (1978). *How children understand stories: A developmental analysis* (Tech. Rep. No. 69). Champaign, IL: Center for the Study of Reading, University of Illinois.

Sutton-Smith, B. (1983a). *Text and context in imaginative play.* Symposium conducted at the meeting of the American Educational Research Association, Montreal (April).

——— (1983b). *Play research: The state of the art.* Address to the International Conference on Play and Play Environments, Austin, TX (June).

Taylor, A. R., and S. R. Asher (1984). *Children's interpersonal goals in game situations.* Paper presented at the annual meeting of the American Educational Research Association, New Orleans (April).

Vandenburg, B. (1981). The role of play in the development of insightful tool using strategies. *Merrill-Palmer Quarterly, 27,* 97–109.

Williamson, P. A., and S. B. Silvern (1990). The effects of play training on the story comprehension of upper primary children. *Journal of Research in Childhood Education, 4,* 130–136.

——— (1989). *"You can't be grandma; You're a boy": Events within the thematic fantasy play context which contribute to story comprehension.* Submitted for publication.

5

"But It Ain't Real!": Pretense in Children's Play and Literacy Development

Amanda Branscombe

A child's use of play is as complex as the ancient Greek theatrical production of Euripides' *The Bacchae.* It exists and has meaning only as the child is in the act of playing. Just as there is no such thing as a literal translation from ancient Greek verse, there is no literal translation of a child's intentions, connections, or constructions made during play. Both use associations, actions, and language to create personal representations and abstractions of reality. Both may use a word, phrase, image, or action to express one thought or an entire event. Both are still as much of an enigma as Dionysos, the protagonist in *The Bacchae,* and his various transformations. Like contemporary translators and directors of Greek drama, as researchers of play, we only translate and interpret what we see and hear based on what we know.

The study presented in this chapter is just such a translation and interpretation. It is a follow-up case study of De and Tutti, two black children whose mother, Charlene Thomas, worked with Shirley Brice Heath and myself in a year-long ethnographic study of De's literacy development when Charlene was a member of my ninth grade basic English class in 1981–82. This study was undertaken to analyze and explain how the two boys construct their own differentiations between reality and pretense through play. Our data indicate that, when children such as De and Tutti are given opportunities to become their own makers of knowledge—art pieces, literacy artifacts, stories, games, and schoolwork—they view play as their work and literacy events as play. Conversely, when children are only allowed to work in schools with adult-prepared environments with materials, routines, and rituals of pretense and imitation directed by adults rather than a child-centered environment anchored in reality and facilitated by adults, they construct notions that schooling "ain't real."

In order to make the above assertions, I, like Susanna Millar (1974), chose to define play "not as a class of activities. . .but as a description of how, when, where, and under what conditions an action is performed." The description of the action and the conditions is a representation of play. Because of this, play has "a certain degree of choice and a lack of constraint from conventional ways of handling objects, materials, and ideas" (p. 21). In effect, through play, children lay claim to (or make a stake in) their environment, which allows them to feel some ownership of and control over it. Through these conditions, children construct notions about literacy that make "connections with art and other forms of invention" (p. 21).

The Story's Beginnings: Charlene as Ethnographer

Because this is a follow-up case study, a brief summary of the original study, which focused on literacy and language learning in a lower socioeconomic black home, seems necessary. Charlene Thomas, De and Tutti's mother, dropped out of school in November 1981, when she was sixteen and a ninth grader in my basic English class. She had missed school the previous year because of her mother's prolonged illness and death and the birth of her first son, De. She decided to drop out because she was pregnant with her second son, Tutti, but she did continue to collaborate with Heath and myself about her children's language learning and daily activities.

Our project consisted of Charlene reading to De, tape recording those sessions, and taking fieldnotes of their interactions and his activities. I occasionally visited Charlene to monitor the project, give her more tapes and materials, and gather the data she had collected. Heath corresponded with the two of us, provided books and materials, and commented on the project's progress. By school standards, Charlene was not literate, from a literate environment, or even a marginal student. A detailed account of her literacy development (Heath, 1984) indicated that, before this project, she had never written a letter, read a book, or succeeded in a formal learning situation.

Neither Heath nor I had any reason to believe that she would follow through with the project, but she did. In late February 1982, she provided us with her first fieldnotes. According to Heath (1984), the fieldnotes contained specific details of De's speech, her attempts to get De to label objects and people in the room, conversations others had with De, and his daily activities.

Heath and I encouraged Charlene to read to De on a regular basis, talk with him about those reading events, and record her impressions of his interest during those events. In June 1982, we discovered that when Charlene had reading sessions with De she made him sit or stand in front of her and say the object pictured in the book. Then she read the story to him as he stood or sat quietly looking at the cover of the book. If he moved during the reading event, she disciplined him. I quickly intervened by modelling a reading session with De. I had him sit by my side or in my lap so that we could both see the pictures and print. Because Tutti was a 'lap baby,' I explained that he should be present during the reading events and involved with the interactions as much as possible.

Charlene adjusted her reading style so that both children were sitting with her, and she noted that reading to De became much easier as a result of that intervention. After that, she began constructing her own strategies for the reading sessions. She started to experiment with times to read to them, ways to hold the book so that all could see, ways to talk to and question them about the stories, and ways (such as pointing to the text) to focus their attention on the print and pictures.

Because of the early reading events and Charlene's interaction with De and Tutti during those events, the children began to develop a predisposition for reading and rudimentary notions about literacy and schooling. Both looked forward to their story time. De retold stories that had been read to him and attempted to write stories, his name, the alphabet, and his numbers. Because of his age, Tutti watched De and listened. But during that time, neither the children, nor Charlene developed their literacy notions to the point that they could be described as proficient practitioners of mainstream literacy events.

In October 1982, I moved and, as a result, maintained minimal contact with Charlene. From 1982 until 1984, however, Charlene continued to take fieldnotes, mail Heath and myself letters and tapes, and visit with me when I stopped by. We lost regular contact with Charlene and the children over the next few years because of my sporadic visits, the children's school schedule, and Charlene's home and work situations.

Several Years Later

"Miss Brask! Did you . . . you brang me any books! You is Miss Brask ain't cha. Yea! You is. Did you brang any books?"

This was De's opening statement to me in March 1988, even though I had not seen him for several years. He, Tutti, his mother, his twin brothers, and his baby sister lived in a six-room frame house with his mother's brothers, friends, and a boarder. I later learned from Charlene that they had been living in that situation for about a year. Before that, she and her family had moved around within the community several times. Each move was precipitated by a crisis—a fire destroying their trailer, a report of parental neglect, relatives telling the family to get out, and so on.

Although the family had moved numerous times, De and Tutti continued to attend the same school. When I asked Charlene about the children's schooling, she explained that the school's staff had added to her problems by retaining De in first grade because he was two points below the system's cutoff score on the Stanford Achievement Test (SAT), was very active and somewhat immature, and had a parent who didn't seem to be interested in his schooling. (She was a cook who worked for hourly wages and couldn't get off work to meet the school's scheduled conferences.) She also recounted that Tutti was viewed as a troublemaker and fighter who couldn't get along with others in his kindergarten class.

Her earlier expectations of school success for her children had been destroyed. According to Charlene, she just wanted to keep De and Tutti from being tested and placed in a special education program like the one she had experienced. Finally, she noted that she could not understand the school system's assessment of De and Tutti because they did well on their schoolwork, report cards, and test scores. Furthermore, she noted that De loved to read. She recounted numerous times when he would sit at the kitchen table and read to Tutti and his twin brothers while she cooked dinner. She said that she took him to the library to get books because she couldn't afford to buy as many as he read.

When I asked if she had any records of De and Tutti's schoolwork, she opened a drawer which contained a two-year collection of their papers, report cards, standardized testing reports, and letters to her about their progress. After examining those and talking with De and Tutti, I too questioned the incongruities between the children's standardized scores, their grades, and their teachers' subjective complaints regarding neatness, correctness, and behavior.

Needless to say, Charlene wanted answers. Because of her interest in her children's education and her concern about De's possible placement in special education, she requested that I evaluate De. Because I was also interested in determining his intellectual development, I agreed. For the assessment, I chose several Piagetian tasks to look at the kind of logical and social reasoning De was using, the Observational Guidelines for Literacy Checklist to look at his attitudes and abilities in reading and writing, and informal interviews with him to determine what was meaningful to him in terms of his learning.

Before I administered the assessment, I informally talked with some of De's and Tutti's teachers to obtain the school's perception of them as students. From the interviews, I learned that De was viewed as an immature child who had been retained because of parental disinterest and the SAT score. Furthermore, the teachers noted that Tutti was a problem because he was in a class of 25 'bad' children from poor homes. At no point in the interviews did the teachers comment about the children's abilities. Instead, they made subjective judgements about the children's home life.

I began the assessment using a Piagetian clinical interview of early logical-mathematical knowledge, which included tasks related to classification, order, and number. From the beginning, it was apparent that De viewed this as a test, and he was quite certain that this time he would not fail because he knew his patterns. Because of the influence of the curriculum of the school, De disregarded my instructions for the task and began making patterns with the pieces. Rather than interpreting this as preoperational graphic behavior, I readministered the task by having him sort the pieces into boxes. With this change, De readily grouped the pieces on the basis of all three attributes, and from that point on the assessment went smoothly. The results of this component indicated that De (at 7.7 years of age) was making the transition from preoperational to concrete operational thought. The only schemes not fully operationalized were the ability to move back to the whole from the parts and the realization of the some-all relationship among classes. This transition is at the upper range of normal intellectual development, and on all other tasks his reasoning was operational.

De's literacy assessment indicated that he had high expectations of print, enjoyed books and stories, had extensive experience with books, retold favorite stories, sought out experiences with books, and experimented with drawing and writing on his own. He used appropriate expression and intonation patterns when he read aloud. Furthermore, De used effective strategies for gaining meaning as he read unknown texts. For example, he used self-monitoring and prior knowledge about genre for constructing the meaning of a story written as a play. He could predict meaning from the book's title, illustrations, and chapter headings. He could make inferences and retell stories. He seemingly had no difficulty with temporal or causal sequences. Finally, he could restate the main ideas of stories, pull detail from texts, and make evaluative statements about stories. His love and respect for books was demonstrated in a number of ways. When Tutti said that he was going to tear up a pre-primer, De responded that he would return it to school so that Tutti could not destroy it. In that same conversation, he noted that he did not like for his twin brothers to read his books because "they scribble-scrabble in them and mess them up." Furthermore, he demonstrated his interest in reading by taking two hours at a local bookstore to read the titles and retell the stories of the books he had read.

The third component of my assessment focused on De's conception of rules. According to Piaget (1962), rules help researchers examine children's social reality. Through the rules of a game, researchers observe whether children have a sense of community (rules we have all decided on and use), reciprocity (turn taking), and socialization (needs met by playing the game). Rules also demonstrate children's ability to take on the perspective of others. I introduced this component of the assessment by asking De to teach me how to play checkers, a game he mentioned that he played at school and home. From this experience, I observed that De, like many young children, lacked the verbal abilities to discuss and describe processes. Although he explained the way to play checkers, he focused on the game's action rather than its opening, context, or complete rule system. De offered rules and strategies for playing as he needed them. Furthermore, he seemed to focus on the power aspects of gaining control through jumping and beating the "bad man" who is the opponent. Whether he was pretending to play checkers like the adults in his home and neighborhood, or whether he had constructed his notions about the game from watching them play is a question I cannot answer. However, checkers is a real game that is played by adults, and De's approach to the game was that of a power struggle in which he has identity, is recognized by others as being an authority, and is in control. Sutton-Smith (1984) has noted such play outside of the school setting. He states that social play among children is about power and control, whereas, supervised school play is about being "flexible, nonliteral, positively affected, and intrinsically motivated" (p. 61). Thus, De's construction of rules seemed appropriate in this context and demonstrated a sense of reciprocity and socialization.

After the evaluation, I was even more perplexed by De's experience with public schooling and his seeming inability to "do school" (Heath, 1983; Dyson, 1984). I was also confused about the school's image of Tutti as a troublemaker. While De was the active 'doer' who could easily exasperate a teacher, Tutti was the quiet child who watched, tagged along, and listened. He never interfered or interrupted and seemed to have a loving disposition that drew people rather than repelled them.

De and Tutti's Constructions of Pretend and Pretense in Play and Literacy

The results of De's evaluation led me to attempt an intervention that might offer both children a positive learning situation. Because the local university's early childhood program offered a summer lab experience for children between four and eight years old, I enrolled De and Tutti. Ironically, this experience proved to be as highly frustrating as De and Tutti's public school experience, but it did answer some of my questions about their attempts to "do school."

The early childhood lab program varies from summer to summer because of teacher assignments and undergraduate students who elected to take the course. To some extent, the quality of the summer experience depends on the college students, their motivation and interest in the program, and their ability to run such a program. Furthermore, it is dependent on their interpretation of the constructivist theory of learning and their implementation of that theory through a thematic teaching approach.

When De and Tutti enrolled in the program, they found that the undergraduate students had selected "The Farm" as their summer theme. The children had seen cows, horses, goats, and sheep at the university's agricultural barns, but neither had visited a farm or studied about it. Because of this, they were eager to attend the program. When they arrived for their first day, De and Tutti discovered the summer lab program's computer and text talker. De quickly learned to operate it so that the text talker made garbled sounds which caused the other children to laugh. Furthermore, he and Tutti figured out a way to play with the computer most of the morning. When the undergraduates made them stop playing with the computer so that other children could have a turn, De and Tutti either stayed in the snack center or drifted around the rooms. When I picked them up after the first morning's session, I expected to hear about the farm. Instead, De asked if he could go early the next day so that he could sign up for the computer, have it make more funny noises, and make the other children laugh. Neither one mentioned the farm. They were establishing their identity, control, and power in the program. They were getting attention, but they were not "doin' school".

After De and Tutti had spent a few days with the computer, one of the professors suggested that I needed to do something with "those kids" because they were "hogging the computer" and creating management problems. I suggested that the students needed to develop an intervention that would work with De and Tutti rather than have me discipline them or take them out of the program.

When I questioned De and Tutti to find out what they thought they were learning in the program, the following conversation took place:

Amanda: What is your favorite story in lab? What kind of stories are you reading?
De: In school?
Amanda: Yeah, in school.
De: Talkin' 'bout summer school or our school?
Amanda: No, summer school.
De: We don't read nothin'... but we say words like teeth when dey point to a picture.
Amanda: Why aren't you reading?
De: I don't know. 'Cause dey think we don't know no words. Sometimes I gets some books off that shelf. I... dey put 'em on the top shelf, and I jump so high... I get 'em. Me and Tutti we climbed in a chair today to get 'em.
Amanda: Well, what are those books about?
De: Animals!
Amanda: What about animals?
De: That school... dey don't be puttin' on real... dey be puttin' on make-believe.
Amanda: What do you mean by that?
De: Dey be puttin' on... make-believe...
Amanda: Well, what's real?
De: Well, I got some real stories. I got a dog book. It real... Jack the Pup... real.
Amanda: What's a make-believe story that you've got?

De: A make-believe one? Jack and the Beanstalk. . . cause Jack
           cain't climb. . . —cause there werent' no magic beans, are
           there? Mama workplace real. She work there (points to a
           local restaurant). Daddy be working two works.

De's comments suggested that the summer lab experience lacked reality
for him. Except for using the computer and making others laugh, he
felt no sense of ownership, control, or belonging. Tutti felt equally
displaced. The theme was apparently meaningless, and the experience
was becoming one of subtle bias rather than learning.

     After the children's conversation about the lab, Charlene and I
talked. We decided to withdraw them from the program because they
were more interested in the building's elevator than the lab experience.
They talked about their own books rather than stories that they were
hearing or reading in lab. When they made puppets with paper plates
or colored stereotypical farm animals on photocopied sheets, they
threw them in the nearest trash can. What I had hoped would be a
positive learning and socializing experience for them was becoming
a repeat of their negative experience in school. To them, the lab
program was pretend school; to the teachers, they were problems.

     During the lab experience, they learned one chant, "The Cat Ate
the Cheese," which they recited in a school-like performance voice
which lacked much of their black intonation patterns and language.

Amanda: Have you learned in chants at school?
De: Yeah. (*Begins in his school voice*) Where's my cheese?
           The cat ate it.
Amanda: What did it say?
De: It says, where's the cat?
           In the house.
           Where the house?
           On fire. . . Fire burnin' it.
           Where the fire?
           Water squashed it.
           Where's the water?
           Pig drankin' it.
           Where the pig?
           Butcher got it
           Where the butcher?
           Road tripped it.
           Where the road?
           Mouse nibbled it,

	Where the mouse?
	Cat chased it.
Tutti:	Where the cat?
De:	Where the cat?
	Eating the cheese.

When questioned about the chant, they explained that you just say it. This was in direct contrast to their chant of "The Gingerbread Man," Tutti's favorite story, which both children offered after reciting "The Cat Ate the Cheese." De began the chant with the following lines:

De:	Here how Gingerbread Man go.
	Run, run, as fast as you can
	You can't catch me
	I'm the Gingerbread Man.

Tutti repeated this chorus, and then he began to tell the story, with De interrupting to add the chorus at the appropriate places. Both children had a sense of control and ownership over this chant. It was play, as was this episode, which followed their Gingerbread Man chant:

De:	(*Using the voice of an authoritative adult*) What you eaten boy?
Tutti:	(Laughs) Crackers.
De:	What kind?
Tutti:	What you think I'm eaten? Boy!
De:	What kind? Boy! You hear me! Boy!
Tutti:	Uhm. . . hum.
De:	You think you better. . . Do thing you better do. . . You hear me talkin' to you!
Tutti:	Uh. . . hum.
De:	Tutti. . . what you eaten? (*Changes voice tone to school voice*)
Tutti:	None yo' busy! Boy!

The game seemed to end, but Tutti opened it again with laughter.

Tutti:	De, De. Look down. Look down here.
De:	Boy! What you done?
Tutti:	See.
De:	Naw. . . Dem mine. You had yo' crackers.
Tutti:	I had bout ten crackers. You ain't got but two. (*Laughs*)

Tutti obviously had tricked De and won their game by getting more crackers. Just as the "Gingerbread Man" story involved the ability to outwit or trick others, Tutti's game had outwitted or tricked De. "The Cat Ate the Cheese" chant lacked the element of trickery and good literature, so De and Tutti viewed it as meaningless. This use of trickery and wit in play was also reported in Heath's (1983) work with the Trackton community in the Carolina Piedmonts. The ability to outwit others allowed the child to get a treat and win the verbal game.

Although one might think that this use of trickery is found only in the black culture, it is not. Literature is filled with stories, poems, and plays based on the main character's ability to figure out the riddle, trick the villain, outwit the suitor to win a true love, or outwit the witch to break a spell.

Tutti's game used the same structure as stories found in fairy tales and children's literature. It was verbal in nature and anchored in reality. It had a desired object (candy, crackers, toys, etc.) that one person had and the other wanted. In order to get that object, De had to outwit or trick Tutti into giving it to him. De used the adult role of authority to try to get the crackers. He was able to demand two packs but lost them back to Tutti when he stopped paying attention to Tutti and the game. As a result, Tutti took the crackers and won.

In the months following the lab experience, the children and I made regular visits to the bookstore and local park. De became more and more interested in looking at toy guns in the toy store next to the bookstore. Tutti, on the other hand, became totally involved with "The Three Little Pigs." In August, he bought his fourth copy. When I asked why, he said that the pictures looked different. De recounted that Tutti would go in his room, read the story as fast as he could and just "say the huff and puff part aloud." As De told this, Tutti laughed. De pointed out that he wouldn't be able to play like that with reading in school. When De was questioned about Tutti's schooling, he said:

De: In first grade, you be eatin' snacks all the time. And drinkin' milk... You don't like milk but it don't matter. You ain't be doin' no work. In second grade... you work.
Tutti: They don't give me nothin'?
De: Naw, in first grade they give... They just do things like walk... learn to walk. You be goin' to be goin' to readin' too.
Tutti: I ain't gonna read.
De: Soon Tutti, you gonna be in that green book I be in.
Tutti: Naw, I ain't gonna read.

De: Yeah, see you just get the book. Den you look at it. Den you don't know dem words, and dey gonna tell you word. Den dey gonna give you a list to take home to yo' mama and she gonna teach it to you. Den you just brang that book home and take it back and brang it home and take it back.

Amanda: What was your favorite story in your reading book, De?

De: Don't have none in it.

Amanda: What do you mean?

De: Don't have no stories in dem books. Just be words you gonna learn. Don't have stories like "Jack the Pup" "Sleeping Beauty" and "Three Pigs."

Amanda: (*Because I did not realize that the basal readers have a limited use of literature in them, I was confused with De's comment.*) What do you mean?

De: Dem books don't have stories. "Goose and the Golden Egg" was the best I read and it were a play.

Tutti: I can already do math.

De: Yeah, but you gonna have to do whole page. Like five plus seven, five plus six, and even up to twenty. You'll see.

In this exchange, De offered his perception of first grade. It was based on his experience. To him, school was not a place to play, read good stories, or have children's wishes acknowledged. It was not a place where he or his brother would have control or ownership. In effect, De's notions of schooling were isolated from the events in his life and his constructions of literacy. In his view, Tutti would not learn to read at school, but at home with his mother. However, the school would teach Tutti to walk in a line. Just as in the summer lab experience, De's conversation lacked connections to his own experiences in his home and neighborhood. It lacked the cohesion that provides listeners with clues to the speaker's context.

When school opened, De's mother convinced the school's administration not to test De for special education. She worked with him on ways to control his behavior. Even though they both had difficulty with his third grade assignments, he made A's and B's. He also made average scores on his SAT. Finally, he improved his conduct grades so that his third grade teacher wrote comments like "a pleasure to teach." When I asked him about school, he explained that he did not like it anymore. He noted that it was like the summer program.

They just be puttin' on. . . .It ain't real. At home we play like we cars sometimes. At school. . .when school goin' on. . .we don't.

At school the teacher stands in front of the room and talks to you. But at home, Mama sit by you and make you do writin' bout stories and stuff. At school we don't write. . . Like writin'. . . we copy off the board.

In the afternoons, as he babysat his brothers and sister, De would spend hours drawing pictures of monsters, cars, army events, firemen putting out house fires, and bicycles. He explained that he could decide what he wanted to draw, how he wanted to draw it, and then whether he wanted to save it or throw it away. His love for art replaced his love for books. It became his play.

Tutti, on the other hand, did quite well in first grade. At the beginning of the year, he was placed in an advanced regular class and succeeded. He loved school and spent his time doing his work as neatly as he could. After he finished his homework, he often watched De draw.

Neither was allowed to play outside on the playground behind their house, because Charlene knew that the children in their project were experimenting with crack and running drugs for local pushers. All of her children had books as well as toy cars, trucks, and trains. Charlene saved the books for the ritualistic times when she or De read to the younger children. Tutti was the only child who did not engage in the ritual. Because of his school record, he was allowed to read from the family's books at any time. Most of the toys were battery operated, so they were usually stored in a closet because of dead batteries. Such circumstances caused De and Tutti to play hide-and-seek or rough and tumble with their little brothers.

Tutti: The Child as Maker

De begged to attend the 1989 early childhood summer lab. After much thought, I agreed to enroll the boys for one week. Charlene was moving to a nearby city at the end of that week, and I thought they could attend while she packed. On the lab's first day, Tutti was waiting for me. De was angry that his good shirts had been packed. He refused to attend if he had to wear a torn shirt. Both children had been attending a city summer day camp for project children which provided a meal, craft activities, games, and swimming. De decided that he would rather continue to attend it than go to the university with a torn shirt. Much to everyone's surprise, Tutti decided to attend the university's program without De. As we drove to the lab program,

Tutti explained that when De couldn't find a good shirt, he decided that he could have more fun at the day camp because he'd get to "run with the big boys" and get candy for winning games.

The 1989 summer lab students and professors had selected butterflies for their theme. When Tutti arrived, one of the undergraduates was using the shared book experience to open the morning session. She had selected a big book about a turtle that captured Tutti's attention the minute he walked through the door. After the opening activities, Tutti asked one of the graduate teachers where he could go to learn about "dem butterflies." She directed him to one of the centers called "The Safari."

Tutti's first remark when I picked him up at the end of the morning was, "Dem our butterflies to study. I want to go tomorrow. I helped make a tree."

Tutti experienced ownership, cooperation, sharing and *real* butterflies that first day. He played with the butterflies, watched them, heard stories, wrote, and then had an opportunity to make something in an unconventional way (a ten-foot-high tree cut from construction paper and taped to the wall).

As he entered the car for his second day, he said, "I helped dem make a tree and put a snake in it yesterday. You think snakes live in trees?"

I responded that snakes often crawled into trees along creek banks. When he looked a bit puzzled, I explained that a tree had to have limbs low enough for a snake to get started on its climb.

"Really!" He said. That response seemed to end his inquiry.

I asked what he thought he'd do that day. He noted that he wasn't sure but would wait and see what "dem girls offered." He walked into the lab and again quickly settled into a student's reading of *The Caterpillar Diary*, which has close-up photographs of the life cycle of the caterpillar and moth.

When I picked him up at 11:30, he said, "I been on a field trip." I responded with: "Oh? Where did you go?"

> Over to a place where they make thread and cloth and stuff.
> (*He was holding two sample patches of fabric.*)
> Yep, when I get home De, he gonna say, "What cha'do today? It was boring weren't it."
> I'm gonna say, "I went to see where they make stuff."
> Den he gonna say, "What stuff?"
> And I gonna say, "Thread. You know thread be white and den dey color it like dis here be blue and light blue."

Den he gonna say, "What be there beside thread?"

And I gonna say, "Dese machines that takes de thread and makes it into cloth like dis here."

(*To me*) Dem machines was on and was making stuff. And dey take thread and weave it together so it look like dis (*points to his patch of the tiger*). Dey weave it like (*puts his fingers so that they are somethat lattice like*).

Den Dede gonna say, "You gonna give me one dem?"

And I'm gonna say . . .

(*Stops and says to me*) Did you know this be a picture of a place here close to where my grand-daddy work? It be de building with a clock on it. Let turn here so you can see it. Look see! Dere it!

Den I'm gonna say, "Naw, I'm gonna put dis patch on my new blue jeans, and dis patch on de back of my new blue jean jacket and get me some blue shoes and go to my new school. Dey gonna think I'm from Auburn. Cause I is."

Den Dede's gonna say, "I'm going tomorrow."

And I gonna say, "Naw you ain't cause you didn't wanta go yesterday."

And he gonna say, "Yes I is!"

And I'm gonna say, "Naw you ain't!" Come get me early tomorrow so we can get dere early and be dere longer. (*He takes his patches and rearranges the designs on his leg, presses the tiger.*)

Dis be a tiger. Silk comes from worms. Dis be cotton.

Den I gonna say, "Dede I knowed how dis tiger be on dis cloth."

He gonna say, "Naw you don't."

And I gonna say, "Yea I do cause dey draw it on white paper and den dey do some other stuff and put a print of dis on the cloth. Everybody at school got one of dis."

He gonna say, "Naw you don't know."

Miss Brask is school where you be like dis? Is I gonna get to come to yo' school?

(*I respond with no. He continues.*)

Dis be fun! I got some real stuff.

(*We pull up to his grandmother's front door.*)

Don't forget to come early tomorrow. Textile . . . dat where it be. Textile.

This playful, make-believe conversation that Tutti enacted between himself and De allowed him to assimilate his recent field trip.

Furthermore, it was the space he needed for relating and connecting his field trip to his previous knowledge about field trips, cloth, machines, and his family and their knowledge. It was the first of several such make-believe conversations he had with different members of his family as we drove to and from the summer lab's program.

The interactive nature of this conversation, which occurred in external reality (Tutti sitting in the car and talking as I listened and drove) seemed to be an example of Winnicott's (1971) space of play which is between internal psychic and external reality. If that is the case, then through these conversations, Tutti used play to relate and connect the different cultural experiences (his home culture and his summer school's culture) he was having. Furthermore, it allowed him to construct his notions about contexts and relate them. Unlike De's conversations about the 1988 lab, his had cohesion, organization, and connection.

The next day, I realized that Tutti was attempting to resolve whether the summer lab experience was a real learning experience or like those he and De had experienced in last year's lab and during the school year. The following fieldnotes describe his struggle. They were recorded as he talked about his lab center's decision to create an environment (the rainforest) where butterflies could live.

What is a rainforest? Is it a real place? Do it have wild aminals? Like what kinds? Do dey live in cages? Do people live there? In what? Do you have pictures of it? Where is it? How come it be there [in the classroom] with butterflies?

I'm gonna stay at my uncle's and come next week. School starts August twenty-fifth, so I have to go the first day then I gonna come back here."

His questioning focused on the reality of a rainforest and then connected with his notions about wild animals being caged at a zoo. He also asked me, an outside authority whom he trusted, whether this study was real. As he closed his nonstop questioning, he answered his own question about returning to the program for another week even though Charlene and De had moved. His decision to return for a second week indicated that he had determined that the lab was a place he could learn.

The next morning, Tutti walked eight blocks in order to attend the program. Because he and his family had spent the night at an uncle's house, he had not been at his home when I went for him. When I picked him up at noon, he reported that he had made a tiger—drawn it on paper on the wall and then colored it. He stated, "They put the paper on the wall, and you draw on it there. At school you get little paper and draw at yo' table."

Later that same day, Tutti was looking at a Phantom comic book when he saw a tiger with the same pose as his. He exclaimed, "This be just like my tiger. Look." I looked and nodded in agreement. He then pointed to another. "This tiger be on a mountain?" I replied that the tiger was on a ledge. He fired back, "Do they have ledges in the rainforest?" I replied that they could.

In this conversation, Tutti talked about the connections he was making between his own representation of a tiger and the comic book's representation. His construction of such a relationship freed him to begin to understand that pictures and print in books are representations of reality. It also allowed him to see that he, like the writers of books, could make such representations. Finally, it served as a connector between the abstract meaning of print and real objects. He demonstrated his construction of the relationship again when he reported that he had also made an ant tree. He explained that he had learned about it from the teachers and from a book. He noted that he named his tree's ants, "Aztec ants...like in the book." Such comments seemed to suggest that Tutti had come to use this book as a source from which he could pull information and make meaning.

Tutti continued to make plants, flowers, ants, and animals and to engage in the large-group time, which consisted of shared reading, shared journal writing, and wrap-up. He also began making friends with the other children in his center, and they soon functioned as a team when they made various objects and animals.

On August 9, 1989, Tutti met me in the hall and exclaimed:

I made a shirt today. I put it on dat frame. De butterfly was on it. She poured orange paint on dat butterfly. I pulled dat ting over de shirt. Real careful then there be de picture. It was hard to pull. Then I had to take it off careful and put it on a table. It take one hour to dry.

I asked him if he had done silkscreening with his shirt. He responded, "Yea, like on dis here shirt. I think dat it like my shirt." Although he changed subjects, he continued without a pause: "I made a coral snake. Dey be poison. Dey even be round here."

Because I had seen it and knew that it was three-dimensional I asked, "Did you stuff it?" He replied,

Naw, some dem did. I painted it. Dey stuff it. It be a stocking
with some stuff from WalMart's in it. I painted de bands (*We drove
through a wooded area*) Dey . . . dem coral snakes be out there.
I ain't gonna go out there. You have to put a thing on your arm
dat be real tight if dem snakes bite you. Then somebody sucks
de poison out. I wonder why . . . do horses lay down to sleep at
night? How?

I attempted to explain that horses do lay down to sleep and how they
do it.

Tutti continued to engage in shared play at the lab. He was not
only representing objects through writing and drawing, but also
through three-dimensional sculpturing. Furthermore, he was able to
do such representation both as a member of a team and on his own.
It seemed that his self-confidence was increasing. For example, he
talked more, asked *I wonder* questions, and even planned what he
would do in the lab the next day.

When one of my teacher friends asked Tutti what he was studying
in the summer lab, he explained that he was studying with the others
in the safari center. He noted that they were all studying about
butterflies, but "I be doin my work in de safari." He elaborated, "I
be doin' my artwork." She explained that she had seen his tiger. To
which he responded, "I be doin a coral snake now. I can draw any
animal I want to dere."

This conversation shows that he viewed his work in his center
as important, something he controlled, something he could shape and
create—and the center as a place he could work. It also showed that
he was unrestrained in his work. Finally, it showed the importance
he placed in working with others. Rather than answering her question
with the topic of study, he answered with the fact he was studying
with others. Then he named the topic. Interestingly enough, he did
not stop at that point, he went on to let her know where his work
was occurring and what his current project was. Such comments
seemed to indicate that he was creating his work environment rather
than having adults create it for him.

Even though Tutti loved to read and have stories read or told
to him, he had never been much of a storyteller. He would add details
to De's retellings about a movie, TV show, family event, or school
happening, but he seldom offered his own. As he gained confidence
through his work at the center, he began to make up stories. One
morning he asked whether I had been to a park at a local lake. I
responded that I had. He began a tale:

I went up to Windy Creek. Dere be alligators up dere. Out in the deep water and long de edge too. Dey look like logs, you know. I was walkin'. . . long de edge. I picked up a log and under it was a little alligator. I throwed dat log down. It were a baby one. It had jaws. They jaws opened wide, and it be white inside. Dey have teeth and bite you. I told Dede, Don't you go over dere. Dere be a alligator over dere. He didn't go neither.

Alligators be in big water places. They be in the water places in the rainforest. Be careful!

His story was anchored in reality. He used a real place, real facts that he had learned about alligators, and real characters. He paired these with a make-believe adventure he and his brother had had. Rather than De being the hero, Tutti warned De and saved him from the jaws of the alligator. Finally, Tutti ended his story by telling his listeners where they could find alligators. He also warned them to be careful of the alligator when they go to large and small bodies of water.

Tutti told me the alligator story after he had made his information book about the coral snake. Like that story, the coral snake book is anchored in reality. Unlike the alligator story, the book is an expository piece about the snake. Its text is presented here in its entirety.

Dazzling
Deadly
Coral
Snake
By Lavoris (Title Page)

The snake has venem. (Page 1 which included the print and a picture of the snake's mouth and tongue.)

This snake can possne and celae people. (Page 2 which included the print and picture of the snake.)

The crayola is red black yellow. (Page 3 which included print and a picture of the snake's mid-section with the rings colored. Tutti used the label on his crayon in an attempt to spell color.)

The rain forest is war he live. (Page 4 which included the print and a picture of trees and rain drops.)

It dose not have no legs and ame (arms). (Page 5 which is a picture of the entire snake along with the print.)

The snake eat anmle. (Page 6 which depicts part of the snake, as well as the print.)

It dose'nt eat plopoe (people). (Page 7 has letters that take up the
entire page, thus no picture.)
The end. (Page 8)
The book is about a snake. (The book's summary which appeared
on the back cover.)

This story used alliteration in its title. It had some degree of
cohesion. It contained specific, factual details that Tutti learned as he
studied about the coral snake, and Tutti presented those details through
his illustrations and print. He determined the book's contents, length,
and appearance. He was its maker.

The same day he told me his alligator story, Tutti read his snake
book to the entire lab group (45 children and 40 undergraduate
students). When I asked him how he felt when he read to that many
people, he said quietly, "They clapped for me. They clapped for me
when I read my book."

These two attempts at making books and telling stories were
Tutti's first tries as a maker of literacy artifacts. According to earlier
fieldnotes, he had not had opportunities to make books or tell stories
in school. He had not had an audience listen to his writings or look
at his artwork. Charlene was the only one who asked him to write,
and his writings from those sessions were formula-like and looked more
like sentences copied from a blackboard or the basal reader than
cohesive stories. Following is an example:

Jack the Pup
He was born 1989.
He was mean.
He got put in the dogpronud.
He got put in there for biting peoples.
He had big teeth.
He was tied up with a chain.

Tutti explained that he had corrected the writing because his
mother made him. Furthermore, he did not use illustrations or enjoy
doing the writing. He claimed that he had difficulty knowing what to
write so he used De's ideas of writing about the puppy. He also stated
that he hoped she would not make him write at home because they
did not write at school.

These comments were in contrast to his interest in writing in the
summer lab. There he wrote everyday. He labeled his artwork and
wrote facts about that work. He wrote in a shared journal and made

books. Finally, he and his team wrote and produced the script for a video of their work and then (with the help of the undergraduate teachers) presented it to the entire summer lab group. Again, he and his team were the makers who worked in their own environment. They were using real materials for meaningful tasks.

Needless to say, Tutti continued to attend the lab. He stayed with an uncle and his great-grandmother because his mother had moved. Each day he would discuss his plans for his work in the lab. The discussions seemed to be unsolicited, external talks with himself. They had some of the characteristics of his imaginary interactive conversations with his family at the beginning of the summer, but these conversations focused on plans for the day rather than explaining past events. The following transcript recounts one such conversation:

I'm gonna make another tiger today. One of dem soft sculpture. It gonna be standing. Like I did my snake. Stuff it and paint it.

I'm gonna make me a monkey tomorrow . . . I mean Monday. It be easy. I can make three may be four things in a morning if we get there early. First, I go to group . . . large group . . . then choice board . . . then get to my work. I can even do five things if I work fast. I can draw a monkey . . . then make a soft sculpture . . . then . . . Tuesday I can do more things.

I reminded him that Tuesday was their fieldtrip to Callaway Gardens in Georgia. His response was, "Mean we can't work in the safari?"

When I asked Tutti to help me understand how much this lab experience had meant to him, he compared it to the day camp he and De had attended at the beginning of the summer.

This camp is better than that other one. They didn't do nothing. It was boring. If you got in trouble you had to go in the corner. Since there weren't nothing to do you stayed in the corner. Then when you go outside and somebody be bad . . . everybody be comin inside. Here don't nobody stay in the corner. You be doin stuff.

Then I asked him whether he thought this experience was school, camp, or something else. He thought for a moment and then said,

It be play. See, you go and read and do stuff in de large group. Den you go to de choice board and choose your work. Den you

do yor art. Art. . . dat be my work. Then you do your journal and
have snack. Play. . . you know. . . It be play. It be fun! You be
learnin bout art and soft sculpture and tigers and books and stuff.

During his first visit with his mother and De, he told them:

I be doin art. I drawed a tiger and made a baby tiger. I make a
coral snake. I made a book. I got a journal.

When De decided to minimize what Tutti had done by saying that he
could draw a rattlesnake better than Tutti could, Tutti replied that a
coral snake was more poisonous than a rattlesnake. He also explained
to De that he had done lots of drawing at the lab and had even
silkscreened a T-shirt. Finally, he said, "See, you be sorry you didn't
go now. You could have gone. A whole week. It mine now."

The following week, he went on the Callaway Gardens field trip
and came back with stories about what he had learned and seen, but
the next day he was eager to return to the lab so that he could finish
his spider monkey. He valued the trip, but he equally valued his work
and the place where he could do that work.

A few days before the lab ended, he announced that he needed
camouflage clothes for a film. He explained that they were going to
make a movie and have their safari van in it. They planned to use
tranquilizer guns to shoot the animals so that they could cage and study
them.

We gonna make up the parts about the van and the animals, but
we are goin to have a real movie with film and a camera. I ain't
never been in a film."

After we had decided on ways to get his clothes, he began to
inquire about attending this program throughout the year. I explained
that it was only a summer program. He continued to ask to stay in
a school like his summer program. When I pointed out that he could
attend again next summer, he remarked, "Lot can happen between
now and next summer. Can I brang my bike? Could we study about
dogs. . . dey'd be good. Dogs."

I dropped him off so that he and his team could shoot their film.
His teachers, Ms. Ramey and Ms. Smith, had the camera, film, and signs
for "Take One" and "Cut" ready for the group. When I picked him
up, I expected him to tell me numerous stories. Instead, when I asked
about the film he replied, "I be one of 'em." When I asked him to
clarify his statement, he repeated:

I be one of 'em. Before, at school, I weren't in plays. My clothes
or somethin' weren't right...but this time...I be one of 'em.

Through his experience in the summer lab program—the work
of professors like Janet B. Taylor and Steve Silvern, undergraduate
teachers like Pam Smith and Rachel Rainey, and the friendships of
children like Chase, Antonio, and Emily—Tutti constructed more
notions about literacy. He became the maker of his literacy artifacts
rather than the consumer. He paired his culture with the summer lab
program's culture so that he could function within both cultures with
some ease. He had laid claim to his play space and used it to build self-
confidence. Adults had not interfered in that space; rather, they
fostered and encouraged his work within it.

When Tutti left the lab for the last time, he carried two Hefty
garbage bags filled with pictures, objects, books, murals, and soft
sculpture that he had made. As he left, he looked at me and asked,
"Will I ever see 'em again?"

Reflections

Children try to understand the very nature of their world through
interaction in play, the constructions such interactions create, and the
environment in which those occur. When adults prepare a world in
which they want children to demonstrate what they know rather than
allowing children to build, act on, and be in that world, children often
resist. Such resistance causes disfranchisement unless an intervention
helps the children know that the adults' goals are to mold them to fit
into a given culture. When children do not share the adults' cultural
heritage, they are forced to question what is real and what is pretense.
They are also faced with finding a place to answer their questions
through play. Furthermore, they must question deeply whether the
adults' notions of demonstration are for the good of society, the good
of their culture, or the good of those adults who are in control.

De and Tutti have experienced such an adult-prepared educational environment. They have also had opportunities to construct their
own notions about literacy outside of those environments. Their media
to make such constructions have been play, their mother, storybooks,
artwork, and summer school experiences. Because of their
opportunities, they question the reality of many school settings. To
them, schools are "puttin' on" and not helping them with their work.

Because De is older, he entered school and felt the brunt of its
expectations first. Charlene did not view herself as successful enough

to help him learn how the school wanted him to do his work. He experienced the most opposition, failure, and alienation. Rather than continue to have confidence in himself and trust his own ability to demonstrate what the schools wanted him to do, he has retreated into his art and "hangin' with the big boys." He continues to "do school" the way the teachers expect, but considers his social play with the "big boys" his place to gain power, recognition, and control. He maintains that he will finish school, but he no longer feels the expectation or excitement about it that he once did.

Tutti, on the other hand, has learned from De. He listened as De told him what to expect in first grade. He followed De's advice about behavior and learning to read. He watched as De and Charlene worked with De's assignments, readings, and artwork. Because he had the opportunity to do this, he is a maker. He uses play when he reads stories, does his artwork, and talks with others. He uses the methods of literary characters to trick people when they are playing games. He makes his own chants and books. He uses the conventional in unconventional ways. Unlike De—who struggles to fit adults' molds, fails, and then becomes angry and withdraws—Tutti takes adults' molds and makes them fit his needs. To him, schooling "ain't real," but he has constructed ways to use that pretense as a pawn in his play.

In this project, the older brother, De, was the teacher and the family's warrior. He learned how to function in school. Tutti, in effect, apprenticed himself to De and the members of his team in summer lab so that he could make his own notions of literacy once he had learned their notions.

Notes

1. The identification of the subjects of this research has been done with the full written consent of Charlene Thomas. I expect to continue to work with her as we follow the progress of her sons.

2. I wish to extend a special thanks to Shirley Brice Heath and Janet B. Taylor for their help with this chapter.

References

Dyson, A. (1984). Learning to write/learning to do school: Emergent writers' interpretations of school literacy tasks. *Research in the Teaching of English 18.* (pp. 233–64).

Euripides (1987). *The Bacchae* (K. Cavander, Trans.). Minneapolis, MN: The Guthrie Theater. (Original work published 407 B.C.)

Heath, S. B. (1983). *Ways with words: Language, life, and work in communities and classrooms.* Cambridge, England: Cambridge University Press.

————— (1984). The achievement of preschool literacy for mother and child. In: H. Goelman, A. Oberg, and F. Smith (Eds.), *Awakening to literacy.* Exeter, NH: Heinemann Educational.

Kessel, F. and A. Goncu (Eds.) (1984). Analyzing children's play dialogues. *New Directions for Child Development, 25*(4). San Francisco: Jossey-Bass.

Millar, Susanna. (1974). *The psychology of play.* New York: Jason Aronson.

Piaget, J. (1962). *Plays, dreams, and imitation in childhood.* New York: Norton.

Sutton-Smith, B. (1984). Text and context in imaginative play and the social sciences. In: F. Kessel and A. Goncu (Eds.), Analyzing children's play dialogues. *New Directions for Child Development 25*(4). (pp. 53–70). San Francisco: Jossey-Bass.

Winnicott, D. W. (1971). *Playing and reality.* London: Tavistock.

Part III

Educational Applications

6

Classroom Literature Activities and Kindergartners' Dramatic Story Reenactments*

Miriam Martinez, Markay Cheyney, and William H. Teale

Today's early childhood educators can draw on an exciting decade of literacy research as they design and implement programs that provide children with daily opportunities to experience developmentally appropriate and meaningful reading and writing activities. A strong consensus has emerged that literature should be at the core of such programs. But just what types of experiences with stories should children have? It has long been widely accepted that early childhood teachers should read stories to children on a regular basis. Three decades of correlational and observational research studies, as well as recent experimental evidence, have clearly established that storybook reading contributes significantly to young children's literacy development (Sulzby and Teale, 1991). It is also increasingly recommended that children have opportunities to interact independently with stories as a planned part of the early childhood language arts curriculum (see, for example: Morrow, 1989b; Schickedanz, 1986; Teale and Martinez, 1988).

Of these two forms of storybook reading experience—being read stories and interacting independently with stories—far more is known about being read to. A substantial body of literature has helped us gain considerable insight into the nature and effects of storybook readings, both group storybook readings typical of the classroom and the more intimate storybook readings typical of the home (see: Martinez and

Roser, 1991; Sulzby and Teale, 1991; and Teale, 1987 for reviews). Less is known about children's independent interactions with stories, but the potential contribution of such interactions to young children's literacy development is indicated by several lines of research. The literature on early readers, for example, suggests that early readers typically spent long periods of time 'pretend reading' stories to themselves, to stuffed animals, or to pets (see, for example: Clark, 1976; Durkin, 1966; Tobin, 1981). A case study by Teale and Sulzby (1987) that covered a period of more than two years in a young child's life showed that independent re-enactments of books played a significant role in that child's literacy acquisition. In longitudinal studies, Sulzby (1985, 1988) has found that when two- to four-year-old children are asked to read familiar, well-liked stories, they produce speech that could be characterized as an act of reading. She described these readings by a classification scheme that identified 11 categories of emergent storybook reading. The scheme appeared to have developmental properties. Pappas (1987) studied the same types of reading and described the phenomenon as "protoreading." She found that proto-reading played a key role in various aspects of early childhood literacy development, such as learning the registers of written language and vocabulary development (Eller, Pappas, and Brown, 1988; Pappas and Brown, 1987).

We believed that it would be profitable to investigate more fully the role that such re-enactments of books play in facilitating early literacy development and to explore how to structure literacy environ-ments to foster the spontaneous occurrence of children's independent book-handling behaviors. Therefore, we conducted a one-year obser-vational study in three kindergarten classrooms. The study was designed to examine the relationships between the storybook reading program in each of the classrooms and the children's independent interactions with stories. In each classroom, observers documented children's independent uses of books in the classroom library. The children's independent behaviors were then analyzed.

One particular form of story re-enactment was of special note as we sought to understand the role of play in children's independent story reading behaviors. This was the dramatic story re-enactment in which the children spontaneously played a story which had been previously read to them. This form of story re-enactment was intriguing for a number of reasons. First, as we gathered data over the course of the year, it appeared that the spontaneous dramatic story re-enactments were occurring almost exclusively in one classroom. Furthermore, this particular form of story re-enactment appeared to be a highly motivating and involving experience for the children. Finally, there exists a body of research which suggests that dramatic story re-enactment, like children's "pretend reading" of storybooks, facilitates literacy development.

This chapter presents a case study of the kindergarten classroom in which spontaneous dramatic re-enactments of stories were an integral part of the classroom literacy program. In particular, we describe the literacy context that appeared to nurture these re-enactments.

Review of Related Research

Many different experiences contribute to a child's early literacy learning, and evidence continues to be amassed that play can be one of those facilitating experiences. Literacy development and play are intermeshed in a variety of ways. For example, play appears to facilitate the representational abilities that serve as the foundation for literacy development (Isenberg and Jacob, 1983; Pellegrini, 1980; Piaget, 1962, Vygotsky, 1978). Play can provide children with opportunities to explore various uses and functions of print and to practice different literacy skills directly (Isenberg and Jacob, 1983; Jacob, 1984; Morrow, 1989). Last of all, a number of lines of evidence converge to suggest that play fosters a child's emerging sense of story. It is this final intermeshing of literacy development and play that forms the focus of this review.

The Developmental Nature of Children's Narrative Competence

Sense of story refers to one's understanding of the form and structure of stories, an understanding that can be at an explicit or implicit level. Researchers who have described the structure of stories have identified a number of key components common to most stories (Mandler and Johnson, 1977; Rumelhart, 1975; Stein and Glenn, 1979). These researchers describe stories as consisting of episodes which center around problems. These episodes contain key elements—a protagonist *attempts* to achieve a *goal,* there is an *outcome* to the attempt, and the character *reacts* to the outcome. The reader (or listener) who develops an intuitive sense of the organization of stories is clearly at an advantage in that a sense of story facilitates both the reader's processing and recall of stories.

A number of lines of research have revealed that the child's sense of story, or narrative competence, is developmental in nature. First of all, the stories children tell differ distinctly across age levels. Applebee (1978) analyzed the stories told by two- to five-year-olds from the Pitcher and Prelinger (1963) collection, and he found increasing complexity across age levels. Younger children's stories consisted of unrelated 'heaps' of actions and arbitrary 'sequences' of actions. Growth was evident in the older children's stories, which centered around a main character and contained a series of linked events that became increasingly elaborate. Gardner and Gardner (1971) also found increasing competence as they examined first, third, sixth, and ninth graders' story completions and retellings. Sulzby's (1985) investigations of the re-enactments of familiar storybooks also indicated that children's narrative competence is developmental in nature. Finally, investigations of children's sociodramatic play also reveal the developmental nature of children's narrative competence. Sachs (1980) noted that, as children got older, more elements of the mature story (as described by story grammars) appeared in their play, and these elements were better developed.

The Contribution of Dramatic Story Re-enactments to Young Children's Literacy Development

It seems reasonable that children's developing sense of story would emerge through their repeated experiences with narratives (Galda, 1984). These experiences can take many forms for the young child—storybook reading, listening to others telling personal stories, engaging in sociodramatic play, and participating in dramatic re-enactments of stories. Miccinati and Phelps (1980) argue that this latter form of narrative experience, the dramatic story re-enactment, contributes directly to the development of children's sense of story:

> It allows them to sharpen their sense of how a story "works," how the elements of character, plot, action, and setting work together. Through dramatic retelling of a story, children develop what Applebee (1978) calls their "mastery of the underlying conventions which govern the exchange between author and audience."

Pellegrini and Galda (1982) present similar arguments in their discussion of dramatic story re-enactments, or what they term "thematic-fantasy play" (TFP). Citing the work of Brown (1975), who found that children's story comprehension is facilitated through story reconstruction, they argue that TFP helps children "build an internal representation of the story" (p. 444). They believe that TFP is an especially powerful form of story reconstruction because child participants collaborate with others and, in the process of play, must accommodate their story concepts to those of others.

The dramatic story re-enactment has been the focus of a number of investigations. Saltz and Johnson (1974) found that the preschoolers who received TFP training scored significantly better on a story memory task and were better able to connect and integrate events in telling a story. In a follow-up study, Saltz, Dixon, and Johnson (1977) found that preschoolers who had an above-median IQ and who received TFP and sociodramatic play training were better able to relate events and interpret causal relations between events when telling a story depicted by pictures.

Pellegrini and Galda (1982) examined the effects of TFP on children's recall and comprehension of the story played. They found that kindergarten and first- and second-grade children who verbally reconstructed stories through play interactions with peers performed significantly better in retelling the story and on a criterion-referenced comprehension test. Further, those children in the TFP condition who played roles that required more active involvement (i.e., the roles of major characters) performed better on the recall and comprehension measures. Second graders in the play condition did not perform significantly better than peers in the discussion and drawing conditions. Yet, in a further analysis of the second graders' retellings, Galda (1984) found that those who played the story had richer retellings that included more character motivations. She also found evidence of greater understanding of cause-and-effect relationships within the story and greater sensitivity to the emotional responses of characters. Galda concluded that playing a story helped the older children "shift from focus on the physical events in a story to a more psychological, character-oriented focus" (p. 114).

Building on this work, Silvern and colleagues (1986) conducted two investigations to determine whether the facilitative effects of TFP were due to the play itself or to the adult tutoring that occurred in the play conditions in each investigation (see Chapter 4). As they studied children in kindergarten through third grade, the researchers found that the story recall increased with age and that children in the TFP condition performed significantly better on story recall than did children in a control condition. Further analysis revealed that the TFP treatment benefited children up to the age of 6.7. Their second study focused specifically on the effects of adult intervention by establishing two play conditions—(a) *directive,* in which teachers who led play groups were told to take responsibility for making sure that the re-enactment of the story was accurate by narrating, prompting, and directing the action as was needed, and (b) *facilitative,* in which teachers were trained to help children establish the situation so that the children themselves controlled the re-enactment. Silvern and colleagues found that children in the play conditions performed significantly better than did those in the story-discussion condition, but there was not a significant difference between the two play conditions. Thus, TFP itself facilitated development of young children's sense of story, although the most positive role which the teacher can take in promoting children's play remained unclear.

Investigations have revealed that TFP is an activity that fosters many aspects of children's narrative competence—story memory, storytelling, story interpretation, and story recall of re-enacted stories as well as stories not re-enacted. However, the picture is a complex one. Children of different ages appear to respond differently to TFP. Although preschoolers in the Saltz and Johnson study benefited from TFP training, only the more intellectually mature preschoolers in the Saltz, Dixon, and Johnson study benefited from the training. Focusing on older subjects, Pellegrini and Galda (1982) and Silvern and colleagues (1986) also found age to be a factor. In both investigations, kindergartens and first graders benefited from TFP as measured by their story recall, whereas older children did not. However, Galda's qualitative analysis of her second-grade subjects' retellings suggests that these older children benefited from TFP by developing greater sensitivity to the motives and emotional responses of characters.

Consideration of Factors Related to the Implementation of a Program of Dramatic Re-enactments

The dramatic story re-enactment would appear to be a strategy that early childhood teachers could profitably incorporate into the literacy program. However, questions must be answered about how best to implement and sustain a program of dramatic story re-enactments in a natural classroom setting. What features of the literacy context foster the occurrence of TFP? What is the role of the adult in sustaining children's TFP? Our discussion of factors related to the implementation of a program of dramatic re-enactments focuses first on the role of the adult.

Vygotsky maintains that children learn higher psychological processes by participating with adults in activities requiring those processes. He states: "The very mechanism underlying higher mental functions is a copy from social interaction. All higher mental functions are internalized social relationships" (1981). Research certainly indicates that many facets of children's literacy development are facilitated through adult support, including direct interactions with adults. Morrow (1989a) found that children in classrooms where teachers provided literacy-related materials in dramatic play areas and guidance in the use of those materials participated in more literacy activities during play than did children in a control group. Harris-Schmidt and McNamee (1986) found that children learned planning and monitoring literacy strategies while working under the guidance of an adult in writing activities. Evidence also exists that children develop narrative competence by participating with adults in different activities. Sachs (1980) found that parents facilitate the young child's narrative competence by guiding and structuring the child's socio-dramatic play. Storybook reading is a literacy activity which lends itself to fostering narrative competence through child/adult interactions. Examining the storybook reading interaction styles of three kindergarten teachers, Martinez and Teale (1989) identified one style that appeared to be especially apt to promote the development of children's sense of story. This style was one in which the teacher consistently highlighted key story events and character goals, both during and following the reading of the story.

The research on TFP also suggests a need to attend more closely to the role of the adult in promoting dramatic re-enactment of stories. Saltz and Johnson (1974) gathered observational data that gives insight into the impact of TFP training on children's spontaneous play behaviors. The children were observed on 20 different days during the intervention, and all instances of TFP or sociodramatic play were recorded. The researchers found that significantly more TFP subjects participated in dramatic free play than did other subjects. Comparing the first 10 observations to the final 10, Saltz and Johnson found a significant increase in spontaneous TFP for TFP subjects and a drop in spontaneous TFP for control subjects.

Saltz, Dixon, and Johnson (1977) also systematically observed their subjects outside the training situation during free play and counted the occurrences of TFP. Each child was observed on 20 different occasions for one minute per observation. The following percentages of children in each group engaged in spontaneous TFP at least once: TFP group, 57%; sociodramatic-play group, 21%; fantasy-discussion group, 33%; and control group, 18%. The observations of Saltz and Johnson, as well as those of Saltz, Dixon, and Johnson, suggest that TFP does not necessarily occur spontaneously on a widespread basis without adult nurturing. Children's participation in adult-initiated, adult-led TFP appears to foster the occurrence of spontaneous TFP.

Although the studies reviewed thus far provide insights into how to promote dramatic re-enactments in a classroom setting, they also raise questions about the role of adults in fostering TFP. Saltz and Johnson found that preschoolers required extensive adult support in playing stories. Initially, the children in the study enjoyed TFP, but they nonetheless found it difficult. In their early attempts to re-enact the stories, they had difficulty remembering the story sequence and they often remembered only the final scene or the most striking event in the story. In order to facilitate TFP, several changes were made in procedures. The intervention teacher often participated in the dramatization by assuming one of the roles. In addition, the teacher narrated portions of the story while the children re-enacted them; for the portions of the story that were not narrated the teacher provided lines for the children as needed. As the children became more experienced at re-enacting stories with adult support and guidance, Saltz and Johnson found that they became better at following the sequence of the stories and generally became more efficient at TFP.

The necessity of adult intervention and support with older children is less clear. Galda (1982) observed that story dramatizations do not come easily for all children. She recommended that teachers facilitate TFP through the use of questions and suggestions as well as by actually participating as a player in the dramatization. However, Silvern and his colleagues did not find any overall significant differences between facilitative and directive teacher involvement. Their findings also suggested that the target story the children will be re-enacting may be a factor that should be considered. Children who re-enacted unfamiliar stories benefited when the adult assumed a directive role, whereas those re-enacting familiar stories benefited more when the adult assumed a facilitative role. Given the potential benefits of dramatic story re-enactments, these and other issues related to the implementation of this strategy deserve attention.

Dramatic Story Re-enactments in a Kindergarten Classroom

In this section we explore the literacy context in which dramatic re-enactments flourished in one kindergarten classroom by presenting preliminary analysis of data collected as part of the previously described year-long observational study of emergent literacy behaviors in the library centers of three kindergarten classrooms. Although our discussion centers on only one classroom, some comparisons will be made to a second classroom in the study in order to provide perspective on the focal classroom.

Both classrooms were in a school located in an older neighborhood in an urban community. The neighborhood contained families from varied ethnic backgrounds—Hispanic, African American, Anglo, and Asian—and from different socioeconomic status groups. Many of the children in the school were considered at-risk children, including children whose families were below the poverty line, children whose first language was not English, and children whose parents were illiterate. Many other students at the school, however, were from mainstream backgrounds.

Procedures

Data were collected over a period of one academic year in the two kindergarten classrooms. An identical core classroom library of approximately 50 hardback children's books was established in each classroom. The teachers selected the books, which were paid for by the grant funding the project. The core collections contained a mixture of books with predictable structures and ones with nonpredictable structures. The teachers were told they could supplement this core collection in any way they wished.

Baseline data from the classroom library activities were collected in each classroom during the first four weeks of the school year. During this period, the children's use of the library center was relatively unstructured. The children worked without direct adult supervision and were told that they could read books to themselves or to each other.

Following the collection of baseline data, the program intervention was introduced in Ms. Garrett's classroom. Ms. Chavez's classroom served as the control group. Procedures that had been established for the library during the first four weeks were maintained throughout the study in Ms. Chavez's classroom. In the focal classroom, the literature program was organized to encourage independent re-enactments of stories. The control classroom teacher was not directed to take any action to foster the spontaneous occurrence of story re-enactments.

The intervention attempted to induce story re-enactments in Ms. Garrett's classroom in two general ways. First, the investigators worked with the classroom teacher in structuring the storybook read-aloud program to ensure that predictable books were read regularly and that repeated readings of particular books were systematically provided. This emphasis on predictable books and repeated readings was prompted by the findings from a pilot study in another kindergarten classroom indicating that these two variables affected children's independent reading behaviors (Martinez and Teale, 1988).

In addition to restructuring the read-aloud program, the teacher in the intervention classroom also changed the children's routine at the library center one day a week. Based on the results of the pilot study, the investigators and the teacher developed a repertoire of activities that required story re-enactments—e.g., reading to a partner, reading to a stuffed animal, reading while conducting a flannel board presentation of a story, reading and acting out a story. Ways of implementing each activity were discussed with the teacher. The teacher then encouraged the students to participate once a week at the library center in an adult-initiated activity that encouraged an independent re-enactment of a storybook. When the students visited the library center on other days, they were directed (as were the children in the control group) to 'read' books to themselves or each other.

Data Collection

Classroom library observations. Observational data were collected in both classrooms over the entire period of the study. In each library center, two observers were present twice a week for one hour per visit. As small groups of children worked in the center, each observer recorded information on designated children in the group. Several types of information were collected for each child. First, the title of each book selected by the child was recorded. This information enabled the researchers to describe children's book selections in the library center. The observers also recorded the way(s) in which each book was used by the child, as well as any book-related social interaction involving other persons present in the library center (e.g., leafing through the book, systematically and silently studying illustrations, 'reading' the story to a partner, etc.).

Performance samples of emergent reading. In addition to descriptions of students' emergent reading behaviors in the classroom, data on their emergent reading behaviors and their book-handling knowledge were collected in interview situations. These data will not be reported in this chapter.

Teacher logs. The teacher in each classroom kept a log during the course of the study. In this log, the teacher maintained a record of all books read to the class and described any teacher-initiated activities related to those books (art projects, puppetry, etc.).

Booklists. Each teacher also maintained a list of all books that moved into and out of the library center during the course of the year. Based on inspections of each book on the list, the researchers coded each book on a number of variables—book size (big book or conventional-sized); type of story (story or non-story); type of non-story (informational, alphabet, counting, concept, poetry, other); and structure (predictable or unpredictable). Based on information obtained through the teacher's logs, each book was also coded according to three additional features—(1) the number of times the book was read to the children; (2) the type(s) of response activities, if any, associated with the book (art, class book, experience chart, creative dramatics, choral reading, flannel board, music, puppetry, emergent writing, other); and (3) the type(s) of related activities, if any, associated with the book (flannel board, dramatic presentation, music, puppetry, other). Response activities were those in which children directly participated, either independently or under teacher guidance. Related activities were those in which the children participated as members of an audience, but did not themselves conduct. Thus, a dramatic presentation as a related activity might have the children watching a production by an adult theatre group or older children.

Teacher journal. Beginning in February, when it became apparent that the children in Ms. Garrett's room were getting extremely involved in spontaneous dramatic story re-enactments, Ms. Garrett began to keep a journal in which she recorded her observations related to the children's spontaneous dramatic story re-enactments, as well as interviews with her students about their dramatizations. This journal was kept from February until the end of the school year (early June).

Findings

Our focus in reporting findings is on Ms. Garrett's classroom. However, in order to establish a perspective for understanding what was happening there, it is helpful to begin by comparing the classrooms of Ms. Garrett and Ms. Chavez on a number of key dimensions. Then, we describe Ms. Garrett's classroom in more depth in order to identify components of the literacy context that nurtured the children's spontaneous dramatic re-enactments of stories.

A general indicator of activity is the mean number of book-handling episodes per child in each classroom library. A book-handling episode occurred when a child picked up a book and interacted with it himself/herself, or when the child was read to (either in an emergent fashion or conventionally) by another child. The children in the study were found to have interacted with a book in any one of the following ways: leafing through the book, silently studying the book, engaging in an independent emergent reading or a choral emergent reading, emergent reading to a partner or group, discussing the illustrations in a book with others, acting out a story or portions of a story, or reading a story conventionally. There was little difference in the number of book-handling episodes in the two classroom libraries. In Ms. Garrett's classroom, the mean number of episodes per child over the entire observation period was 77.6; in Ms. Chavez's classroom, 69.4.

Of greater note than the amount of book-handling activity in the two library centers was the way in which the children interacted with books. The activity in Ms. Garrett's library center was a more social experience than the activity in Ms. Chavez's center. There were six categories of book-handling behaviors in which a child interacted with others: emergent reading to a partner, emergent reading to a group, choral reading, discussion of illustrations, story re-enactment, and listening to another person reading. As can be seen in Table 6.1, these six categories accounted for 49.4% of all the children's activities in the library center in Ms. Garrett's classroom, compared to 33.7% in Ms. Chavez's classroom.

Table 6.1

Book Handling Behaviors in the Two Library Centers

Behavior	Garrett		Chavez	
	Number	Percent	Number	Percent
Leafing through book	365	19.6	260	15.0
Silent studying	395	21.2	395	22.8
Emergent reading (independently)	644	34.6	752	43.3
Emergent reading (to partner)	150	8.1	93	5.4
Emergent reading (to group)	33	1.8	11	.6
Choral reading	110	5.9	30	1.7
Discusses illustrations	264	14.2	319	18.4
Dramatic reenactment	175	9.4	16	.9
Conventional reading	14	.8	59	3.4
Listens to someone reading	186	10.0	116	6.7

Another way of noting contrasts in the social dimensions of interacting with books in the two classrooms was to examine the activities that involve reconstructing a story. Four categories of story reconstruction were social in nature (emergent reading with a partner, emergent reading to a group, choral emergent reading, and dramatic story re-enactments), one was nonsocial (independent emergent reading), and one could have been either (conventional reading). In Ms. Garrett's room, independent emergent readings (a nonsocial form of story reconstruction) accounted for 34.6% of the total behaviors compared to 43.3% in Ms. Chavez's room. By contrast, emergent reading to a partner, to a group, or chorally accounted for 15.8% of the activity in Ms. Garrett's library center and only 7.7% in Ms. Chavez's classroom.

Finally, of particular note was the difference in the occurrence of spontaneous dramatic story re-enactments in the two classrooms. In Ms. Garrett's library center, there were 175 documented instances of dramatic re-enactments (9.4% of the total library center activities), compared to 16 instances (0.9% of the total library center activities) in Ms. Chavez's center.

Why were book interactions in Ms. Garrett's classroom library more social in nature than those in Ms. Chavez's room? What factors fostered the occurrence of dramatic story re-enactments in Ms. Garrett's room? These were guiding questions in this study, and in seeking answers we examined the global context in which literature was shared with the children in the two classrooms. A number of key differences provided insights into why the children interacted with books in such different ways in their respective library centers.

In general, Ms. Garrett's classroom appeared to be the more literature-oriented of the two classes. One way in which this was evident was in the number of books that the two teachers made available in the classroom library. During the course of the study Ms. Garrett introduced a total of 558 books into the classroom library, and 454 of these books were available on a long-term basis (i.e., for one month or longer). By contrast, Ms. Chavez introduced a total of 136 books in her library center, 118 of which were available on a long-term basis.

The emphasis on storybook reading was also different in the two classrooms. Ms. Garrett read to her children 375 of the storybooks that were placed in the library center, whereas Ms. Chavez read 110 of the books in her library center. (Both teachers also read stories to their students that were not made available for the students' use in the library centers. However, since these were not available for the children's independent use, they were excluded from our analysis.) Furthermore, in Ms. Garrett's classroom, the children had far more *intensive* experiences with stories. Reading a story repeatedly to children is one way to provide an intensive experience with a story. Of the 373 storybook readings in Ms. Garrett's classroom, 251 were repeated readings of a storybook. In Ms. Chavez's classroom, 109 of the 174 storybook readings were repeated readings.

A teacher can also make children's experiences with a story more intense by providing them with the opportunity to respond to the story in multiple and diverse ways—through creative dramatics, through music, through art, through writing, and so on. Table 2 depicts the frequency of response activities in each classroom. In Ms. Garrett's room, the children were invited by the teacher to respond to 67 of the stories read aloud. For 27 of these stories, more than one response activity was provided. In Ms. Chavez's classroom, response activities accompanied 23 of the stories read aloud, with only two of these stories accompanied by more than one response activity.

The social nature of the literature experience in Ms. Garrett's classroom was also evident in the types of response activities that accompanied stories. Table 6.2 shows that, of the 117 response activities in Ms. Garrett's classroom, 61 were social experiences (composing a class book or experience chart, music, choral reading, creative dramatics, flannel board story, puppet story). Twenty-five response activities occurred in Ms. Chavez's classroom, with only the 8 creative dramatics activities being social in nature.[1] Of particular note in Table 6.2 is the difference in the occurrence of teacher-initiated, teacher-led creative dramatics activities in the two classrooms. There were 20 instances of such activities in Ms. Garrett's classroom compared to only 8 in Ms. Chavez's classroom. Thus, the more social nature of the storybook experiences in Ms. Garrett's room was one factor that could be related to the occurrence of spontaneous dramatic re-enactments in her classroom.

In addition, Ms. Garrett, through the use of repeated readings and response activities, frequently provided her students with intense experiences with stories. These experiences helped make the stories more accessible to the children. A final comparative variable that might be related to the occurrence of dramatic story re-enactments in the classroom library center was that Mrs. Garrett's library and her read-aloud log contained many more predictable books than did Ms. Chavez's. Mrs. Garrett's library held 87 predictable books, and 45 of those books had been read aloud at least once. The corresponding figures for Ms. Chavez were 40 predictable books in the library, with 34 of those books having been read aloud. Many researchers and early childhood educators have noted that books containing highly

Table 6.2

Frequency of Response Activities

Type of Activity	Garrett Frequency	Chavez Frequency
Class book	3	0
Experience chart	3	0
Emergent writing	28	1
Music	12	0
Choral reading	16	0
Creative dramatics	20	8
Art	22	15
Flannel board	3	0
Puppetry	4	0
Other	6	0

predictable plots or repetitive, cumulative, or rhyming language patterns can be more easily remembered by young children; and ease of recall might well be related to dramatic re-enactments of stories.

Ms. Garrett's Classroom

Dramatic story re-enactments were a popular activity in Ms. Garrett's classroom. In this section we focus on a number of factors that appeared to be related to the occurrence of these re-enactments.

It would seem that the more familiar children are with a story, the easier it would be for them to reconstruct it. Hence, it was expected that increased familiarity with a story would foster the occurrence of dramatic re-enactments of that story. Chi-square analyses on the data reported in Table 6.3 indicated that the number of times a story was read to the children was significantly related to the occurrence of dramatic story re-enactments: $x^2(10) = 238.6$, p < .001. Only 10.9% of the dramatic re-enactments occurred with stories that Ms. Garrett had read only once, whereas more than half (59.8%) of the dramatic re-enactments occurred with stories that had been read to the children five or six times. Reading a story more than six times appeared to have relatively little effect on the occurrence of the children's dramatic story re-enactments.

Predictable story structures also appeared to give children access to books. A Chi-square analysis showed that story predictability was significantly related to the occurrence of dramatic story re-enactments:

Table 6.3

Relationship between Number of Readings
and Occurrence of Dramatic Re-enactments

Number of Times Story Was Read	Percentage of Dramatic Re-enactments
1	10.9
2	7.5
3	1.4
4	10.9
5	37.7
6	21.9
7	2.7
9	6.2
10	0.8

$x^2(2) = 39.6$, p < .001. When acting out stories, the children in Ms. Garrett's room chose books with predictable structures 78.1% of the time. Of particular note was the frequency with which the children chose to act out big books. The big books in Ms. Garrett's classroom library were all highly predictable and very short, a combination of features that seemed to make them highly accessible. Although only 11 (2%) of the 558 books in Ms. Garrett's classroom library were big books, 10% of the total dramatic re-enactments centered around big books.

Ms. Garrett heightened attention to books through the use of response activities, which in turn appeared to increase the likelihood that the children would spontaneously re-enact a story. Chi-square analysis of the data in Table 6.4 indicated that the occurrence of a response activity with a story was significantly related to the occurrence of dramatic story re-enactments: $x^2(9) = 163.2$, p < .001. In fact, 70.5% of the dramatic re-enactments in Ms. Garrett's classroom occurred with stories that were associated with a response activity of some sort. Many of the stories that the children re-enacted were associated with more than one response activity. Of the 31 titles re-enacted by the children, 15 had been accompanied by a response activity, and 13 of these 15 titles had been accompanied by between two and five response activities.

These data clearly indicate that story predictability, story familiarity, and the number and type of response activities are related to the occurrence of dramatic story re-enactments. Through analysis of her journal, Ms. Garrett identified a number of other factors operating

Table 6.4

Percentage of Dramatic Re-enactments across Response Activity Types

Type of Response Activity	Percentage of Instances of Dramatic Re-enactments
No response activity	29.5
Art	8.2
Class book	21.2
Creative dramatics	26.7
Choral reading	8.9
Flannel board	4.1
Music	0.7
Puppetry	0
Emergent writing	0.7
Other	0

within her classroom that may also have worked to motivate the children to re-enact stories in the classroom library. First of all, singing was an important activity in this classroom, and the children were encouraged to do dramatic renditions of songs which included putting motions to the songs the class sang. Likewise, when participating in choral readings during story time, the children were invited to express themselves in dramatic ways and to use gestures and voices that were appropriate to story characters. Also, creative dramatics were even used in conjunction with "word bank" activities. The children in Ms. Garrett's classroom kept "word banks"—boxes that contained words of special interest to them. They dictated the words to Ms. Garrett, who wrote them on cards. As it turned out, the children often chose to include the names of story characters in their word boxes, and they frequently chose to dramatize a story character as part of the word bank activity. Dramatic play was also nurtured through the use of themed dramatic play centers—a store, a hospital, a beauty parlor, and so on. Finally, in order to facilitate trouble-free story re-enactments, Ms. Garrett taught her children special strategies such as running or hopping in place and pretending to touch rather than actually doing so. By teaching the children such strategies, she was able to give them the freedom to engage independently in dramatic story re-enactments when visiting the classroom library without fear of major disturbances.

Ms. Garrett identified one final factor that she felt was especially important in nurturing dramatic re-enactments. In November, in an attempt to encourage spontaneous dramatic re-enactments in the library center, she began to seek others who could model story re-enactments for her kindergartners. One opportunity to provide her students with models occurred in December when she took her class to see a scripted dramatization of *The Emperor's New Clothes* presented by an adult theatre group. Also, in November, she began collaborating with a second-grade teacher in her school. With the help of university practicum students assigned to her classroom, the second-grade teacher organized groups of second graders to present a series of unscripted story dramatizations for the kindergartners. Three of these dramatizations occurred in November, one in December, one in January, and one in March. The second graders presented productions that were complete with sets and props and sometimes left these items behind for the kindergartners to use. This modeling appeared to pay off: 22.6% of the children's dramatic re-enactments centered around stories that had been enacted for them by either the adults or the second graders.

Any attempt to understand the literacy context that nurtured the occurrence of spontaneous dramatic re-enactments in Ms. Garrett's room would be incomplete without a view across time. The month of September was devoted to collecting baseline data. During this period, Ms. Garrett took no steps to foster the occurrence of emergent readings or dramatic story re-enactments, and observers in the library center documented no instances of dramatic re-enactments. In October, Ms. Garrett initiated the program described earlier that was designed to promote the occurrence of emergent reading in all forms including dramatic story re-enactments, and indeed, during the period of October through December the children in Ms. Garrett's classroom did begin to engage in story re-enactments independently in the library center. However, the children's participation in dramatic re-enactments was barely beginning during this period. The observers documented the occurrence of only 30 dramatic story re-enactments from the beginning of October to mid-December—a rate of five per week. It was not until the spring that the children appeared to become immersed in dramatic re-enactments. From January through April, the observers documented the occurrence of 145 dramatic re-enactments in the library center— an average of almost ten per week. In her journal, Mrs. Garrett documented the occurrence of many more dramatic re-enactments during other times during the day and on days when there were not observers in the classroom. It appeared that the momentum behind dramatic re-enactments built slowly during the early part of the year until the children in Ms. Garrett's classroom moved to 'center stage' during the spring of the year. Once on center stage, they chose to stay. Spontaneous dramatic story re-enactments became an integral part of the literature program in this classroom.

A Final Word

Ms. Garrett and her kindergartners were a community of readers. They read stories together, the wrote about stories, they sang about stories, and they acted out stories. The social spirit of their literacy experiences was also evident in the children's activities with books independent of their teacher. In their visits to the classroom library center, more often than not the children chose to *share* literature; and one form this sharing took was the dramatic story re-enactment. The research on TFP indicates that participation in dramatic re-enactments of stories facilitates many aspects of children's narrative competence. Although this research has focused on adult-initiated re-enactments, the research of Silvern and colleagues indicates that adult direction is not *the* crucial component of the TFP experience. Rather, it is the actual participation in reconstructing the story that appears to facilitate the development of narrative competence. In light of this, the *spontaneous* occurrence of dramatic re-enactments in Ms. Garrett's classroom library center assumes special significance. In their visits to the library center, the kindergartners in her room frequently chose an activity that clearly contributed to their literacy development. Comparing the activity in the library centers of Ms. Garrett and Ms. Chavez, it becomes evident that the occurrence of dramatic story re-enactments cannot be taken for granted. The children in Ms. Chavez's classroom engaged in dramatic story re-enactments very infrequently. It appears, then, that these re-enactments must be nurtured if they are to become an activity of choice in the classroom library center. Teachers can do this by involving children in numerous intensive social experiences centering around stories.

Notes

* The research reported on in this chapter was supported by a grant from the Research Foundation of the National Council of Teachers of English. Thanks go to the children, teachers, and administrators of San Antonio Independent School District whose cooperation made this work possible.

1. Discussion of a story is also a social response activity. However, the teachers did not systematically document in their logs the discussions that occurred during or after a storybook reading, perhaps taking for granted the occurrence of such discussion.

References

Applebee, A. N. (1978). *The child's concept of story: Ages two to seventeen.* Chicago: University of Chicago Press.

Brown, A. L. (1975). Recognition, reconstruction, and recall of narrative sequences by preoperational children. *Child Development, 46,* 156–166.

Clark, M. M. (1976). *Young fluent readers.* London: Heinemann Educational Books.

Durkin, D. (1966). *Children who read early.* New York: Teachers College Press.

Eller, R., C. Pappas, and E. Brown (1988). The lexical development of kindergartners: Learning from written context. *Journal of Reading Behavior, 20,* 5–24.

Gardner, H., and J. Gardner (1971). Children's literary skills. *The Journal of Experimental Education, 39,* 42–46.

Galda, L. (1982). Playing about a story: Its impact on comprehension. *The Reading Teacher, 36,* 52–55.

———— (1984). Narrative competence: Play, storytelling and story comprehension. In: A. D. Pellegrini and T. D. Yawkey (Eds.), *The development of oral and written language in social contexts* (pp. 105–117). Norwood, NJ: Ablex Publishing Corporation.

Harris-Schmidt, G., and G. D. McNamee (1986). Children as authors and actors: Literacy development through 'basic activities.' *Child Language Teaching and Therapy, 2,* 63–73.

Isenberg, J., and E. Jacob (1983). Literacy and symbolic play: A review of the literature. *Childhood Education, 59,* 272–275.

Jacob, E. (1984). Learning literacy through play: Puerto Rican kindergarten children. In: H. Goelman, A. Oberg, and F. Smith (Eds.), *Awakening to literacy.* Exeter, NH: Heinemann Educational Books.

Mandler, J. M., and N. S. Johnson (1977). Remembrance of things parsed: Story structure and recall. *Cognitive Psychology, 9,* 111–151.

Martinez, M. G., and N. L. Roser (1990). Research on teaching specific aspects of the English language arts: Children's responses to literature. In: J. Flood, J. Jensen, D. Lapp, and J. Squire (Eds.), *Handbook of research on teaching the English language arts.* Urbana, IL: National Council of Teachers of English and International Reading Association.

Martinez, M. G. and W. H. Teale (1988). Reading in a kindergarten classroom library. *The Reading Teacher, 41,* 568–572.

———— (1989). Classroom storybook reading: The creation of texts and learning opportunities. *Theory into Practice, 28,* 126–135.

Miccinati, J. L. and S. Phelps (1980). Classroom drama from children's reading: From the page to the stage. *The Reading Teacher, 34,* 269–272.

Morrow, L. M. (1989a). *Increasing literacy behavior during play through physical design changes.* Paper presented at 39th Annual Meeting of the National Reading Conference, Austin, TX (December).

———— (1989b). *Literacy development in the early years.* Englewood Cliffs, NJ: Prentice-Hall.

Pappas, C. (1987). Exploring the textual properties of "protoreading." In: R. Steele and T. Threadgold (Eds.), *Language topics: Essays in honour of Michael Halliday* (pp. 137–162). Amsterdam: John Benjamins.

Pappas, C., and E. Brown (1988). The development of children's sense of the written story language register: An analysis of the texture of "pretend reading." *Linguistics and Education, 1,* 45–79.

Pellegrini, A. D. (1980). The relationship between kindergartners' play and achievement in prereading, language, and writing. *Psychology in the Schools, 17,* 530–535.

Pellegrini, A. D., and L. Galda (1982). The effects of thematic-fantasy play training on the development of children's story comprehension. *American Educational Research Journal, 19,* 443–452.

Piaget, J. (1962). *Play, dreams, and imitation.* New York: W. W. Norton.

Pitcher, E. G., and E. Prelinger (1983). *Children tell stories: An analysis of fantasy.* New York: International Universities Press.

Rumelhart, D. E. (1975). Notes on a schema for stories. In: D. Bowbrow and A. Collins (Eds.), *Studies in cognitive science* (pp. 211–236). New York: Academic Press.

Sachs, J. (1980). The role of adult-child play in language development. In: K. H. Rubin (Ed.), *Children's play. (New directions for child development, No. 9).* San Francisco: Jossey-Bass.

Saltz, E., D. Dixon, and J. Johnson (1977). Training disadvantaged preschoolers on various fantasy activities: Effects on cognitive functioning and impulse control. *Child Development, 48,* 367–380.

Saltz, E., and J. Johnson (1974). Training for thematic-fantasy play in culturally disadvantaged children: Preliminary results. *Journal of Educational Psychology, 66,* 623–630.

Schickedanz, J. A. (1986). *More than the ABC's: The early stages of reading and writing.* Washington, DC: National Associaton for the Education of Young Children.

Silvern S. B., et al. (1986). Young children's story recall as a product of play, story familiarity, and adult intervention. *Merrill-Palmer Quarterly, 32,* 73–86.

Stein, N. L., and C. G. Glenn (1979). An analysis of story comprehension in elementary school children. In: R. O. Freedle (Ed.), *Advances in discourse processes.* Vol. 2, *New directions in discourse processing* (pp. 53–120). Norwood, NJ: Ablex Publishing Corporation.

Sulzby, E. (1985). Children's emergent reading of favorite storybooks: A developmental study. *Reading Research Quarterly, 20,* 458–481.

——— (1988). A study of children's early reading development. In: A. D. Pellegrini (Ed.), *Psychological bases for early education* (pp. 39–75). Chichester, England: John Wiley.

Sulzby, E., and W. H. Teale (1991). Emergent literacy. In: R. Barr, et al. (Eds.), *Handbook of reading research* (Vol. II). New York: Longman.

Teale, W. H. (1987). Emergent literacy: Reading and writing development in early childhood. *Thirty-sixth Yearbook of the National Reading Conference: Research in literacy: Merging perspectives, 36,* 45–74.

Teale, W. H., and M. G. Martinez (1988). Getting on the right road to reading: Bringing children and books together in the classroom. *Young Children, 41,* 10–15.

Teale, W. H., and E. Sulzby (1987). Access, mediation, and literacy acquisition in early childhood. In: D. A. Wagner (Ed.), *The future of literacy in a changing world* (pp. 111–130). New York: Pergamon Press.

Tobin, A. W. (1981). *A multiple discriminant cross-validation of the factors associated with the development of precocious reading achievement.* Unpublished doctoral dissertation, University of Delaware, Newark.

Vygotsky, L. S. (1978). *Mind in society.* Cambridge, MA: Harvard University Press.

——— (1981). The genesis of higher mental functions. In: J. V. Wertsch (Ed.), *The concept of activity in Soviet psychology,* (pp. 144–188). White Plains, NY: M. E. Sharpe.

7

Preparing the Classroom Environment to Promote Literacy during Play

Lesley Mandel Morrow and *Muriel Rand*

Research in environmental psychology indicates that physical environment plays a critical role in the classroom learning experiences of children (Rivlin and Weinstein, 1984). Especially in the field of early literacy, many new insights into pedagogy have evolved out of recent research (Morrow, 1989). With this infusion of new ideas and strategies for pedagogy and documentation of their effectiveness in classroom practice, it has become apparent that physical environment is an essential, supportive, and active influence on the learning and teaching of early literacy. Yet, in spite of the evidence in favor of carefully planned classroom environments, environmental planning of classrooms gets little care and attention and is sometimes completely overlooked. Far more emphasis is placed on planning instructional strategies and curriculum development.

This chapter reviews research evidence that demonstrates the influence of physical classroom design on young children's learning. It focuses specifically on the role of free-play activities in promoting early literacy development, showing how a planned physical environment in early childhood classrooms can increase literacy behavior during free-play periods. In particular, it indicates how dramatic play areas and library corners can be designed to increase children's voluntary use of literacy materials and participation in literacy activities.

Effects of Physical Environment
in Early Childhood Classrooms

Although most of the research evidence is rather recent, the importance of carefully designed physical environments in fostering young children's learning is not new in theory. Pestalozzi's "object lessons" were built on the value of manipulative experiences, and Froebel's "gifts" and "occupations" were systematically planned, as was Montessori's "prepared environment" (Morrison, 1988). Piaget also emphasized that youngsters need to interact with materials in order to learn.

Most recent research considering environmental variables in the ecology of early childhood classrooms can be subcategorized by major focuses on various aspects of the classroom environment. This chapter will summarize research in three such subcategories: spatial arrangements, kinds of materials, and uses of different activity centers.

Spatial Arrangement

A number of studies indicate that spatial arrangements in classrooms can send children complex messages. Some studies underscore the effects of spatial definition. Comparing the effects of large open spaces and smaller partitioned spaces within the same overall area, Field (1980) found that the smaller partitioned spaces facilitated more optimal school behaviors than did large open spaces. Those behaviors included peer and verbal interaction, fantasy play, and associative/cooperative play.

Nash (1981) compared randomly arranged classrooms (in which equipment and materials were placed haphazardly) to spatially planned classrooms (in which rooms were intentionally organized to foster learning outcomes). For purposes of this comparison, daily schedules, activity choices, and patterns of interaction were kept similar in the two kinds of rooms. Results indicated that children in the spatially arranged rooms showed more creative productivity; produced more complex shape, color, and number patterns with materials; and made more use of oral language, listening, and prereading materials than did children in the randomly arranged rooms.

Moore (1986) found similar results in a study of the effects of well-defined and poorly defined spatial settings on the social and cognitive behavior of children. Children in the well-defined settings exhibited more engaged and exploratory behaviors and more social interaction and cooperation than did children in moderately or poorly defined settings.

Another indication that manipulating classroom activity areas can affect the behavior of preschoolers, Kinsman and Berk (1979) found that joining the block and housekeeping areas of a classroom brought increases in mixed-sex grouping in three- and four-year-olds and in relevant, constructive use of the block area by girls.

Montes and Risley (1975) found that even such a simple classroom design element as storage is important in affecting the use of materials. They observed that storing toys on open shelves rather than in storage boxes led to easier selection by children and more time spent playing.

Activity Centers and Materials

It is expected that because early childhood classrooms are usually arranged into activity centers, those different areas foster different kinds of behavior. Shapiro (1975) noted higher levels of both social interaction and aggression in the block and doll areas. Shure (1963) and Rosenthal (1973) observed that the block area was used most frequently and the book area used least frequently. Morrow (1987) and Morrow and Weinstein (1982, 1986) found, however, that library corners greatly increased students' voluntary literacy activities when teachers designed attractive, accessible areas and stocked them with large and varied selections of books and other reading materials as well as literature manipulatives such as feltboard stories, taped stories, and puppets.

The types of materials available in classroom centers can also affect children's behavior. Two studies in which thematic play materials were introduced into the dramatic play areas of a laboratory school classroom (Dodge and Frost, 1986) and of a preschool classroom (Woodard, 1984) demonstrated more elaborate and longer play sequences among children than when thematic materials were not present.

Pellegrini (1982) also examined differences in children's use of language in various activity areas. Engaged in the dramatic play area, children encoded ideas more explicitly into language and depended less on contextual assumptions to convey meaning than when they played in the block area—an important ability in the development of early literacy and communication skills. In further research, Pellegrini (1983) found that both the housekeeping and the block areas elicited more individual and multifunctional uses of language than did other activity areas in the classroom. In an experimental setting, however, playing with dramatic props elicited more imaginative language than playing with blocks alone.

Teacher behaviors, too, apparently are influenced by physical environment. Kritchevsky and Prescott (1977) observed that teachers in higher-quality spaces were more likely to be sensitive and friendly toward children, to encourage children in self-chosen activities, and to teach consideration for the rights and feelings of others. Teachers in poorer-quality spaces, by contrast, were less involved, less interested, more insensitive, more restrictive, and more likely to teach arbitrary social rules.

The studies cited above clearly show the importance of carefully designed classroom environments. The physical space of the classroom affects the behavior of both students and teachers. Used effectively, manipulation and design of space can be a powerful tool in teaching and learning.

Play and Cognitive Development

Evident in several of the studies just reviewed, environmental manipulation can encourage child-centered free-play activities, and those activities, in turn, can result in greater peer interaction and more active involvement of individual children. Vygotsky (1966) theorized that play arises from a child's generalized but unrealized desires, manifest in a detachment of meaning from objects and actions. During play, the child transfers meaning to a pivot object or action, and that transfer becomes an intermediate step toward using symbolic thought. Play, then, provides opportunities for children to develop and use abstract thought that is free from perceptual constraints.

Piaget (1962) also stressed the importance of play in the child's cognitive development as a way of assimilating new information and consolidating past experience through symbolic means. Children benefit from the social interaction needed to organize and sustain dramatic play in particular (Rubin, 1980). The accommodation and negotiation needed to resolve conflict during such social interaction leads to cognitive growth.

In support of such ideas, Pellegrini (1980) identified a relationship between the levels of kindergartners' play and their achievement in prereading, writing, and language. Symbolic play and other forms of play that required higher levels of cognitive demand were found to be predictive of high scores on standardized achievement tests. Similar connections have been demonstrated between play and language development and between play and such areas of literacy development as story comprehension, writing ability, and the functional use of literacy during play.

Literacy Development and Play

Garvey (1977) has pointed out the vital role that oral language plays in maintaining dramatic play episodes. Complex communication involves planning, negotiation, prompting, directing, and narrating during play (Garvey and Berndt, 1977). In an attempt to use planned sociodramatic play to increase language ability, Lovinger (1974) found that both the quantity and complexity of verbalization among preschoolers increased after a play treatment period. Dansky (1980) described having used experiences in adult-guided play to improve childrens' verbal comprehension, production, and organization.

More recently, Levy, Schaefer, and Phelps (1986) manipulated classroom environment over a three-month period to include thematic play areas and dramatic props. Boys in the classroom improved in their Peabody Picture Vocabulary Test scores more than would have been expected without changes in the classroom. That result was attributed to a change in design which increased the boys' participation in sociodramatic play.

Experimental research projects have also increased the amount of dramatic play among children in efforts to improve story comprehension and production. One reason for the proposed connection is that children improve their understanding of story structure (Mandler and Johnson, 1977) through creating play episodes which then improve recall and production of story narratives. Play training intervention often provides thematic-fantasy play sessions in which familiar fairy tales are played out by children.

Two studies (Saltz and Johnson, 1974; Saltz, Dixon, and Johnson, 1977) found that disadvantaged preschoolers trained in thematic-fantasy play showed a greater increase than did a control group in story recall, story interpretation, and storytelling. Similar results were found for kindergartners and first graders trained in thematic-fantasy play (Pellegrini, 1982). Children in the play condition performed better in story comprehension, recall, and sequencing than did those in adult-led story discussion groups.

Silvern and colleagues (1986) found that thematic-fantasy play facilitated recall of a story that had been acted out for children up to 6.7 years old (see Chapter 4). Further investigation revealed that children involved in directing the play episode were most likely to improve in comprehension of the original story (Williamson and Silvern, 1988).

Christie and Noyce (1986) have delineated possible connections between emergent writing abilities and play, especially the idea that sustaining solo discourse without audience input is important in developing writing skills. Among young children, solitary-constructive and dramatic play provide practice in such solo discourse. These researchers also highlight other narrative writing skills evident in play:

- Developing story lines (as in storytelling) supports writing fluency.
- Planning to 'play' stories promotes narrative organizational skills.
- The clarity of expression needed to transform roles and props during play and avoid ambiguity encourages precise vocabulary.

Finally, Christie and Noyce stress the value of a writer's ability to generate a large number of ideas, another ability that play facilitates (Dansky, 1980).

Dramatic play, then, can promote skills that are helpful in the development of writing ability, in addition to providing a natural context for writing-related experiences. Naturalistic observations of preschool children and teachers during symbolic play revealed that teachers promote writing development by modeling functional writing during play sessions and by introducing new functions of print (Schrader, 1988). Play can be an important resource in the development of emergent writers.

Literacy Behaviors in the Context of Play

It is quite evident, then, that play supports development in several different areas of literacy. Dramatic play offers a meaningful context for the growth of language abilities, story understanding, and early writing competencies. Observations of natural classroom environments indicate that play provides children with the opportunity to incorporate new information into play behaviors and to elaborate and extend what they already know or can do into new contexts (Isenberg and Jacob, 1983). Play supports literacy behaviors even in very young children. Roskos (1988) observed preschoolers during play periods engaged in such activities as paper or text handling, storytelling, and early reading and writing. During play, children demonstrate such literacy skills as directionality, print processing, and comprehension. Their knowledge of literacy routines and recognition that literacy serves purposes are clearly evident during play. Play allows children the active involvement essential for the practice, elaboration, and extension of emerging literacy abilities.

Adult Guidance During Play

The role of the adult is one of the most crucial variables in the play context of a preschool classroom. One of the basic principles of Vygotsky's (1978) theory is that children learn higher psychological processes through their social environment, but optimally with adult guidance. Vygotsky described a child's "zone of proximal development" as midway between functioning with the support of an adult or more capable peer and functioning independently. Within this zone of proximal development lies the greatest opportunity for a child's cognitive development. In Vygotsky's view, social context provided by the adult enables the child to perform at a higher level than is possible with neither adult nor context.

Holdaway's (1979) view of literacy development is similar, with the adult providing an "emulative model" for literacy behavior. The child first observes that behavior, then carries it out in a collaborative effort—encouraged and assisted by the adult—and eventually reaches independence. Thus, 'natural' learning is in reality shaped and supported by adult intervention based on the child's needs and current level of ability.

Research shows that physical environment plays an important role in affecting children's behavior during play. Play is capable of involving children in literacy behavior. Adults are important in designing and guiding the contexts and learning experiences that are involved. In preschool classrooms, teachers may provide optimal learning by their modeling, scaffolding, and support of literacy development.

Increasing Literacy Behavior Through Physical Design Changes

Children's play is a rich opportunity for the use and development of literacy concepts and skills. The two play settings described in the following paragraphs are based on two different research studies, both of which demonstrated increased literacy activity among children during free-play time—activity brought about by design changes in the physical environment of the classroom.

Literacy Activity in Dramatic Play

In the first setting, Morrow (1989a) investigated ways of increasing literacy behavior during play through physical design changes. The purpose of the study was to determine if children's use of literacy behaviors during free-play time could be increased by including reading and writing materials in the dramatic play area. Thirteen middle-class, suburban kindergarten classrooms (which included 170 children overall) were assigned to one of four conditions, three experimental and one control.

In Experimental Group 1 (E1), the following literacy materials were added to the block and dramatic play areas: stacks of paper of different sizes and types; book-making materials such as construction paper, a stapler, and ready-made blank booklets; magazines and books; pencils, felt-tip markers, colored pencils, and crayons. The various materials had their own separate storage containers in special places. They were introduced by the teachers, who physically displayed each material or tool and suggested how each might be used during free-play time. Suggestions included writing stories, reading books, writing notes to friends, and reading to dolls. It was pointed out that paper and pencils could be used to write recipes, make shopping lists, and take telephone messages. Teachers reminded the children about the materials at the beginning of each free-play period, encouraging and guiding their use.

Dramatic play areas in Experimental Group 2 (E2) were designed to represent veterinarians' offices. Each had a waiting room with chairs and a table filled with magazines, plus books and pamphlets about pet care. On the wall were posters about pets, lists of doctors' hours, a "No Smoking" sign, and a sign that read, "Check in with the nurse when you arrive." Each nurse's desk or table contained forms on a clipboard for patients to fill out, as well as a telephone, address and telephone books, appointment cards, and a calendar. Doctors' offices were supplied with patient folders, prescription pads, white coats, masks, gloves, cotton swabs, toy doctors' kits, and stuffed animals. Finally, all the materials introduced into E1 areas were replicated in E2 areas.

E2 students were also guided by the teacher in the use of the various materials, though guidance focused thematically on their use during free-play time in the veterinarian's office. For example: "You can read to pets in the waiting areas or fill out forms at the nurse's desk. The doctor can fill out forms about the condition of a patient or prescription forms for medicine. The nurse can look up dates and fill out appointment cards."

Treatment in Experimental Group 3 (E3) replicated everything in E2, including the veterinarian theme in the dramatic play area, with one major exception: Although the teachers mentioned the presence of literacy materials, they offered no guidance in their use. Furthermore, they mentioned the materials only when they were initially placed in the dramatic play areas.

Teachers in the Control Group implemented no changes at all in dramatic play areas, nor did they make any suggestions concerning literacy behaviors that could be practiced during play. The areas were set up typically and traditionally as kitchens and included no literacy materials whatsoever.

Classes in all four groups had regularly scheduled free-play periods of at least 30 minutes a day during which children were allowed to choose their own activities. Before intervention, none of the teachers had made any specific environmental provisions or suggestions for literacy activities during play.

To establish baseline data, children in all groups were observed during free-play time twice a week for three weeks prior to intervention. The number of children engaged in literacy behaviors during those periods and the kinds of literacy behaviors in which they engaged were noted. The physical design changes described for the three experimental groups were then implemented, with a one-week pause in observation to allow novelty to wear off. Observations during free-play time then resumed twice a week for another three weeks. Observers kept anecdotal records of literacy and play behaviors during the free-play periods and collected samples of children's writing efforts during play.

Statistical analyses of data collected during this study project demonstrated significant differences between groups in the amount and type of literacy behaviors during play. Before intervention, observers found very few instances of any kind of literacy behavior during play. During intervention, experimental groups showed significant increases in literacy behaviors, particularly in paper handling and in attempted and pretended reading and writing. The control group showed no differences at all from pre- to post-intervention. Of the three experimental treatments, the unguided thematic play treatment (E3) produced the smallest increase in literacy activity. Increases in literacy behaviors among students in the guided but un-themed treatment (E1) were especially strong in writing. Students in the teacher-guided thematic group (E2) displayed the greatest increase of all in voluntary literacy behaviors.

Guided Use of Literacy Materials

As noted, classroom groups guided in the un-themed use of literacy materials (E1) noticeably increased their voluntary literacy behaviors, especially writing. The kinds of writing behaviors observed were predominantly individual in nature, although some children worked together. Activities tended to focus on exploration and experimentation with writing and writing materials. For example:

> Jaclyn used the colored markers to draw a rocket, then labelled it "ROGT."

> Michael made rows of letters across the paper, mostly M's neatly in line.

The E1 children did not typically integrate writing behavior into their other play activities:

> Veena looked up and asked, "What does NSPAMA spell?" The teacher replied, "What do you think it spells?" Veena answered, "I don't know. Maybe *pumpkin*. Look, Katy, I spelled *pumpkin*," and she continued writing.

> Jessica sat in the dramatic play area with papers and markers, writing all the words she knew how to spell, as Krista watched.

> Dawn used the pencils to write one long word that consisted of random letters, each in a different color.

These examples show that the writing behaviors were not dependent on the play area context and could have taken place with similar materials anywhere in the classroom. In some instances, however, E1 children did initiate a play theme which included literacy behavior:

> Michael, Kristen, and Dawn were playing school with Michael as teacher. Kristen and Dawn gathered papers and pencils to do their "homework," and later Dawn wrote a note to the teacher.

> Sarah, Maisha, and Cecilia used the paper and markers as part of playing "house." They pretended to write notes and complete their homework for school the next day.

> Sarah wrote a letter to her postman, using attempted writing which resembled print. She then found an unused milk crate, turned it upside down, and put her letter in the slot.

Play themes which incorporated literacy behaviors in the E1 group were very limited, usually to playing "house" or "school" and often

Figure 7.1

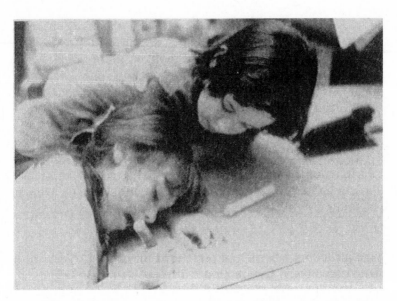

Jessica sat in the dramatic play area with the paper and markers writing all the words she knew how to spell, as Kristen watched.

motivated by teacher guidance, as can be seen in the following example.

> The student teacher showed the children the "blue books" provided for the children to write in, and explained that she used them at college to take tests. Taylor took one of the booklets and said, "I'm writing my name. I'm going to school, now." Jonathan added, "I'm in school, too." Maisha said, "Take your homework, honey," and the play continued along these lines.

Again, there was much more writing than reading observed in the E1 group. Children seemed quite attracted to writing, although no specific function or theme for writing was suggested. Most of the reading among E1 youngsters was, like the writing, isolated from play context and could have occurred in any activity area. Typical reading behaviors included browsing through books:

> Tyree picked up a book and pretended to read it to Sean, who listened attentively. Sean reminded Tyree to start at the beginning, and asked him who the author was.

The telephone and telephone book prompted more reading behaviors in a play context than did books in general:

> Matt talked on the telephone and paged through the phone book looking for numbers. Claire came over and said, "You read the numbers, and I'll dial the numbers," while thumbing through the phone book.

In summary, the literacy behaviors found in the guided literacy materials group (E1) were predominantly writing behaviors not linked to any particular play episode. Nor did the materials motivate many play themes except for a small number of episodes of playing house and school. There was little functional use of literacy. Literacy behaviors that were observed tended to involve exploration and experimentation with materials and practice with familiar literacy skills such as writing letter characters and words for practice rather than to communicate ideas.

Guided Thematic Play. Observations in the classroom in which literacy materials were regularly related by teachers to the veterinarian theme (E2) showed strikingly different results. Only occasionally did children use literacy materials solely for the sake of exploration or skill practice. Almost all literacy behaviors observed were related to the play theme.

Writing was quite prevalent and used functionally to communicate ideas within the contextual theme. For example:

> Preston wrote out a prescription on the pad in scribble writing and, as he wrote, said, "You make sure you take 100 of these every hour until you're better. Keep warm and go to bed."

> Rebecca brought her dog to Carolyn, explaining in detail her dog's broken leg as Carolyn wrote down the information. Rebecca said, "No, doctor, let me write it." She took the pencil, wrote down some lines, and said, "There, that's it," and continued to play.

> John, pretending to be the doctor, took an animal's blood pressure, then wrote down the numbers on the patient's chart.

> Adriana, Jessica, and Keturah took out the files and a sheet of paper and went to the table. They talked about the sick animals and discussed how they had to write down what was wrong with the animals for their owners to know.

Many such episodes occurred because teachers supported the children's play episodes by entering the play and modeling for the children:

> Adriana and Jessica took their files to the table and interviewed the pets' owners. They gave the teacher an animal and told her it was sick. Then they asked the teacher for her name, the animal's name, what was wrong with the animal, and what her mother thought. The teacher was directed to see the doctor. The children asked the teacher how to spell the names and wrote them on the chart.

The children's beginning conceptual framework for the relationship between reading and writing and the functions that literacy serves can be seen in the following examples.

> Joshua filled out an appointment card, including a time, and said, "This is your card to tell you when to come back."

> Israel filled out an appointment card for one of his patients and read it aloud to the patient so that he would remember it. Then he said to the teacher, "I need you to sign this so your pet can go home."

Figure 7.2

DOCTOR	SERVICE	ROOM	
DATE		Note progress of case, complications, consultations, change in diagnosis, condition or discharge, instructions to patient.	

John is pretending to be the doctor. He took the teddy bear's blood pressure and wrote down the numbers on the patient's chart in number-like forms.

Michael sorted through papers and began writing, pretending he was a doctor. He looked up his patient's ailments in a book so he would know what to do.

In the following example, Joshua shows his understanding of how written and spoken language relate:

Joshua said as he was filling out an appointment card, "You know what I'm going to do? I'm going to write his name in dog language. How do you spell *Ruff?*"

Reading behaviors also occurred to a great extent in the thematic play group. Like the writing behaviors, these activities tended to relate to the play theme and to serve functional purposes. A typical activity involved reading in the waiting room, as in these examples:

Meredith sat in the waiting room reading to her monkey. Katie joined her with a cat and at first pretended to read quietly to herself. Then she noticed Meredith reading to her monkey and she began to read to her cat.

Israel said, "Look, I can read this. It says, Pet's name. I think I'm gonna read my teddy bear a book. It will make him feel better."

The pamphlets and flyers in the waiting room suggested to the children the idea of reading for information, and many episodes like the following took place.

Rebecca was drawing a picture of a sick fish. Later, she browsed through the materials looking for a cure for her fish.

Danny shuffled through the new flyers, looking at the writing and pointing to the captions beneath the pictures. He pointed to the words "Veterinarian Clinic" on a wall poster, then to the same words in the book. He showed them to Wade.

Tiffany and Brian sat on the floor looking through the pamphlets. They spent some time with each one and paused over some as though attempting to read the information. Nick wandered over and picked up a flyer to see what was so interesting.

Children also showed evidence of the background knowledge they brought to episodes and of their awareness of environmental print:

Jason took a sticker which said, "SONY TV" and put it on a piece of paper, saying that we need to buy a new TV for one of the hospital rooms.

In summary, the guided thematic play treatment produced an increase in literacy behaviors which were dramatically different from those in the paper and pencil (E1) group. There was more focus on the functions of literacy, with children exploring the role of literacy as a means of communication. There was less emphasis on the actual forms of literacy in terms of writing letter characters or words simply for their own sake or for practice. Finally, the thematic materials generated more reading behaviors which were incorporated into play episodes.

Figure 7.3

While the nurse is on the telephone writing down a date for a patient's appointment, Tiffany waits for her and passes the time by reading a magazine.

Unguided Thematic Play. The importance of the teacher's role in environmental changes becomes apparent in comparing results of the unguided thematic play treatment of this study (E3) with those of guided thematic play (E2). Children in the unguided situation seemed to explore the literacy materials with no incorporation into the play context of the veterinarian's office. For example:

Children put on surgical caps and used them in the block area, continuing to build.

Nicole sorted the papers into different colored piles.

Lauren drew pictures on the paper with markers.

Adam browsed through a book.

Dennis drew pictures on a prescription pad.

The materials did not stimulate the rich thematic play episodes found in the E2 treatment. Although the E3 increase in literacy behavior was statistically significant, there was relatively little of it in comparison and virtually none of the functional uses of literacy observed in the guided group.

Literacy in the Library Corner During Free Play

A second setting for which play can serve as a context for literacy development among young children is the classroom library corner. It is unfortunate that so few early childhood classrooms have library corners, and those that exist are more often than not poorly designed, unattractive, and relatively inaccessible (Morrow, 1982). As a consequence, such areas have been little used by children for literacy activities during free-play time (Morrow, 1982; Rosenthal, 1973; Shure, 1963). Morrow (1987) and Morrow and Weinstein (1982, 1986) determined that appropriate physical design and teacher-directed activities significantly increased children's voluntary use of library corners during free-play periods as well as children's participation in literacy activities.

Note that the latter studies had two major components in common: the physical design of library corners and teacher guidance. Partially partitioned from the rest of the room to give a feeling of privacy, library corners were located for purposes of these studies in quiet areas of classrooms. They were visually and physically accessible and large enough to accommodate at least seven children at a time. Children were free to take materials out of the corners and use them in other parts of the rooms. Corners contained regular bookshelves as well as open-faced bookshelves which displayed books in full cover, many of them books that teachers had read to the children.

The corners held from five to eight books per child, representing three to four different grade levels and a cross-section of genres in children's literature: novels, picture storybooks, poetry, biography, informational books, realistic stories, traditional literature (fairy tales and fables), and children's magazines. Books in the library corners were color-coded for easy identification. The corners also contained bulletin boards with hooks, rings, and index cards so children could keep records of books they had read. Pillows, rugs, stuffed animals, and other soft items were placed in the corners. Corners were stocked with feltboards, roll movies, puppets, materials for making books, Viewmasters with story wheels, headsets and cassette players for taped stories, 'Read' posters, checkout systems for books, and such private spots for reading as boxes to crawl into (Morrow, 1985).

With such design, materials, and teacher encouragement and guidance, library corners significantly increased in popularity during free-time periods, and children independently involved themselves in many literacy activities. The atmosphere was active, involved, social, and cooperative. In all cases, teachers introduced literacy materials to the students, guided their use, and at least mentioned those materials to students at the beginning of each free-play period.

Some children worked alone, others with single friends, and still others in groups. The variety of activities was due in great measure to the variety of materials available and to the directions and encouragement of the teachers who supported children in independent work— urging them to explore, experiment, and solve problems. During a 20-minute observation of any of these rooms, one could see something like the following:

At the listening station, four boys congregated to use the headsets and taped stories. Each also had his own copy of the book that was on the tape. They followed along in their books, tracking with their fingers as the narrator read the book to them. With certain repetitive phrases, as in *The Little Engine that Could,* one could hear the boys' spontaneous chanting: "I think I can, I think I can, I think I can."

Not far from that table, Jeannie had gathered a few children on the floor around her and taken on the role of teacher. She said, "Now, I'm the teacher and you be the children." She was at the easel that held a "Big Book" version of *The Little Red Hen.* With pointer in hand, she pointed to the words as she read. The other children helped her with phrases from the story at appropriate times: " 'Not I,' said the dog. 'Not I,' said the cat. 'Not I,' said the goat." When she finished the story, Jamie asked if he could be the teacher now.

John, Jennifer, Elizabeth, and Adam were all curled close to each other, leaning on pillows in the library corners, reading their books. Tim and Tiffany were reading the same book together. Some of the children had taken stuffed animals to read to.

A puppet show was in progress about *The Ginger Bread Boy* as children acted it out. One of them read the story, serving as narrator. Anthony and Ben did a feltboard version together, and Ivory and Charlene cooperated in telling a roll movie story.

Children independently checked books out of the library corner during free time to take home. They also noted stories they had read on the bulletin board provided for that purpose.

Evan worked on a book he had been writing for several days, one he will add to the library corner. Josh could be seen in the private spot, a three-sided box with a blanket in it, reading comfortably and peacefully. The classroom teacher, observing that all the children were actively and constructively involved, sat down with her own novel to read.

When interviewed and asked what they liked about the library corners, children commented on the following features as those they most enjoyed:

- comfortable seating, such as throw pillows, rocking chairs, and rugs
- wide varieties of reading materials, such as novels, picture storybooks, newspapers, participation books, and magazines
- the system of recording books they had read
- ability to check out books
- materials for writing and binding books
- the regular featuring of new books
- headsets and taped stories
- feltboards with story figures.

In additon to physical features, children also said they liked the opportunity to use the library corner during free time. They enjoyed the chance to choose whatever books they wanted to read, to read to friends, and to be read to by the teacher. They liked not being rushed when reading, allowing them to look at books all the way through.

Figure 7.4

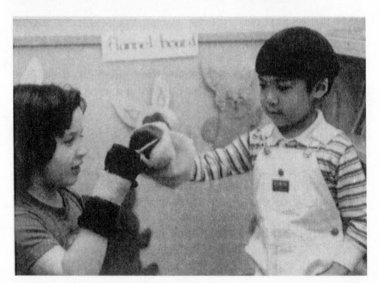

When in the library corner during free-play, Kim relaxes while reading a book and leaning on a comfortable pillow. John and Jennifer use the puppets to tell a story.

Lesley Mandel Morrow, *Literacy Development in the Early Years: Helping Children Read and Write,* © 1989, p. 60 and p. 88. Reprinted by permission of Prentice-Hall, Inc., Englewood Cliffs, N.J.

Conclusions

The changes in physical design implemented in the studies reviewed in some detail here were effective in increasing levels of voluntary literacy behaviors of children during play. The data behind those studies support the recommendations of others concerning the powerful impact of design changes on behavior. Altman and Wohlwill (1979) point out that young children are quite sensitive to modification of the environment. The present studies clearly indicate that teachers should not overlook the physical setting of the classroom in their preoccupation with curricular and interpersonal concerns. By providing well-designed environments, teachers are able to facilitate literacy behaviors and quite probably enhance cognitive development as well. The studies summarized here certainly indicate that the effort involved in providing literacy materials and thematic settings in dramatic play areas plus well-designed library corners yields gratifying results.

It is interesting to note that different settings and conditions generate different behaviors. The teacher-guided thematic play setting, for example, produced a wide variety of functional uses of literacy. The book-paper-and-pencil treatment encouraged a great deal of writing and the opportunity for exploration and experimentation. The library corner created interest in books and a variety of activity because of the range of manipulatives and materials available.

The settings most successful in increasing literacy activity were those in which teacher guidance was a strong component. Although physical design changes play a dramatic role in affecting children's behavior, where teachers introduced materials and frequently made suggestions for their use, children participated in more literacy activities in greater variety than in any other setting. Theories covered in the literature review at the beginning of this chapter are supported by the results of the study projects described. Vygotsky's (1979) theory that children learn higher psychological processes through social environment, especially with adult guidance, has been reinforced. The adult provides a social context that enables the child to perform at a higher level than before. The adult then steps back to let the child explore, experiment, and practice what has been learned. Holdaway (1979) describes the process as a supportive adult providing a model for what is to be learned—a process the child first observes, then carries out in collaboration with the adult (profiting from encouragement and assistance), then practices as a newly acquired behavior, and finally carries out independently.

Play functions as a means by which the child learns to use symbolic, abstract levels of thought (Vygotsky, 1967); develops representational thought; assimilates new information; and consolidates through symbolic means (Piaget, 1962). Because the settings described in this chapter increased voluntary involvement of children in literacy activities, it seems appropriate and beneficial that teachers prepare their classroom environments to include literacy materials in play centers and to design library corners that will stimulate interest in reading. Such play contexts give young children the invaluable opportunity to learn, practice, and gain confidence in the forms and—more importantly—the functions of literacy.

References

Altman, I., and J. Wohlwill (1979). *Children and the environment*. New York: Plenum.

Christie, J., and R. Noyce (1986). Play and writing: Possible connections. In: B. Mergen (Ed.), *Cultural Dimensions of Play, Games and Sport*. Champaign, IL: Human Kinetics.

Dansky, J. (1980). Cognitive consequences of sociodramatic play and exploration training for economically disadvantaged preschoolers. *Journal of Child Psychology and Psychiatry, 21*, 47–58.

Dodge, M., and J. Frost (1986). Children's dramatic play: Influence of thematic and non-thematic settings. *Childhood Education, 62* (January/February), 166–170.

Field, T. (1980). Preschool play: Effects of teacher/child ratios and organization of classroom space. *Child Study Journal, 10*, 191–205.

Garvey, C. (1977). *Play*. Cambridge, MA: Harvard University Press.

Garvey, C., and R. Berndt (1977). Organization of pretend play. *Catalogue of Selected Documents in Psychology, 13*, 246–252.

Holdaway, D. (1979). *The foundations of literacy*. Sydney: Ashton Scholastic.

Isenberg, J., and E. Jacob (1983). *Playful literacy activities and learning: Preliminary observations*. (ERIC document ED 238–577). Washington, DC: Educational Resources Information Center

Kinsman, C., and L. Berk (1979). Joining the block and housekeeping areas: Changes in play and social behavior, *Young Children, 35*, 66–75.

Kritchevsky, S., and E. Prescott (1977). *Planning environments for young children: Physical space.* Washington, DC: National Association for the Education of Young Children.

Levy, A., L. Schaefer, and P. Phelps (1986). Increasing preschool effectiveness: Enhancing the language abilities of 3- and 4-year-old children through planned sociodramatic play. *Early Childhood Research Quarterly, 1,* 133–140.

Lovinger, S. (1974). Sociodramatic play and language development in preschool disadvantaged children. *Psychology in the Schools, 11,* 313–320.

Mandler, J., and N. Johnson (1977). Remembrance of things parsed: Story structure and recall. *Cognitive Psychology, 9,* 111–151.

Montes, F., and T. Risley (1975). Evaluating traditional day care practices: An empirical approach. *Child Care Quarterly, 4,* 208–215.

Moore, G. (1986). Effects of the spatial definition of behavior settings on children's behavior: A quasi-experimental field study. *Journal of Environmental Psychology, 6,*(3), 205–231.

Morrison, G. (1988). *Early childhood education today* (4th ed.). Columbus, OH: Merrill.

Morrow, L. (1982). Relationships between literature programs, library corners and children's use of literature. *Journal of Educational Research, 75*(6), 339–344.

————— (1985). *Promoting voluntary reading at school and home.* Bloomington, IN: The Phi Delta Kappa Educational Foundation.

————— (1987). Promoting inner-city children's recreational reading. *Reading Teacher, 24,* 266–276.

————— (1989a). *Literacy development in the early years: Helping children read and write.* Englewood Cliffs, NJ: Prentice-Hall.

————— (1989b). *Increasing literacy behavior during play through physical design changes.* Paper presented at the National Reading Conference, Austin, TX (December).

Morrow, L., and C. Weinstein (1982). Increasing children's use of literature through program and physical design changes. *The Elementary School Journal, 83*(2), 132–137.

————— (1986). Encouraging voluntary reading: The impact of a literature program on children's use of library corners. *Reading Research Quarterly, 21,* 330–346.

Nash, B. (1981). The effects of classroom spatial organization on four- and five-year-old children's learning. *British Journal of Educational Psychology, 51,* 144–155.

Pellegrini, A. (1980). The relationship between kindergarteners' play and achievement in prereading, language, and writing. *Psychology in the Schools, 17,* 530–535.

———— (1982). The construction of cohesive text by preschoolers in two play contexts. *Discourse Processes, 5,* 101–108.

———— (1983). Sociolinguistic contexts of the preschool. *Journal of Applied Developmental Psychology, 4*(4), 389–397.

Piaget, J. (1962). *Play, dreams and imitation in childhood.* New York: Norton.

Rivlin, L., and C. Weinstein (1984). Educational issues, school settings, and environmental psychology. *Journal of Environmental Psychology, 4,* 347–364.

Rosenthal, B. (1973). *An ecological study of free play in the nursery school.* Doctoral dissertation, Wayne State University. Dissertation Abstracts International, 1974, 34(7–A), 4004–4005. (University Microfilms No. 73–31, 773).

Roskos, K. (1988). *A summary of an exploratory study of the nature of literate behavior in the pretend play episodes of four- and five-year-old children.* Unpublished manuscript.

Rubin, K. (1980). Fantasy play: Its role in the development of social skills and social cognition. In: K. Rubin (Ed.), *Children's play.* San Francisco: Jossey-Bass.

Saltz, E., D. Dixon, and J. Johnson (1977). Training disadvantaged preschoolers on various fantasy activities: Effects on cognitive functioning and impulse control. *Child Development, 48,* 367–380.

Saltz, E., and J. Johnson (1974). Training for thematic-fantasy play in culturally disadvantaged children: Preliminary results. *Journal of Educational Psychology, 66*(4), 623–630.

Schrader, C. (1989). Written language use within the context of young children's symbolic play. *Early Childhood Research Quarterly, 4,* 225–244.

Shapiro, S. (1975). Preschool ecology: A study of three environmental variables. *Reading Improvement, 12*(4), 236–241.

Shure, M. (1963). Psychological ecology of a nursery school. *Child Development, 34,* 979–992.

Silvern, S., et al. (1986). Young children's story recall as a product of play, story familiarity and adult intervention. *Merrill-Palmer Quarterly, 32*(1), 73–86.

Vygotsky, L. (1966). Play and its role in the mental development of the child. *Soviet Psychology, 12*(6), 62–76.

———— (1978). *Mind in society: The development of higher psychological processes.* Cambridge, MA: Harvard University Press.

Williamson, P., and S. Silvern (1988). *The contribution of play, metaplay and narrative competence to story comprehension.* Paper presented at the Annual Meeting of the American Educational Research Association, New Orleans (April).

Woodard, C. (1984). Guidelines for facilitating sociodramatic play. *Childhood Education, 60,* 172–177.

8

The Influence of Literacy-Enriched Play Centers on Preschoolers' Conceptions of the Functions of Print

Susan B. Neuman
and Kathy Roskos

Literacy is, above all, a practical activity. Children develop increasing competence in reading and writing by engaging in purposeful activities. In this respect, children's emerging literacy has important parallels to their developing conceptions of oral language. Halliday (1975), for example, described that the very beginnings of language come from the child's problem-solving behavior to serve evolving functional needs in varying contexts of language use. From this perspective, the learning of both spoken and written language may be thought of as a by-product of striving for these other functional goals.

Too often, however, the first teachings in literacy in preschool and kindergarten classrooms are not grounded in the child's own experiences and, as a result, they often lack meaning. Skills are taught in a systematic, sequential manner and measured in decontextualized settings apart from any functional purposes. Unfortunately, such practices undervalue children's existing understanding of literacy as a meaning-based activity and place control of the manner and rate of learning in the hands of teachers rather than children (Hall, 1987).

In contrast to these traditional practices, play can be a more productive and natural way for literacy awareness to develop. As children discover and invent literacy through play, they are developing important generalizations about written language as a sense-making activity. They are also beginning to find stability and order in the form of written language in the everyday context of its functional uses (Harste, Woodward, and Burke, 1984). One of the most important aspects of play is the fact that it encourages children to elaborate and integrate behaviors by performing tasks in diverse instrumental settings. For example, Jacob (1984) reported that young Puerto Rican children used literacy in a variety of functional ways, including such activities as pretending to construct and use shopping lists, buying goods with food stamps, and getting prescriptions from a doctor. Similarly, Roskos (1988), in describing the play activities of eight preschoolers, found that children used reading and writing to legitimate their pretend play, to express themselves, and to record information within play events.

These kinds of interactions are fostered by play environments designed to be facilitative and supportive of the development of young children's acquisition of literacy. In this chapter, we describe first how play centers can be enriched in the functional uses of print, and then we detail the effects that these environmental changes had on the quality of literacy demonstrations in the social play of a sample of preschoolers.

A Description of Literacy-Enriched Play Centers

It has been shown that the physical environment can have a substantial effect on children's play behaviors (Neill, 1982; Polloway, 1974). To design changes that promote higher social and cognitive forms of play is a complicated process, one that requires information from a child's point of view as well as an understanding of the impact of different environmental settings. Therefore, to prepare for making changes in children's play environments, we decided to first examine preschoolers' conceptions of the functions of literacy in their existing play settings.

The Functions of Literacy for Preschoolers

Over a two-month period, we observed 50 children, ranging in age from three to five years, during their voluntary, self-selected, free-play time. Our purpose was to examine the salient characteristics of literacy from a child's point of view and to describe the common functions that reading and writing serve at these age levels. Our analysis yielded the five categories of functions for preschoolers listed in Table 8.1 (Neuman and Roskos, 1989).

The exploratory, interactional, and transactional functions were most commonly found in the preschoolers' play activities. Children demonstrating the exploratory function used reading and writing to manipulate and investigate various objects in their environment.

Table 8.1

A typology of the functional domains of literacy
as evidenced in children's spontaneous play

Domain	Kinds of Functions	Examples
Exploratory	— To experiment with print	Jackie writes 'o', 'h', 'a'
(The "how does it work?" function)	— To handle literacy-related materials	"We're opening all these envelopes"
	— To figure out how to do	"It says open right here"
Interactional	— To play a game	"Let's play cards"
(The "between you and me" function)	— To communicate with others	"I'll give something to you (a note). It's about you coming over. You have to come over."
	— To share information	"Would you read this to me?"
Personal	— To express oneself	"I write the word love. I like to write it."
(The "for me" function)	— To claim ownership	"This is my picture."
	— To aid memory	"I have to make a list of phone numbers."
Authenticating	— To verify information	"You see, Susan, it's saying 'Happy Arbor Day.'"
(The "Legitimating" function)	— To act grown up	"We have to have all our taxes and I'm filling the taxes this year."
	— To endorse	"They have to come to the doctor's by noon to make an appointment."
Transactional	— To label	"This doesn't say 'stacho."
(The "between me and text" function)	— To communicate about	Pointing to book, "I'm over on this page."
	— To construct meaning from text	Tells teacher that the picture book says "I love you."

Examples included playing with envelopes, using a typewriter, and handling paper and pencils. The interactional functions focused on literacy for communication and social purposes. Here, children used reading and writing to spend time with others, to play games, and to record information in play. The transactional function emphasized the uses of literacy as a means to negotiate meaning between print and the user. Children used reading and writing to label or name items and to make events more meaningful in play. The uses of literacy for personal reasons included more egocentric behaviors like expressing oneself or claiming ownership. And finally, the authenticating function involved literacy actions such as verifying information or taking the role of an adult in daily literacy-related activities.

These categories of functions were considered when designing literacy-enriched play centers for continued examination of play as a context for literacy. Our purpose was to incorporate materials that were familiar to young children in order to stimulate sustained interactions and play without directly superimposing particular play themes in these centers.

A Play Environment: Considering the Given

We were allowed to experimentally reorganize the physical environments of two preschool classrooms, each of which was designed for approximately 20 children in a racially mixed school. The classrooms were similar in size and shape, located in close proximity to one another, and included identical play centers: housekeeping, blocks, manipulatives, book corner, and art. The diagrams in Figure 8.1 illustrate the design of the play environments prior to the literacy enrichment.

In general, the traditional play centers in each of these preschool classrooms seemed ill-defined with few closed spaces and partitions. None of the play centers was labeled: Rather, each was identified by the types of props located there. For example, the book corner contained several shelves of books but could hardly be defined as a library center, which might include a check-out desk and a variety of print materials. In addition, written language was not a dominant feature in either classroom. There was limited labeling of concrete items and limited access to books, pencils, and other literacy-related items. Few written messages were available at a child's eye level, and there was little environmental print in the play areas. For example, the kitchen area included few real grocery items containing print such as cereal or Jello boxes.

Figure 8.1

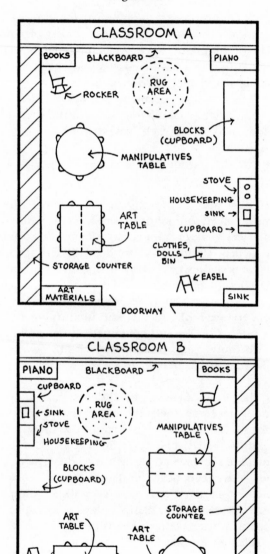

Design of the play environments prior to the literacy enrichment.

To prepare for the restructuring of these classrooms into more literacy-enriched environments, the physical layout of each room was studied. In addition, the kinds of play areas and key play props—along with the types of functions we found children engaged in during literacy-related play—were considered. Because changes in the physical play environment may affect children's play behaviors more broadly (Zifferblatt, 1972), it was important to attempt to modify and enrich existing play centers while taking into account the spatial density and the arrangement of space in each play setting.

A Literacy Enriched Environment: Carving, Categorizing, Labeling and Rearranging

Based on our study of the existing play centers, our redesign of the classrooms involved four kinds of physical environmental changes. First, all the play centers were more dramatically carved away from one another and clearly defined by using semifixed features such as cupboards, screens, tables, and written signs. Hanging mobiles were also installed to designate the various play areas. Each mobile, with the play center's name printed on it, was shaped in a form representative of that center. For example, the mobile identifying the library was shaped like a pile of books and contained the word library in dark, black print. We found that, hung at the children's eye level, these mobiles were often used as references for the writing of specific letters and words.

Second, labeling of items in the general environment was increased. For example, seashells located in the art area were labeled. Storage bins for blocks were marked according to the size blocks (small, large, long, short) that belonged in each. Baskets containing manipulatives were also labeled according to the type of manipulative they contained—i.e., Lego, beads, and Snap'n'Lock blocks. In general, key items in each play area were marked with a printed name.

Third, we developed four distinct play centers in each preschool classroom—a post office, a library, an office, and a kitchen. These four centers were selected for several reasons. For example, because they resembled the preexisting play centers in some ways, they were already somewhat familiar to the children. They could also be directly and easily linked to common literacy-oriented real-life activities outside preschool. Therefore, it was likely that these new centers would have a high degree of familiarity for the children. In addition, we felt it was important to include centers with certain generic qualities. From our point of view, more generalized play centers would provide more opportunities for children to create their *own* play themes that might incorporate reading and writing. In this way, the children would be able to demonstrate their existing knowledge about literacy on their own terms. In other words, rather than superimpose on the children particular play themes that might prompt literacy demonstrations, we sought to provide centers that might encourage both higher quality play and reading and writing behaviors.

Fourth, the physical space was rearranged. The post office and the library were placed adjacent to one another on one side of the room and the office and kitchen on the other side of the room. This arrangement facilitated movement between centers and encouraged the development of sustained play themes, such as those centered around home and work or going to and from the library in a community. The diagrams in Figure 8.2 illustrate the redesign of the play environments for enrichment purposes.

Inserting Literacy Props

Having designated the specific play areas to be enriched, the next step was to include literacy props in each center. These decisions were guided by a number of criteria which had emerged from our earlier work (Neuman and Roskos, 1989; Roskos, 1988).

Appropriateness. The appropriateness of the literacy props was determined by the question, Have we observed the prop being used naturally by children in their spontaneous play? For example, we had observed much spontaneous use of a variety of different kinds of printed matter such as catalogs and magazines, but not many workbooks. We also took into account some safety precautions. Staplers, large paper clamps, and sharply pointed pens were excluded from the centers because of the difficulty in monitoring their uses with young children.

Authenticity. The authenticity of props selected for each center was determined in response to the question, Is this a real item that children might naturally find in their environment? For example, we preferred to use actual printed forms from schools, businesses, and stores instead of "pretend" forms with teacher-made labels. Real file folders, recipe cards, pamphlets, sign-up sheets, memo pads, cookbooks, grocery items, and coupons, were placed in the play areas. Based on our experiences, children were often familiar with these items and had sufficient background knowledge to incorporate them into their play.

Utility. The key question to determine whether an item might be useful in the play context was, Does this prop serve a particular function

Figure 8.2

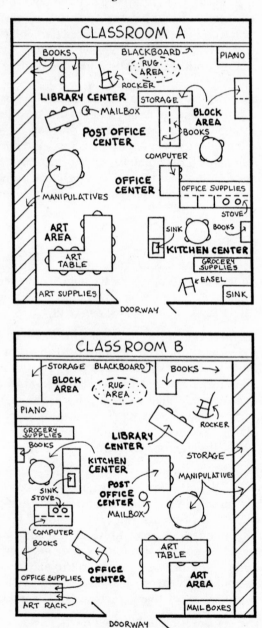

Design of the play environments after the literacy enrichment.

for children in their everyday life? Because we were interested in discerning children's views of literacy, we attempted to include props that involved print in common day-to-day activities. For example, props associated with mailing a letter, envelopes, writing instruments, stamps, and stationary were made available in close proximity to one another. Props associated with literacy-related routines common in the community were also selected for inclusion in these centers—checking out a book, making a grocery list, reading and copying a recipe, and writing a telephone message. Other items that might be regarded as functional to children included taking food orders, reading a menu, and reading a map.

Based on these three criteria, literacy-related materials, as itemized in Table 8.2, were placed in each play center.

Table 8.2

Literacy Props Used to Enrich Play Centers

Kitchen Area
Books to read to dolls or stuffed animals
Telephone books and telephone
Emergency number decals on telephone
Cookbooks/recipe cards/labeled recipe boxes
Small plaques with verses and decorative magnets
Magazines
Personal stationary and envelopes
Food coupons
Grocery store food ads
Play money
Empty food, toiletry, and cleaning containers
Small message board or blackboard
Various types of calendars
Note pads

Office Play Area
Calendar and appointment books
Telephone Books and telephones with buttons
Message pads of various types and pencils
Signs, i.e. Open/closed; Bank open/closed; Window; Please;
    Thank you; Form a line
Magazines and books for a waiting area
Assorted pamphlets, brochures, fliers, charts
File folders and different sized paper
Racks for filing papers
Index cards cut into appointment cards

Table 8.2 *continued*

Business cards
Date and other stamps and stamp pads
Business stationary and envelopes
Assorted forms
Play money and check-like pieces of paper
Ledger sheets
Typewriter
Post-its
Hand calculator
Computer keyboard
In/out trays (labeled)
Clip boards

Post Office Play Area
Pencils, pens, markers
Envelopes of various sizes
Assorted forms
Stationary supplies
Stickers, stars, gummed stamps
Post Office Box for letters
A tote bag for mail delivery
Calendar
Telephone and telephone book
Bins or slotted devices to sort mail
Signs related to Post Office, e.g. about zip codes
Empty small stamp books
Open/closed signs
Computer labels
Post Officer hat
Stamps and stamp pads

Library Corner
Library book return cards
Stamps for marking books
A wide variety of children's books
A wide variety of magazines
Book marks
Pencils
Paper
A sign-up sheet and sign-out sheet
Stickers to mark books or shelves
ABC Index cards
File boxes
Telephone

Effects Of Literacy-Enriched Play Centers
On Children's Involvement With Print

To determine the potential effects of these literacy-enriched play centers, we conducted an exploratory study analyzing the play of the 37 preschoolers in both redesigned classrooms. Two major questions guided our investigation. First: were children engaging in more literacy demonstrations during their play as a result of the inclusion of these materials in play centers? And second: did these reading and writing activities take on greater purposefulness, becoming a more integral part of the children's imaginative play?

Before the literacy-enrichment phase of the project, the 37 preschoolers (ranging in ages from 4.2 to 5.7) were individually administered the *Sand* form of Clay's (1979) Conventions About Print (CAP) test. Two observational measures were used to assess children's literacy activities during their spontaneous free play. The first measure, developed by Singer and Singer (1980), was designed to analyze the average number of literacy demonstrations children naturally engaged in during their free-play. Observers were trained to select a particular child and record all actions and language (verbatim) for a ten-minute period on four separate occasions. A total of 40 minutes of observation was recorded for each child over a period of one month. These protocols were analyzed for evidence of literacy demonstrations, which we defined as instances of reading- or writing-like behaviors. Such demonstrations included scribbling, marking on paper, pretending to read, book-handling, or attending to print in some manner, for example:

Julia is sitting at a table with another little girl and making a birthday picture for her friend, Andrea. It is a design of all different shapes and colors and a red heart. She is writing, "Happy Birthday, Andrea—Love, Julia."

The second observational measure was designed to qualitatively analyze the nature of the preschoolers' play with literacy. Eight hours of play were recorded on videotape and analyzed by two observers. Play frames—play that is bound by a location and a particular focus or interaction (Bateson, 1955; Garvey, 1977; Sutton-Smith, 1979)—were established and literacy-related frames isolated for further analysis.

Following these procedures, the physical environments of the classrooms were enriched with literacy-related materials. The actual redesign of the play environments in each classroom and enrichment of the key play centers took approximately six hours and occurred during nonschool hours.

Children's reactions to these physical design changes were enthusiastic. One little girl exclaimed, "We just love this." During this exploratory time, teachers and aides were encouraged not to intervene or restrict any areas, but rather to allow the children to move freely through all centers during free-play periods.

No formal observations occurred during the first month as children adjusted to the physical design changes in their new environment. We did, however, occasionally videotape the play areas in order to obtain some advanced information on how they were being used, as well as information on the children's interactions with print. But we waited a full four weeks before beginning to systematically observe, once again, the number and the quality of children's engagements with literacy during play. *Stones,* another form of the CAP test, was also administered to each child.

Literacy Demonstrations in Play

Although our study was exploratory in nature, the results clearly indicate that physical design changes in preschool classrooms can, indeed, affect children's engagement in reading and writing activities during play. Findings reported in Table 8.3 suggest that children's scores on the CAP test rose signifiantly over a two-month period, as did the average number of literacy demonstrations engaged in during play. Although it is impossible from this study to suggest a causal relationship (i.e., that literacy demonstrations *caused* higher CAP scores), the results make a compelling argument for the inclusion of literacy props in preschool play centers. With access to relatively simple, inexpensive materials, young children spontaneously used almost twice as much print for play purposes than they did before our intervention.

Of course, more controlled experimental studies are needed to determine whether these findings—based on an action research model—can be generalized to other preschool settings. Our data do, however, support the view that "literacy-rich" and littered-with-print school environments encourage children's interactions with literacy.

Examining the Functions of Literacy in Play

Our second question focused on a qualitative assessment of children's uses of literacy in play: How did these literacy-enriched play

Table 8.3

Effects of a Literacy-Enriched Play Environment:
Mean Score Differences

Variable	Prior to enrichment		Following Enrichment	
	$\overline{X}$	SD	$\overline{X}$	SD
Literacy Demonstrations	1.51	1.95	2.83*	2.9
Conventions About Print (Clay, 1979)	9.16	3.9	11.51**	3.77

* p < .01
** p < .001

environments affect preschoolers' understandings of the functions of reading and writing? Beyond certain quantitative changes in the number of literacy demonstrations, were there also qualitative changes in the ways children used literacy? Although researchers have argued against looking for particular benefits or payoffs of play, several important advantages have been noted consistently in the parallel field of oral language. For example, Cazden (1976) has argued that children explore and elaborate on the phonological, syntactic, and semantic rules of language through play. Extending this argument, Dauite (1989) posits that play is a "form of thought" for children—involving the critical thinking skills of analysis, synthesis, and evaluation which can then be applied to writing. Consequently, as children used literacy through play, might they also have been constructing more complex ideas about its functions in our redesigned environment?

To examine the functional dimensions of literacy, play frames before the literacy enrichment were compared with those that followed four weeks after the physical design changes occurred. Insights from previous research had alerted us to the multidimensional nature of the term *function* (Blumler, 1979; Heath, 1980; Neuman, 1980). For example, function has been used to denote: (a) purpose or reasons for reading and writing, such as for communication (Downing, 1979); (b) perceptions of written language, as in, "What is reading?" (Johns, 1986); and (c) context, or situation-of-use of written language, which serves to make encounters with print meaningful (Harste, Woodward and Burke, 1984). Although we were sensitive to these dimensions, rather than conforming to any existing definitions, we allowed for specific indicators of functions to emerge from our analysis of the 16 hours of videotaped play. In this respect, our purpose was to describe the meaning of function from the child's point of view. Therefore, in an attempt to extend our understanding of the categories of functions as illustrated in out typology in Table 8.1, we now asked the question, What makes literacy functional for young chldren on their own terms?

The following analysis, which describes literacy demonstrations during play before and after our intervention, illustrates the nature of function in literacy-related play. We will argue that the concept of function is more multifaceted than the mere delineation of the uses of reading and writing for young children. In literacy-enriched environments, sustained, purposeful interactions that integrate reading and writing behaviors occur within play frames. Consequently, children's play begins to reflect more than just literacy *demonstrations.* Rather, they are literacy *events,* occasions in which written language is part of the nature of participant interactions (Heath, 1982). Thus, rather than being incidental to the play, reading and writing are integral parts of the play itself, not only contributing to the creation of a more coherent play theme, but also revealing more clearly young children's conceptions of the functions of these activities.

Qualitative Changes in the Functions Of Literacy in Play

Although it is difficult to detail all the complexities and deep meanings of the nature of function in reading and writing activities, a number of important indicators of change emerged from our analysis of literacy demonstrations in play frames before and after our intervention.

Literacy in Play Became More Useful

As might be expected, we found that children's reading and writing behaviors became more purposeful in the literacy-enriched environment. Before the experiment, demonstrations often occurred as isolated events apart from the general stream of play behavior. For example, in one play frame, Dana moved from playing in the kitchen corner to the art table, where she began to write letters on drawing paper. Then she moved back to the kitchen—within 45 seconds.

In contrast, following our literacy enrichment, Dana's engagement in play with Hilary in the post office center lasted for 22 minutes. The example illustrates the utility of writing in play:

Dana and Hilary are sitting at the table in the post office center. They are writing and making marks on paper. They seem to be preparing to send letters.

Hilary: "Now we have to sign our names."

They each sign their names at the bottom of their messages. They smile at each other as they shuffle their papers. They each get an envelope from the boxes at the front of the table, fold their papers and put them aside. They watch each other as they do this. Then they move toward the mailbox at the corner of the table, and mail their letters.

Children also used reading and writing in extended play for conveying information ("fireproofing a building"), following a recipe ("This is how to make Jello"), filling out taxes ("You did 'em wrong last year"), and calling the mayor.

Literacy in Play Became More Situation-Based

Sustained literacy interactions tended to occur in a known context or situation that was familiar to children. Before any changes were made in the physical environment, the play contexts were created by the children themselves. For example, in one particular play activity, Scott chose to spend time in the book corner. He moved to the book area, took a book out, looked at it for 55 seconds, then returned it and went off to play in another center.

In our enriched environment, however, books are placed in the context of a library, where children can play at being a librarian and develop some of the behaviors associated with borrowing books at the library. For example:

Scott and David are pretending to be librarians. Their friend, Aaron, arrives in the center.

Scott: "You don't buy books here, you only borrow 'em."

Aaron: "Yoo-man, I borrowed this scary book for four days."

They all begin to look at the book. Aaron is turning the pages left to right. They look at the book quietly at first, and then Aaron starts to retell the story. "Here comes the bad guy." After reading, Aaron places the book on the table. David flips through it to retrieve the card, then puts the book in a holder and shouts out to Aaron, "Come to the library again."

The generic contexts of library, office, kitchen, and post office offer children a broad spectrum of potential play themes. For example, some children pretended to be clerks in the office play center, while others transformed this same center into a police headquarters, using the same props—a computer keyboard, paper, and index cards—in ways related to their own particular play theme.

Literacy in Play Became More Unified and Sustained

Before intervention, literacy demonstrations often appeared to be rather brief exchanges between children or their teachers. The majority of these demonstrations (eleven in all for the total eight hours of pre-enrichment videotaped play) lasted for less than one minute. In one exchange, for example, Brian was involved in the purposeful activity of writing an "alphabet newspaper." He shared the paper with his teacher and his friend, Scott, then moved on to another activity. The total activity, including his composing and his interactions with others, took approximately 50 seconds.

We would argue that, in literacy-enriched settings, such demonstrations appear to become more connected and more integral to the play itself. In other words, there is a greater density in the number of demonstrations—practically a chain reaction or webbing effect. As a result, it becomes almost impossible at times to isolate one demonstration from another:

> Brian and Michael are in the office center. Brian is seated at the desk, and Michael is playing with the computer keyboard. Brian grabs a book and Michael joins him.
>
> Michael: "Look what I found" (pointing to an object). "Guess who stole it?"
>
> Brian: "Who?"
>
> Then Brian points to the print in the book and talks to Michael as if using the print as reference. He moves his finger back and forth over the print.
>
> Michael: "What about the robbery?"
>
> They talk back and forth and Brian keeps referring to the print with his finger as if it is confirming what Michael is saying about the robbery. Brian raises his arm and says, "Freedom. .fightin' crime. . ." He then gets a pencil and starts writing notes.

As the play and literacy demonstrations become more unified, children reveal their definitions of literacy artifacts and practices in a naturally occurring, child-centered context. As the link between these instances of reading and writing behaviors increase, so too do they begin to take on an event-like status, becoming pressed into service for larger goals or intents.

Literacy in Play Became More Interactive

Children experiment with the meanings of language through transformations, including variation, association, and contrast (Dauite, 1989). For example, in mother-baby play, children create scenarios in which they associate Mother with specific behaviors (such as disciplining a young child), and they highlight role contrasts between the authority figure of Mother with the seeming helplessness of the child. The interactive characteristics of the play allow children to explore or try out alternatives based on their views of the social world.

The interactive nature of group play is particularly important for young children who come to school with varying conceptions of and levels of reading and writing behaviors. These conversational interchanges help to refine their beliefs about this relatively unfamiliar activity of literacy through experiences that are supportive and nonevaluative.

Our analysis indicated that, before these classrooms were redesigned, more than half of the literacy demonstrations involved children in solitary play. For example, in one play activity lasting about one minute, Adam looked at a book on dinosaurs. In another activity lasting approximately 40 seconds, Brandon wrote his name while drawing and coloring at the art table.

We found a great deal more interaction occurring between children in literacy-enriched play centers. For example:

David runs over to the teacher and says: "Mrs. G., will you come and buy books?"

Mrs. G.: "Are they for sale?"

David runs and whispers to Scott: "Somebody's comin' to buy books." Mrs. G. comes over with pretend money.

Scott: "You don't need to buy 'em."

Mrs. G.: "David asked me to buy a book."

Scott: "But this is a library. All you need is a library card. What book do you want? You can have one for four days."

They help her look for a book. Mrs. G. selects *Where the Wild Things Are*. Scott then "marks" a card with a stamp. David records the same information on a larger paper. Scott tells her that the check mark refers to the day she needs to bring the book back.

To this play frame, Scott brought a pretty detailed scenario of a library schemata which he shared with David, who appeared to be less familiar with these routines. Through social participation and interaction, children are drawn into the uses of literacy in ways that nurture and develop their conceptions of its functions (Galda, Pellegrini and Cox, 1989; Vygotsky, 1978).

Literacy in Play Became More Role-Defined

Role enactments are a natural concomitant of social play among preschoolers. Adopting common roles in play is important on a number of dimensions. It indicates an awareness of role-appropriate behaviors and role relationships (Johnson, Christie, and Yawkey, 1987). For example, when Hilary grabbed a mailbag to play postmaster and shuffled through mail to give Dana a letter, she was demonstrating her knowledge of the stereotypic behaviors associated with an important person in her community.

Because we saw very little interactive literacy-related play before implementing our physical design changes, we found few opportunities for children to take on roles that involved any reading and writing activities. The inclusion of materials in the new centers, however, sparked role-taking that included literacy in many of the pretend play frames. For example:

Brian and Michael are pretending to be police. Brian is sitting at the table looking at a book. Brian is pointing at the print with his finger, then says, "There's a fire. We gotta go get every cop that we have."

Michael agrees and proceeds to describe something about fire in detail. Brian pretends to read aloud to Michael as if giving him some vital information or directions. They continue talking about needing "a lot of cops and putting out fires."

Aaron comes over and asks whether he "can be a cop." The two other boys ignore him referring to the print in the book and following along with their fingers. They all together discuss fires.

Brian then returns to the book and pretends to read by reciting the alphabet. He takes out a magnifying glass and uses it to help him read in greater detail.

In this play frame, the boys combined the roles of firefighters and police officers (and perhaps, detectives) into what might be called crisis management. At the same time, however, they were demonstrating the importance of reading for extracting information and authenticating role definitions. This type of play appears to lend a greater coherence and meaning to literacy within play than the isolated demonstrations we had seen earlier—children scribbling for brief seconds on paper or quickly glancing at a book in a corner.

Summary

On the basis of this exploratory research, we would argue that children's creative and imitative engagement with reading and writing activities in play may be an important developmental activity in the process of becoming literate. Through their play actions, children are demonstrating—from their point of view—that literacy is a social process and that it comes about by one's engagement in literacy acts. We hypothesize that, by encouraging children to make sense of print on their own terms, literacy emerges as a more useful activity—a means to many kinds of ends, serving a wide range of real functions. Bettleheim and Zelan (1981) suggest the importance of these first lessons in literacy:

We teach children to read in the hope that what they read will have meaning for them. But a skill that was not intrinsically meaningful when we first learned it is much less likely to become deeply meaningful later on [p. 42].

This research attempted to combine what we viewed as the functions of literacy based on children's conceptions with materials that would facilitate their engagement in extending the functions of reading and writing. It is important to note, however, that some of the preschool teachers appeared concerned with all of the literacy materials in the play environments. A number expressed concern that the design changes were "overwhelming" and perhaps not good for the children. The literacy enrichment, according to informal reports, involved "too much paper," "too many books," and "too much access to pencils and markers."

Based on our qualitative analysis, however, our restructuring of the environment did not appear in any way to either restrict pretend play or create a more school-like environment. Rather, we believe that by including appropriate, authentic, and functional props and writing materials in young children's play centers, we are welcoming them into the "literacy club" (Smith, 1983), and thus—in a very real sense—empowering them as thinkers and learners.

References

Bateson, G. (1955). A theory of play and fantasy. *Psychiatric Research Report, 2,* 39–51.

Bettleheim, B. and K. Zelan (1981). *On learning to read.* New York: Knopf.

Blumler, J. (1979). The role of theory in uses and gratifications studies. *Communications Research, 6,* 9–36.

Cazden, C. (1976). Play with language and meta-linguistic awareness. In: J. Bruner, A. Jolly, and K. Sylva (Eds.), *Play—Its role in development and evolution* (pp. 603-608). New York: Basic Books.

Clay, M. (1979). *The early detection of reading difficulties: A diagnostic survey with recovery procedures.* Portsmouth, NH: Heinemann Educational Books.

Daiute, C. (1989). Play as thought: Thinking strategies of young writers. *Harvard Educational Review, 59,* 1–23.

Downing, J. (1979). *Reading and reasoning.* Edinburgh: W. and C. Black.

Galda, L., A.D. Pellegrini, and S. Cox (1989). *A short-term longitudinal study of preschoolers' emergent literacy.* Paper presented at the American Educational Research Association Conference, San Francisco (April).

Garvey, C. (1977). *Play.* Cambridge, MA: Harvard University Press.

Hall, N. (1987). *The emergence of literacy.* Portsmouth, NH: Heinemann Educational Books.

Halliday, M.A.K. (1975). *Learning how to mean: Explorations in the development of language.* New York: Elsevier North-Holland.

Harste, J., C. Woodward, and V. Burke (1984). *Language stories and literacy lessons.* Portsmouth, NH: Heinemann Educational Books.

Heath, S.B. (1982). What no bedtime story means: Narrative skills at home and school. *Language in Society, 2,* 49-76.

Jacob, E. (1984). Learning literacy through play: Puerto Rican kindergarten children. In: H. Goelman, A. Oberg, and F. Smith (Eds.), *Awakening to literacy* (pp. 73–83). Portsmouth, NH: Heinemann Educational Books.

Johns, J. (1986). Students' perceptions of reading: Thirty years of inquiry. In D. Yaden and S. Templeton (Eds.), *Metalinguistic awareness and beginning literacy* (pp. 31–40). Portsmouth, NH: Heinemann Educational Books.

Johnson, J.E., J.F. Christie and Yawkey, T.D. (1987). *Play and early childhood development.* Glenview, IL: Scott-Foresman.

Neill, S. (1982). Experimental alterations in playroom layout and their effect on staff and child behavior. *Educational Psychology, 2,* 103–109.

Neuman, S. B. (1980). Why children read: A functional approach. *Journal of Reading Behavior, 12,* 333–336.

Neuman, S.B. and R. Roskos (1989). Preschoolers' conceptions of literacy as reflected in their spontaneous play. In: S. McCormick and J. Zutell (Eds.), *Cognitive and social perspectives for literacy research and instruction.* Thirty-eighth Yearbook of the National Reading Conference. Chicago, IL: National Reading Conference.

Polloway, A.M. (1974). The child in the physical environment: A design problem. In: G. Coates (Ed.), *Alternative environments* (pp. 370–381). Stroudsburg, PA: Dowden, Hutchison, & Ross.

Roskos, K. (1988). Literacy at work in play. *The Reading Teacher, 41,* 562–567.

Singer, J. and D. Singer (1980). *Television viewing and imaginative play in preschoolers: A developmental and parent-intervention study.* Progress report to the Spencer Foundation.

Smith, F. (1983). *Essays into literacy.* Portsmouth, NH: Heinemann Educational Books.

Sutton-Smith, B. (1979). Introduction. In: B. Sutton-Smith (Ed.). *Play and Learning* (pp. 1–6). New York: Gardner Press.

Vygotsky, L. (1978). *Mind in society.* Cambridge, MA: Harvard University Press.

Zifferblatt, S. (1972). Architecture and human behavior: Toward increasing understanding of a functional relationship. *Educational Technology, 12,* 54–57.

9

Symbolic Play: A Source of Meaningful Engagements with Writing and Reading

Carol Taylor Schrader

Young children use symbolic play to better understand their life experiences (Piaget, 1962). "They project themselves into the adult activities of their culture and rehearse their future roles and values" (Vygotsky, 1978, p. 129). In a literate society, such experiences include encounters with functional writing and reading (Taylor, 1983). For example, young children may see adults and older children writing and reading notes, grocery lists, checks, and so on. Such observing youngsters then re-present these activities in their symbolic play (Isenberg and Jacob, 1983; Jacob, 1984; Schickedanz, 1978; Schrader, 1989).

This chapter reports two naturalistic research studies of play and early literacy. The first study examines the written language used by young children within the context of symbolic play. The second explores ways in which early childhood teachers can facilitate early literacy development by functioning as participants within the context of children's spontaneous symbolic play.

Study 1: Written Language Used in Play

The development of children's oral language was studied by Halliday (1973, 1978) from the functional-interactional perspective of language in use. Attention was focused on what language can do and what the child can do with language. Meaning intent, meaning potential, and meaning exchange were found to characterize children's language interaction with others. Halliday identified a set of seven functions of oral language a child uses in "learning how to mean":

1. Instrumental ("I want"): satisfying material needs
2. Regulatory ("Do as I tell you"): controlling the behavior of others
3. Interactional ("Me and you"): getting along with other people
4. Personal ("Here I come"): identifying and expressing the self
5. Heuristic ("Tell me why"): exploring the world around the inside one
6. Imaginative ("Let's pretend"): creating a world of one's own
7. Informative ("I've got something to tell you"): communicating new information (Halliday, 1973)

According to Halliday, the initial functions are instrumental, regulatory, interactional, and personal; these are then followed by the heuristic and the imaginative. Eventually the child adds the informative function.

The implications of the sociolinguistic view for early literacy teaching and learning were addressed by Halliday (1978). He contended that literacy is an extension of the functional potential of oral language. Furthermore, in order for children to learn to read and write, Halliday believes they must make sense of the functional extension that writing and reading provide.

Study 1 was based on assumptions derived from sociopsycholinguistic research—that written language development is occurring before schooling and that written language develops in ways similar to oral language (Schrader, 1989). It was further assumed that children's uses of written language could be viewed from Halliday's functional-interactional perspective. Also, because children use symbolic play to facilitate understanding of their life experiences, it seemed reasonable to expect that they would attempt to incorporate written language into their symbolic play. The question raised for study was, In what ways do prekindergarten chlidren use written language within the context of their spontaneous symbolic play?

Method

Participants. The participants were seven prekindergarten children from an early childhood education center. The children ranged in age from 5 to 5.5 years. All were from middle-class families, they had had similar school literacy experiences, and their native language was English. Their spontaneous playgroup at school included children who ranged in age from 2 to 6, also from middle-class families. Four children in the playgroup were from minority racial and ethnic groups. Most of the parents were college-educated professionals, although some were graduate students.

Procedures. The naturalistic research paradigm was deemed appropriate for the investigation (Lincoln and Guba, 1985) because it enabled the researcher to observe the children's use of written language as a holistic process within meaningful contexts and purposeful experiences. It also provided rich descriptive data about the participants' naturally occurring behaviors within the educational setting.

Triangulated data collection was accomplished by several procedures. Videotaping spontaneous symbolic play served as the primary means for data collection. The children had had previous experience with being videotaped at school. An initial week of researcher visits and videotaping allowed the children to ask questions and accept the changes in their classroom. The videotapings were supported with field notes taken by the observing teacher, who had prior in-service training in the meaning-centered model of written language teaching and learning. She had also implemented the model with her students in her early childhood classroom. She understood the purpose of the study and her responsibilities as research assistant. Her role was that of a nonparticipant observer. She sat at the edge of the play area, noted the writing behaviors of the participant children, and recorded her observations according to procedures recommended by Bogdan and Biklen (1982, pp. 74–93). The children's written language productions during the videotaped events were collected to document the youngsters' intended use of written language in their play. The observing teacher discussed with each child the content and purpose of his or her writing to further verify the meaning.

Data were collected on 15 days during a three-week period. Children designated as participants within the spontaneous play group were targeted for videotaping. Housekeeping, post office, and office centers were set up for use during the first 2 weeks. An animal hospital center was added for the third week (Table 9.1).

Analysis. The videotapes were transcribed by the researcher in a typescript of the children's oral language, writing behaviors, and corresponding actions. These typescripts were then compared with the observing teacher's field notes and the children's writing and explanations of meaning intent.

Table 9.1

Play Settings

Center: The House

Description of Contents: The housekeeping area contained equipment and props traditional to such an area: stove, sink, refrigerator, kitchen accessories, table, chairs, cradle and blankets, shelves, dolls and accessories, dress-up clothes, and telephone. Added to this, however, were literacy materials: housekeeping magazines, local newspaper, telephone book, checkbooks with checks, paper, and pencils.

Center: The Office

Description of Contents: The office consisted of a 2' × 4' carrel supplied with two chairs, two telephones, two telephone books, business stationery, envelopes, business forms, cash receipts, checks, paper clips, rubber bands, file folders, junk mail, scissors, paste, and pencils. The area was walled on three sides by cardboard. A sign reading "The Office" and a picture of people working in an office were posted on the walls.

Center: The Post Office

Description of Contents: The post office consisted of a 3' × 4' shelf enclosed on three sides with red Kraft paper. The shelves were supplied with envelopes, plain paper, stickers, stamp-sized paper, paste, scissors, and pencils. The top shelf served as a counter and was equipped with a mailbox and a scale. The mailbox had a slot in the front and a large opening in the back. It was covered on five sides with pictures depicting mailing activities. The area was walled on three sides by cardboard. Pictures of mail carriers at work were posted on the walls. A sign reading "Post Office" and labels reading "mailman" were also posted on the walls.

Center: The Animal Hospital

Description of Contents: The animal hospital contained a 2' × 4' table, stuffed toy bear and mouse, a stethoscope, jars of cotton balls and Q-tips, two children's animal picture books, four x-rays, plain paper, and pencils. The animal hospital was walled on three sides by cardboard. A sign reading "Animal Hospital" and "Veterinarian," a picture of a doctor with a stethoscope, and dog and cat pictures were posted on the walls. Two chairs were placed at one end of the table.

A particular coding scheme was suggested by the sociolinguistic theoretical approach to this study—that of analyzing the children's uses of written language according to Halliday's (1973, 1978) seven functions of language in use (Bogden and Biklen, 1982, pp. 155–170). The coding categories that follow are an adaptation of Halliday's language functions as they evolved during data analysis:

1. Instrumental ("I want.")
   to satisfy one's materials needs, to obtain goods and services.
   Ex.: Writing a list
       Writing a check
       Writing an order

2. Regulatory ("Do as I tell you.")
   to control the actions and behaviors of others and/or self.
   Ex.: Writing plans for future actions
       Writing a sign
       Writing directions or instructions
       Writing an assignment
       Writing prescriptions

3. Interactional (" Me and you.")
   to interact with others, to participate in social relationships.
   Ex.: Writing letters, postcards, notes

4. Personal ("Here I come.")
   to identify and express personal feelings and attitudes.
   Ex.: Writing one's name
       Writing about me
       Writing a diary

5. Heuristic ("Tell me why.")
   to explore the world, to discover, to seek information, and
   to solve problems.
   Ex.: Writing questions

6. Imaginative ("Let's pretend.")
   to create a world of one's own.
   Ex.: Writing a story
       Writing poetry

7. Informative ("I've got something to tell you.")
   to communicate new information to someone who does
   not already possess that information.
   Ex.: Writing memos, bulletins, signs
       Writing reports
       Writing labels, nametags
       Writing a newspaper
       Writing textbooks or resource books
       Writing money
       Writing name, address, phone number

Results

The children's knowledge of written language functions was demonstrated not only as they worte for real-life purposes, but also as they read their writing and discussed the meaning of their written language with their classmates and teacher. The children further verified the meaning intent of their writing by their actions. Consequently, the researcher was able to identify and classify the children's written language productions according to Halliday's seven functions served by language. The children wrote for instrumental, regulatory, interactional, personal, and informational purposes. They were not observed using the heuristic or imaginative functions of writing. Examples from the profusion of data collected are presented here.

Instrumental function. Children wrote checks for specific goods and services. Jace, for example, sat at the kitchen table, wrote a check for the animal doctor for $100, and mailed it at the post office. Carrie wrote a check for $15 for macaroni and cheese and grape juice (see Figure 9.1).

Figure 9.1

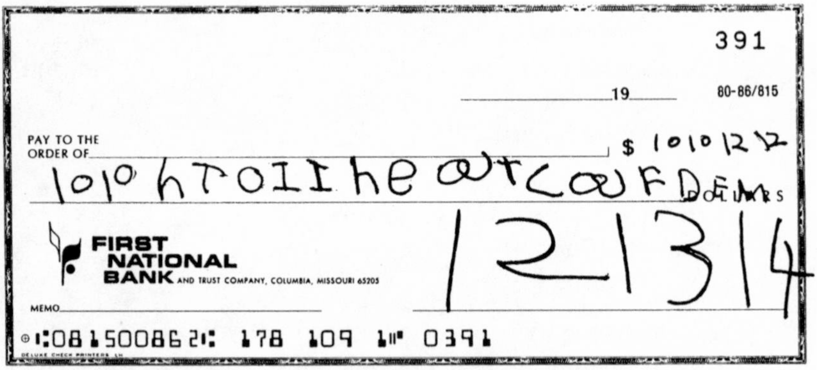

Carrie's check for $15 for macaroni and cheese and grape juice.

Regulatory function. Brian wrote that he had a five o'clock appointment with Dr. Neice because he was sick. Andy wrote assignments and said, "I'll be the judge. I have to assign all these assignments. Sheesh!" Brian put checks in three envelopes and wrote, "Don't open this." on each one. He also wrote and posted a "closed" sign. When he removed the sign, he announced that the office was now open. Thomas examined a toy bear and wrote instructions: "Come back to the doctor next week." He explained that the bear had a really bad cut on his paw.

Interactional Function. Amber wrote several letters, put them in envelopes, mailed them, and read each one to the teacher. One such letter said, "Hello Goldie, I hope you don't mind. I have to go to school some days, but I'll always come home. Love, Amber" (see Figure 9.2). She wrote "605" on an envelope and explained, "That is my number that my office is." Andy wrote a message, placed it in an envelope, licked and sealed the envelope, then took it to the post office and put it in the mailbox. He said, "Here guys, mail this to . . . mail this to Judge 28 . . . 606." His message read: "Please come to Kansas City. Love, Andy."

Personal Function. Jace drew around his foot, made a nose and legs, and said it was a dinosaur. He wrote his name on his drawing. Thomas drew a picture and said, "It's someone wrestling. He got beat up." Then he wrote his name on his paper.

Informative function. Several children wrote on paper to indicate that it had monetary value. Amber, for example, wrote on a check and said, "It's a check for $100 to me. I am to cash it at the bank and spend it." Thomas wrote alphabet cards (see Figure 9.3). He became a teacher to the baby doll by putting a pencil in the doll's hand, showing it how to write, and saying, "That's a good *N*, Baby." Brian entered the house and talked on the telephone. He then wrote on a card and left it under the telephone receiver. This sign said, "Telephone broken." Children also wrote their names, addresses, and telephone numbers as information for others.

Discussion and Implications

These data indicate that, when literacy materials are available to them, young children are able to use five of Halliday's seven functions of language for writing within the context of their symbolic play. Thus, the study provides empirical support for Halliday's contention that written language learning is an extension of the functional potential of oral language development. The findings, however, are inconsistent with Halliday's developmental sequence for oral language in that the children were not observed writing for heuristic or imaginative purposes, although they did use the informative function. It is likely that the children used written language to carry out only those

Figure 9.2

Amber's letter to Goldie. ''Hello Goldie, I hope you don't mind. I have to go to school some days, but I'll always come home. Love, Amber.''

Figure 9.3

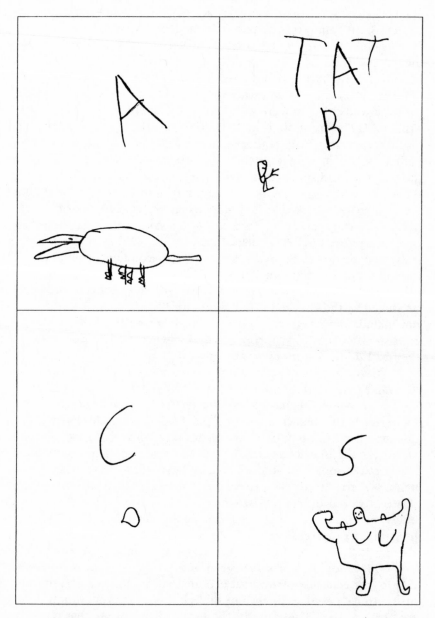

Thomas's alphabet cards. "A for Alligator, B for Bear, C for Circle, and S for Strongman."

functions with which they had had some experience. They relied on oral language for the heuristic function—to question each other. It may be that these youngsters had not experienced written language used for this purpose. Further research is needed to explain the absence of this function.

These children were not observed using the imaginative function of written language. In an earlier investigation (Schrader, 1987), five four-year-old children were asked on two separate occasions to draw a picture and write about it. Each child readily drew, wrote, and read his or her writing—using the imaginative function to produce stories. For example, Courtney wrote, "The ghost mouse went deep, deep in the water to find some rocks, and he couldn't find um. He went to the rock store except they did not have any more rocks left. He found his own sparkly rock that he found when he went looking high up in the sky. The sparkly rock was up on the sky, and he dropped that one on his little toe." The lack of imaginative writing in the present study may be due to the realistic literacy environments provided for the children. In accordance with Halliday's model of context/text relations, the lifelike contexts of discourse directly affected the texts produced by the children. They wrote for life-like functions that did not include the imaginative function of story writing. The children consistently used role-appropriate oral and written language which they had derived from everyday life.

These data also support Halliday's theory that the context of discourse (field, tenor, and mode) is influenced directly by the social context in which language is produced. In the housekeeping center, for example, the subject matter or topic (field) of the children's written discourse pertained to grocery shopping, bill paying, and personal letter writing. In the animal hospital, the children discussed illnesses, injuries, and prescriptions. The interpersonal relationships between children (tenor) differed from center to center. In the post office, the youngsters related to each other as post office workers and customers; in the housekeeping center, they related as family members. The children used the written channel (mode) of language for role-appropriate writing such as letters, checks, prescriptions, signs, and so on.

This study supports Pellegrini and Galda's (1986) recommendation that educators manipulate contextual variables as part of their instructional practices to enable children to use different functions of written language. These results, however, demonstrate that teachers can easily manipulate not only the mode of discourse but also the field and tenor. Providing writing materials in symbolic play centers enables and encourages children to use the written mode of discourse. The field, or topic of discourse, and the tenor, or relationships between children, can also be easily manipulated by the play settings and props.

It is the teacher who exerts the most influence on the classroom social environment. Teachers using a functional-interactional approach to language development are concerned with the social process involved, with language as a form of interaction, and with the functions that language serves in the life of the young child. The teacher's role as preparer of the classroom is an important one, because children learn the language they experience around them. It becomes necessary, therefore, for early childhood educators to create literacy environments which lend themselves to facilitating such learning.

Consider the traditional housekeeping corner, which is often unused by five-year-old chidren. The addition of literacy materials can give it new meaning for such youngsters. The office is also found in many classrooms, but it can be enhanced with a variety of literacy materials. Most early childhood programs present a unit on community workers, including the mail carrier. The post office center, too, can be enhanced with a rich supply of writing materials. All children have experiences with doctors and some with veterinarians as well. Youngsters' emerging concepts of a veterinarian as a writer and reader can be facilitated in the play center.

The data from this study and from Pellegrini (1984) demonstrate that learning centers such as those described here can elicit from preschoolers functional uses of language. Therefore, this study provides support for teachers who choose to provide their young students with symbolic play experiences to enable them to learn how written language is meaningful and useful. The encounters with written language described here can be an important part of the curriculum. They would enable young children to make sense of writing and reading, to expand their awareness of the functions of written language, and to facilitate their literacy learning.

Study 2 stemmed from the notion that teachers who wish to attempt to influence the amount and quality of children's symbolic play with literacy materials may do so by moving in and out of the play centers, by making comments and suggestions, and by modeling role-appropriate behaviors.

Study 2: Symbolic Play as a Curricular Tool

In play training studies (Feitelson and Ross, 1973; Lovinger, 1974; Rosen, 1974; Saltz and Johnson, 1974; Saltz, Dixon, and Johnson, 1977;

Singer, 1973; Smilansky, 1968), teachers actually joined in the children's play, took a role, demonstrated using objects as symbols, and modeled role-appropriate behavior and language. Some limitations, however, were placed on these teachers. In Smilansky's (1968) study, for example, teachers were cautioned "not to influence the content of the child's play, but rather to aid the child in its fuller elaboration" (p. 95). Intervention by the teacher was limited to suggestions, comments, questions, and demonstrations. The teacher encouraged and enabled the child to do what the child had wanted to do.

Theoretical support for the teacher as participant is provided by Vygotsky (1978). He identified a "zone of proximal development" as the "distance between the actual developmental level as determined by independent problem solving and the level of potential development as determined through problem solving under adult guidance or in collaboration with more capable peers" (pp. 86–91). It is the area in which a child can solve problems by working with others, especially adults. This is the area Vygotsky feels is especially important in a child's learning—the area where a child, with help, can go beyond his or her present developmental level. Adult/child interaction, then, becomes crucial in that it provides necessary assistance as the child stretches beyond his or her level of development. Vygotsky views learning as a profoundly social process, emphasizing dialogue and the varied roles that language plays in instruction and mediated cognitive growth. Thus, Vygotsky's theory implies that teacher/child interaction within play settings in the form of suggested ideas, posed questions, or noted observations can enable the child to progress in learning.

Teachers of young children are currently under a great deal of pressure from school administrators and parents to use inappropriate formal teaching techniques and to overemphasize achievement of narrowly defined academic skills (NAEYC, 1986; Elkind, 1986). Many teachers limit the amount of symbolic play because they do not fully understand how they can legitimately use play to accomplish educational objectives. They cannot explain how symbolic play facilitates learning in the academic areas, nor do they know how to function effectively within the context of the child's play.

Empirical research is needed to test assumptions and theories and to demonstrate ways in which symbolic play functions as a valuable teaching and learning medium during early childhood. More specifically, evidence is needed to support the teacher's participation in symbolic play and its use as a curricular tool for teaching and learning writing and reading during the early years.

Thus, the purpose of Study 2 was to explore the teacher's use of symbolic play as a teaching/learning medium for early literacy development (Schrader, 1990). The study also attempted to answer the question, In what ways can teachers facilitate early literacy development by functioning as participants within the context of young children's spontaneous symbolic play?

Method

Participants. Four prekindergarten teachers from three early childhood education centers were selected as participants in the study. Each of the teachers had a college degree in elementary education. Two worked in a university laboratory preschool, and the other two worked in private community preschools. All three facilities were in the same small midwestern community. The children who attended the preschools were three-, four-, and five-year-olds from middle-class families. A few children were from minority racial and ethnic groups.

The role of the teacher. The teachers' role was that of participant observer. Each one participated spontaneously in the play experiences with the children. After a writing event, the teacher recorded her observations of what a child had written and read. These observations were shared with the researcher.

Teacher participation was not intended to control or direct the content of the children's play but only to assist the children in extending their play more fully. Teachers were instructed to first listen and observe to determine the child's intentions. They could then use comments, questions, suggestions, and modeling to help the child go beyond his or her level of development.

Teacher training procedures. To be able to ascertain the child's intentions, the teachers had to operate from a knowledge base of the natural development of literacy in young children. Consequently, teachers were exposed to the sociopsycholinguistic theory of early written language development during a three-part workshop. Research findings were discussed, instructional principles were abstracted from theory, and demonstrations of how these principles translate into practice were provided.

Data collection procedures. The naturalistic inquiry paradigm (Lincoln and Guba, 1985) was employed for the study. This approach was deemed appropriate for several reasons. Literacy teaching and learning are holistic social processes. Naturalistic inquiry permits observation of these processes as they occur in the classrooms; provides rich, descriptive data of adult/child interactions; and enables the researcher to observe links between teacher practices and effects on the child's developing writing and reading abilities.

Triangulated data collection was accomplished by (1) video-tapings and audiotapings of the teachers' and children's behaviors and language during symbolic play; (2) children's written language productions; and (3) teacher-recorded observations of children's writing and reading behaviors.

The teachers were videotaped and audiotaped for eight days during two weeks as they participated in symbolic play with the children. The play times were scheduled during the mornings for 30 minutes per day. The same housekeeping, post office, and office play centers were used in each of the four classrooms. Children were free to enter or leave these centers as they chose.

Analysis. The teachers' and children's oral language, writing and reading behaviors, and corresponding actions were transcribed from the videotapes and audiotapes by the researcher. These typescripts were then compared with the participating teacher's recorded observations and the children's writings.

Vygotsky's theory of the zone of proximal development suggested a particular coding scheme—that of analyzing each teacher's interaction style as either "extending" or "redirecting" (Bogdan and Biklen, 1982, pp. 155–170; Cazden, 1972, pp. 125–127; Tamburrini, 1982). Extending teacher behaviors are those which take their cue from the child and are based on the teacher's assessment of what the child is paying attention to and is trying to accomplish. The teacher interacts with the child only after first ascertaining the nature of the child's intentions. She then meets the child's idea with a relevant—but different—idea. Thus, she not only focuses on the child's idea but also extends that idea beyond the presumed meaning of the child and introduces more varied elements related to that meaning. Redirecting teacher behaviors are those which ignore what the child is paying attention to and trying to accomplish. The teacher requires the child to shift his or her focus of attention to an idea that is unrelated in meaning to that of the child's intentions. This style frequently results in the play activity becoming nonplay—the child loses control.

The effects of the teachers' interaction styles on the child's developing writing and reading were studied. The guiding question was, How effective were the teacher and child in negotiating the child's zone of proximal development in interactive writing events?

Coding decisions for each teaching/learning episode were based on three sources of data—the videotapes and audiotapes, the children's written language productions, and the participating teacher's recorded observations. Analysis was cross-checked by a second researcher who was selected for content area and process expertise. Consensus was reached for all examples.

Results

The teachers' interaction styles were revealed not only by their language and behaviors during teaching/learning episodes, but also by a diagnosis of children's intentions and subsequent language and behaviors. Each teacher demonstrated both extending and redirecting styles, but to different degrees. All four teachers used considerably more extending style than redirecting style. Tables 9.2 and 9.3 summarize for each teacher the percentage per day of occurrences of each style of interaction. Examples were selected for illustration.

Table 9.2

Percent Per Day of Extending Style Interaction

	Teachers			
Day	Carlene	Barbara	Debra	Carla
1	100	75	100	83
2	94	75	100	77
3	92	53	81	60
4	82	56	78	90
5	88	53	83	77
6	91	50	45	67
7	83	60	70	92
8	100	82	71	67

Extending Style Interaction. Charlene consistently used the extending style of interaction (see Figure 9.4). She would approach children who were engrossed in their play by asking, "What are you working on?" and then continued on the basis of the children's explanations: "I'm writing a letter." or "I'm writing a check." Charlene then asked questions which led children to talk about the content and purpose of their writing: "Who are you writing to? What are you telling them?" She regularly invited children to read their writing to her and to show where they had written what they were reading: "Can you

Table 9.3

Percent Per Day of Redirecting Style Interaction

Day	Teachers			
	Carlene	Barbara	Debra	Carla
1	0	25	0	17
2	6	25	0	23
3	8	47	19	40
4	18	44	22	10
5	12	47	17	23
6	9	50	55	33
7	17	40	30	8
8	0	18	29	33

read to me what that says?'' or ''Where does it say that?'' Children responded by pointing to and reading their writing. Charlene later read two children's writings to other interested children.

She extended episodes by making suggestions for continued writing: ''Did you write the address on the envelope?'' ''You could buy a stamp.'' ''You could write a check for it.'' ''You could fill out the order form'' (to order a book). ''How about if you make her a ticket?'' ''It would probably be nice if you invite them all.'' ''Why don't you look it up in the phone book?'' ''You probably need to write his name on the envelope so you'll know it's his.''

During two episodes, Charlene approached the children with a more specific question: ''What company do you work for?'' When the children indicated that they worked for a bank and a telephone company, the teacher proceeded to do business with those companies. She opened an account at the bank and deposited funds. She ordered telephone repair service at the phone company. Both episodes involved writing and reading by the children.

Cody: (*Sits at office desk handling papers and writing.*)
T: What company do you work for?
Cody: Uh. . . We work for the bank a little while.
T: You work for the bank?
Cody: Yeah.
T: Okay. How about if I open an account and you fill out the form?
Cody: Okay.

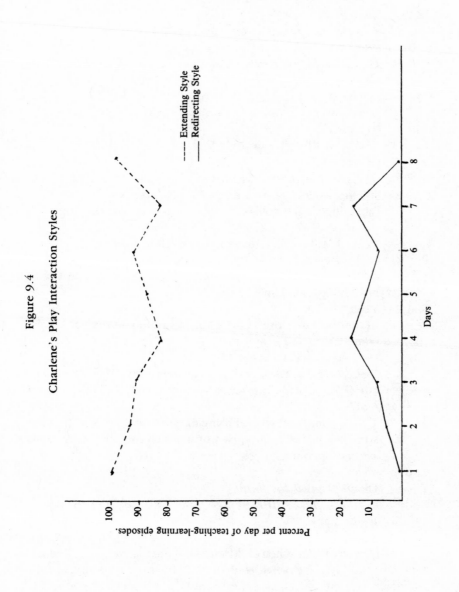

Figure 9.4

Charlene's Play Interaction Styles

----- Extending Style
——— Redirecting Style

T: Okay. Here's the form. (*Hands paper to Cody.*) First you need to write down my name.

Cody: How do I?

T: You can just write it the way you'd like to.

Cody: I don't. . . I don't write very good.

T: That's okay. You write the best you can. What you think you should.

Cody: (*Writes.*)

T: Write my name down. . . on the form. . . Mrs. Smith.

Cody: (*Writes.*)

T: And then I'll tell you my address.

Cody: (*Writes.*)

T: (*Dictates her address and phone number slowly.*)

Cody: (*Writes each part as the teacher dictates.*)

T: Can I deposit ten dollars in my savings account? Did you open it up?

Cody: Yeah. I still. . . We need a check. Okay?

T: Okay. Here's my ten dollars. (*Hands check to Cody.*) Open my account. Did you sign your name so I know that I have my savings account?

Cody: Yeah.

T: In that way any time I need to put money in the bank I can come here. And you'll mark it down for me.

Cody: Do I supposed to keep this ten dollars?

T: Yes, you keep the ten dollars and you give me the form.

Cody: Oh. (*Puts form in envelope, licks and seals it, hands it to the teacher.*) Here.

T: Thank you. Now when I bring my money, I'll bring my form so that you can write down how much money I have in my savings account.

Cody: Okay.

T: Okay? (*Leaves the bank.*)

Cody: (*Talks to child sitting next to him.*) This lady gots ten dollars in the bank.

There were times when children asked the teacher to spell words for them, and Charlene provided them with the requested information. However, when children said they could not write, Charlene's usual response was, "Write whatever way you'd like to." or "Write it the way you want to." Children would then rely on their own concept of written language and write.

Redirecting Style Interaction. Barbara consistently used the redirecting style of interaction (see Figure 9.5). When she approached playing children, she ignored what they might have been working on and redirected their attention to a writing activity of her choosing: "I'd like you to write me a story. Okay? Write me a story." "I need some assistance with my taxes. It's time for me to fix my income tax. Can you fix that for me?" "You might need to write some orders for your store. I'm ready for your order for your supplies at your store. Would you write out the order for your supplies, please, so I'll know what to get for you?" "Come and write me a receipt, please. I came to get a receipt for my package that I mailed. Would you write me a receipt, please?" "Would you make a list for her? Where's her list?" "Would you write the menu down for me, please?" "I need to have you fill out a form for me." "Would you write down the schedule of your office, please?" "Would you write a note to Mrs. Smith?" "Would you write a letter to my mother?" "Would you write a letter for me while I'm waiting, please?" Barbara directed children to "write a letter" several times during each day.

Even though many of the above examples were stated as requests, they functioned as redirectives. The children responded by going along with their teacher to the extent that they were able to understand the meaning of the writing activity. Some children rejected or ignored her redirections. There were times when Barbara pressed children to write—and sometimes showed them how to write using cursive-like lines.

Angie:	(*Sits at table in house, handles papers, uses phone.*)
T:	(*Talks across room.*) Are you ready to um . . . to write your letter for Easter?
Angie:	(*No response.*)
T:	I'll come over and we'll write for Easter. (*Goes to house, sits with child at table.*) Now, do you write a letter to the Easter Bunny?
Angie:	(*No response.*)
T:	I wonder what he would do if we wrote a letter to him.
Angie:	(*No response.*)
T:	Do you think he'd like to get a letter?
Angie:	(*No response.*)
T:	I think he would. Let's . . . You write a letter, and I'll write a letter to him. Okay? (*Talks to other children.*) Now what are you going to say to the Easter Bunny, Angie?

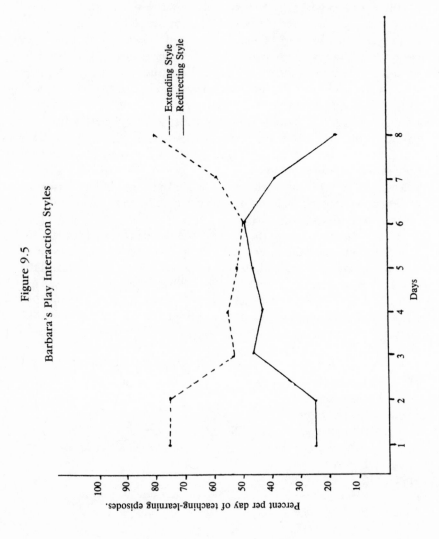

Figure 9.5

Barbara's Play Interaction Styles

Extending Style
Redirecting Style

Days

Percent per day of teaching-learning episodes.

Angie: I don't know. (*Shrugs shoulders.*)

T: Where would you like to have him leave your Easter eggs?

Angie: (*No response.*)

T: (*Makes cursive-like lines on paper as she talks.*) "Dear Easter Bunny, I will be at my house on Easter Sunday. I will have company at my house. I hope you will leave me some Easter eggs. And if you have any extra Easter eggs would you please leave some eggs for my company? I will have six people at my house. I love you Mr. Easter Bunny. Mrs. Ray." Okay, now then, you write your letter. (*Points to Angie's paper.*)

Angie: (*Watches teacher, does not write.*)

T: See I just made pretend. That's pretend writing. Because I talk faster than I write. So then I make pretend writing. Can you make pretend writing?

Angie: (*Watches teacher, does not write.*)

T: (*Talks to other children, returns to Angie.*) Okay. What are you going to say in your letter, Angie?

Angie: I can't think of anything.

T: Oh, you don't want the Easter Bunny to come to your house?

Angie: (*Nods yes.*)

T: Why don't you tell him that? Why don't you tell him you'd like to have him come visit you.

Angie: I don't know what to write.

T: Oh, okay. The Easter Rabbit doesn't care what you write. He just likes to get mail. See, he likes to have you write any kind of letter.

Angie: I'm gonna draw some Easter eggs on here.

T: Okay. That'll be fine.

Discussion and Implications

The study demonstrates that teachers can use symbolic play as a teaching/learning medium for early literacy development. The study also revealed ways in which teachers can facilitate early literacy development by functioning as participants within the context of young children's spontaneous symbolic play. Teachers in play settings are able to interact with children to make specific information available to them and to expand the learning possibilities inherent in the play situations. Teachers are able to help children use literacy-related play materials in new ways. They can model functional writing and introduce new functions of print through suggestions. Children can be exposed to literacy concepts simply with a word, a question, or a momentary interaction provided by the teacher. When teachers respond to children's play, they have the opportunity to provide just those learning experiences which are meaningful to children.

Early childhood teachers evidently vary in their ability to function spontaneously and creatively in relation to the ever-changing play engaged in by children. They are constantly called upon to respond to a number of variables and to make situational decisions. They cannot use preplanned lessons. This requires teachers to focus not on teaching per se, but on the process of learning—which belongs to the child. Consequently, teachers must exercise self-control when participating in children's symbolic play. They must refrain from pressuring children to cooperate with the teacher's own preconceived priorities.

This study shows that teachers can be trained to assist children in play that involves writing and reading. Teacher education programs are needed which will not only provide educators with information enabling them to create play settings in which children can explore functional written language, but also to become familiar with teaching/ learning strategies that will enable them to function effectively within those play settings.

This study provides empirical support for Vygotsky's theory of the zone of proximal development. Teachers interacting with children in the play settings were able to help those children go beyond their present developmental levels. The adult/child interaction provided necessary assistance that enabled the children to progress as writers and readers.

Vygotsky's research led him to three practical conclusions (1978, pp. 116–119). The results of this study provide not only support for those conclusions, but also clues to how early childhood educators should organize the complex teaching/learning process.

1. *"If early childhood educators are to provide writing experiences during the preschool years they should be organized in such a way that writing and reading are necessary for something. They must be something the child needs. They must be relevant to life."* This study demonstrates how classroom literacy environments can provoke functional, meaningful writing experiences. The house, post office, and office enabled children to write for real-life purposes, to read their writing, and to discuss their writing with classmates and teachers. Participating teachers had opportunities to contribute information about the uses of written language and help children make sense of writing.

2. *"The writing and reading should be meaningful for children, an intrinsic need should be aroused in them."* This study indicates not

only that writing and reading events occur in children's symbolic play, but that the children's motivations to write and read are intrinsic and serve no other objectives. Children who have control over a play situation can be expected to self-select writing and reading activities that are meaningful to them.

3. *"Writing should be taught naturally. The activity should be engaged in the course of children's play, and writing should be "cultivated" rather than "imposed". Natural methods of teaching reading and writing involve appropriate operations on the child's environment. Reading and writing should become necessary for her in her play."* This study demonstrates that natural literacy development can be cultivated within the context of children's symbolic play. Providing literacy-rich play settings for children enables them to represent through symbolic play literacy activities with which they have had experience and are working to understand. Teachers then have many opportunities to interact with their students and extend their writing by introducing more varied experiences.

These findings led to a particularly important pedagogical conclusion. Preschool and kindergarten is the appropriate time for teaching and learning writing and reading. The best method, however, is one in which both processes are found in children's symbolic play.

References

Bogdan, R. and S. Biklen (1982) *Qualitative research for educators: An introduction to theory and method*. Boston, MA: Allyn and Bacon.

Cazden, C. (1972). *Child language and education*. New York: Holt, Rinehart & Winston.

Elkind, D. (1986). Formal education and early childhood education: An essential difference. *Phi Delta Kappan, 67,* 631–636.

Feitelson, D. and G. Ross (1973). The neglected factor—play. *Human Development, 16,* 202–223.

Halliday, M.A.K. (1973). *Learning how to mean: Explorations in the development of language*. New York: Elsevier North-Holland.

——— (1978). *Language as social semiotic: The social interpretation of language and meaning*. Baltimore, MD: University Park Press.

Isenberg, J. and E. Jacob (1985). Playful literacy activities and learning: Preliminary observations. In: J. Frost and S. Sunderlin (Eds.), *When*

Children Play. Wheaton, MD: Association for Childhood Education International.

Jacob, E. (1984). Learning literacy through play: Puerto Rican kindergarten children. In: H. Goilman, A. Oberg, and F. Smith (Eds.), *Awakening to literacy*. Exeter, NH: Heinemann Educational Books.

Lincoln, Y. S. and E. Guba (1985). *Naturalistic inquiry*. Beverly Hills, CA: Sage.

Lovinger, S. (1974). Socio-dramatic play and language development in preschool disadvantaged children. *Psychology in the Schools, 11,* 313–320.

NAEYC (1986). Position statement of developmentally appropriate practice in programs for 4- and 5-year-olds. *Young Children, 41,* 20–29.

Pellegrini, A. (1984). The effects of classroom ecology on preschooler's functional uses of language. In: A. Pellegrini and T. Yawkey (Eds.), *The development of oral and written language in social contexts*. Norwood, NJ: Ablex Publishing Corporation.

Pellegrini, A. and L. Galda (1986). The role of theory in oral and written language curricula. *The Elementary School Journal, 87,* 201–208.

Piaget, J. (1962). *Play, dreams and imitation in childhood,* New York: Norton.

Rosen, C. (1974). The effects of sociodramatic play on problem-solving behavior among culturally disadvantaged preschool children. *Child Development, 45,* 920–927.

Saltz, E. and J. Johnson (1974). Training for thematic-fantasy play in culturally disadvantaged children: Preliminary results. *Journal of Educational Psychology, 66,* 623–630.

Saltz, E., D. Dixon, and J. Johnson (1977). Training disadvantaged preschoolers on various fantasy activities: Effects on cognitive functioning and impulse control. *Child Development, 48,* 367–380.

Schickedanz, J. (1978). "You be the doctor and I'll be sick": Preschoolers learn the language arts through play. *Language Arts, 55,* 713–718.

Schrader, C. T. and S. Hoffman (1987). Encouraging children's early writing efforts. *Day Care and Early Education, 15,* 9–13.

———— (1989). Written language use within the context of young children's symbolic play. *Early Childhood Research Quarterly, 4,* 225–244.

———— (1990). Symbolic play as a curricular tool for early literacy development. *Early Childhood Research Quarterly, 5,* 79–103.

Smilansky, S. (1968). *The effects of sociodramatic play on disadvantaged preschool children*. New York: Wiley.

Tamburrini, J. (1982). Play and the role of the teacher. *Early Child Development and Care, 8,* 209–217.

Taylor, D. (1983). *Family Literacy.* Portsmouth, NH: Heinemann Educational Books.

Vygotsky, L. (1978). *Mind in society.* Cambridge, MA: Harvard University Press.

10

Materials and Modeling: Promoting Literacy during Play*

Carol Vukelich

Although the topic of play has been of interest to researchers and educators for many years, attention has only recently been directed toward children's literate behaviors during play. A computer search of articles published within the past five years with literacy and play as descriptors revealed some 2,000 articles on play, with nine of these articles focusing on literacy in play. Because "play is the business of childhood" (Bruner, 1978, p. 96), this great interest in children's play is not surprising. But what of this new interest in children's literate behaviors during play?

Early investigations of children's literate behaviors and play focused on the relationship between children's behavior during play and their performance on various measures. For example, Pellegrini (1980) found a positive relationship between the cognitive level of kindergarteners' play and their achievement on literacy-related standardized achievement tests. In other studies, researchers provided young children with training in thematic-fantasy play and discovered that the children's performance in such literate behaviors as story comprehension, recall, sequencing, memory, and interpretation improved (e.g., Pellegrini, 1982; Saltz and Johnson, 1974; Saltz, Dixon, and Johnson, 1977; Silvern, et al., 1986). Although these early investigations provide documentation of the role of play in children's development of literate behaviors, they did not examine children's self-sponsored literate behaviors during play.

The initial investigations of children's literate behaviors during play focused on children's oral language—specifically, children's ability to use role-appropriate language during the portrayal of social roles. Researchers (Cook-Gumperz and Corsaro, 1977; Snow, et al., 1986) examined children's ability to use in-role language and discovered that even quite young children use appropriate role register features during play. These researchers contend that children can use role-appropriate language in their symbolic play because they have abstracted the language from their everyday social interactions. Other researchers (Snow, et al., 1986; Sachs, Goldman, and Chaille, 1985) have documented the importance of exposure to roles in real-world settings on children's use of role-specific oral registers. Collectively, these two studies' findings support French and colleagues' (1985) point that children talk best when they know what they are talking about.

But is the ability to use role-appropiate language really a literate behavior? Pellegrini (1985) argues that this ability is one of the important components of narrative competence, which is an aspect of literate behavior as defined by Heath (1982), Olson (1977), and Scribner and Cole (1978). These researchers define narrative competence as the ability to comprehend and produce characters' actions, motives, goals, and language which are consistent with a particular story line or genre, and they suggest that narrative competence is important in children's reading comprehension. Pellegrini (1985) argues that, because during symbolic play children are reconstructing narrative-like "scripts" by having abstracted characters' actions, goals, and language from real-world activities and experiences, "the appropriate enactment of roles and the generation of role-appropriate language in symbolic play, then, should be related to narrative competence," and subsequently to literacy (p. 112).

In the past few years, investigators have begun to describe additional literate behaviors—such as paper handling, early reading, and writing—demonstrated by young children in typical play settings (Jacob, 1984; Roskos, 1987). Researchers have also examined how children develop hypotheses about the forms and functions of written language as they engage in symbolic play (Neuman and Roskos, 1988). These studies indicate that, even in environments with few literacy materials, young children use their symbolic play situations to practice the conventions of print and extend their understandings of the functions of literacy. Children's inclusion of these literate behaviors in their play in environments with few literacy materials suggests that enriching the play environment with literacy materials might increase the number of their literacy demonstrations and enhance children's understanding of the forms and functions of print.

Early childhood educators have recently begun to advocate that teachers demonstrate their knowledge of literacy to children by guiding play through participation (e.g. Morrow, 1989; Schickedanz, 1986). These educators support Holdaway's (1979) view of the importance of a supportive adult who helps guide natural learning by emulating appropriate behavior, providing the child with encouragement and assistance as he or she attempts the behavior, and then permitting the child to perform the behavior independently. To date, the data describing the impact of adults' demonstrations on young children's literate behavior are from home-based studies (Heath, 1980; Taylor, 1983; Teale, 1986, 1987). These researchers' findings suggest that children's observation of adults reading and writing for specific purposes and adults' periodic direct explanations of literacy events while they are engaged in them are important for children's developing understandings of literacy. It is now incumbent upon educators advocating a similar role for classroom teachers to articulate the specific ways they expect children to benefit from teacher modeling of literate behaviors in classroom play settings.

The intent of the present study was to determine if the amount of time young children engage in literate behaviors during their classroom free-play time (a time of engagement in self-sponsored activities with peers of the child's choice) can be increased through: (a) the inclusion of numerous theme-appropriate reading and writing materials in the dramatic play area and (b) the use of adult modeling of the literate behaviors typically associated with the included materials.

Method

Subjects

The 38 children involved in this study attended a public kindergarten in a middle-class suburb. All subjects were taught by the same teacher in the same classroom. Seventeen of the subjects (10 boys and 7 girls) attended the morning kindergarten session; 21 subjects (12 boys and 9 girls) attended the afternoon session.

Procedure

Research Assistant Training. Before beginning the project, the research assistants (undergraduate students and a graduate student) were provided information about the potential importance of enriching classroom dramatic play settings with literacy materials, and they were trained in data collection procedures and appropriate techniques for modeling literacy events for young children (Schickedanz, 1986). The undergraduate assistants were then assigned to one of two groups and directed to design, subject to the approval of the author, a thematically appropriate, literacy-enriched dramatic play setting. Because of the classroom teacher's thematic topics of study during the two intervention weeks, the two settings chosen for development were a bank and a flower shop. Because a new theme or topic was introduced each week in this classroom, the length of the children's use of each literacy-enriched dramatic play setting (one week) was determined by the teacher's curriculum plan.

Data Collection. Each day, the children had two opportunities to engage in free play—upon their arrival in the classroom and during the scheduled free-play period. Data were collected using a time-sampling procedure during these two play periods. The length of free-play time varied daily, with the teacher controlling the play period duration.

For data collection purposes, the classroom was divided into three areas: (a) the rug area with games and books on shelves, the blackboard, a listening center, and two informative charts; (b) the table area with a writing center, a sand table, a computer, and two paint easels; and (c) the dramatic play area. During the free-play period, a research assistant was assigned to each area. At the beginning of each two-minute segment during each free-play period, each assistant scanned her area, recorded the names of the children in the area, and described their behavior. All observations were made from an unobtrusive sideline section of the area.

Reliability for the recording of the names of the children and their behaviors was established by having a second observer serve as a second recorder in each area at least twice per free-play period at times unknown to the primary observer. The inter-rater reliability was 96 percent. The identified children's behaviors were always described similarly. Differences occurred between observers in identifying *which* children had chosen to engage in activities in the area. Children missing from one recorder's observations were typically described by the other observer as "looking into area" or "walking through area." In no instance was the missing child identified by the other observer as engaged in a behavior which would be categorized as a literate behavior.

Data were collected for three days in the pre-enrichment or baseline period. During this period, the classroom remained as the teacher had designed it. Potential free-play literacy materials present in the classroom included games, books, writing materials in the writing center, literacy materials typical of a home in the dramatic play center (e,g., a telephone memo pad, a telephone book, and blank pads of paper for recording grocery lists), chalk for chalkboard writing, a computer, charts for classroom attendance and classroom job assignments, and drawing and painting supplies.

Intervention. Following the baseline period, the undergraduate research assistants transformed the dramatic play setting into a bank. Literacy materials in the play setting included such items as checks, deposit slips, withdrawal slips, bank pamphlets, instructions on how to use the automated teller machine, a log for recording banking activities, signs (e.g., "Open," "Closed," "Do Not Enter," "Banking Hours," "How to Complete a MAC Card Application Form"), money equivalent posters, loan application forms, and credit card application forms. All other areas of the classroom remained as they had been during the baseline period. After allowing one day for the children to adjust to the novelty of the dramatic play changes, data were collected using the procedures described. On the third and fourth days of the bank dramatic play setting, one undergraduate research assistant entered the setting once each five-minute period of each free-play period to model literacy in the manner recommended by Schickedanz (1986). The assistant selected one literacy materials—e.g., a blank check or a credit card application form—and played the role of a bank customer. The author listened carefully to randomly selected modeling episodes to ensure that modeling—not directing—of the behavior associated with the literacy material was taking place. On the second day of this procedure (the fourth day of the bank dramatic play setting), after again allowing the children to adjust to the novelty of teacher modeling, data were collected as described. On the final day of the bank dramatic play setting, the children played in the bank without adult modeling, and data were collected as described.

This same procedure was used for the second dramatic play setting—a flower shop. Literacy materials placed in this setting included message cards, order forms, seed packages, directions for how to win a plant, receipt forms, posters (on how to care for plants, how to plant seeds, and the prices of flowers), signs, (e.g., "Open," "Closed," and "Win a free plant"), telephone message pads, brochures, a floral arrangement, ordering books, and a phone book.

Data Analysis

Literate behaviors were defined as: (1) reading, which included looking at print, pretend or actual reading, book or pamphlet handling, matching cards with print, and shuffling through text materials (e.g., papers, pamphlets, or cards) in search of a specific paper or card, and (2) writing, which included drawing with crayons or paints, scribbling, copying, producing text using invented or conventional spellings with pencil or paintbrush, and manipulating paper with pencil in hand.

Using the observation notes, two raters categorized the children's described behavior as being engaged in a literate activity or not. Interrater reliability was 100%. Because the length of the free-play period varied—from 18 to 40 minutes in the morning session and 15 to 54 minutes in the afternoon session—the percentage of time spent by each child in literate behaviors during each day's free play (time totalled for the two free-play periods per day) was determined.

Research Design. The major focus of this study was to compare children's literate behaviors during free play in two settings (before literacy enrichment and during literacy enrichment) and three time periods (before, during and after modeling during literacy enrichment). Therefore a repeated-measure design was used. The separate observations of time children spent engaged in various literate behaviors were the repeated factors. Session—morning or afternoon—was the grouping variable. The dependent variable was the percent of time spent in literate behaviors during free play. Main effects of the percent of time the two groups of subjects spent engaged in literate behaviors during the pre-enrichment and the literacy-enriched (bank and flower shop) conditions and the percent of time the two groups of subjects engaged in literate behaviors during freeplay across both and within each literacy-enriched dramatic play setting before, during, and after adult modeling were determined. Significant interactions were examined, post hoc, according to simple effects analyses.

Results

Literate Behaviors During Free-Play

The first set of analyses examined the impact of the inclusion of the two literacy-enriched dramatic play settings on the two groups of children's time spent in literate behaviors during free play. The means and standard deviations for the percent of time spent in literate behaviors by the two groups (morning and afternoon) in the two conditions (baseline and literacy-enriched) are presented in Table 10.1. The analysis indicated there was a significant group by condition interaction, $F(2, 34)$ 17.81 $p < .000$.

Table 10.1

Means (and Standard Deviations) for Percent of Time Spent in Literate Behaviors in the Baseline and Literacy-enriched Conditions

Groups	Baseline	Literacy-enriched
Morning	36.59 (23.99)	25.36 (12.93)
Afternoon	4.88 (4.52)	13.33 (7.27)

Post hoc analyses were done within each condition, across the two classes, and within each class across the two conditions to determine where differences occurred. The first two analyses, univariate analyses of variance, revealed that the morning session children spent a significantly greater percent of time engaged in literate behaviors during free play in the baseline condition, $F(1, 35)$ 35.34 $p < .000$, and in the literacy-enriched condition, $F(1, 35)$ 12.90 $p < .001$, than did the afternoon children.

Two additional analyses, post hoc t-tests, indicated significant differences in the percent of time spent in literate behaviors in the two conditions within each class. The afternoon session children spent a significantly greater percent of their free-play time engaged in literate behaviors in the literacy-enriched condition than they did in the baseline condition ($t = 5.31$, $df = 21$, $p < .000$). The morning session children spent a significantly greater percent of their free-play time engaged in literate behaviors in the baseline condition than they did in the literacy-enriched condition ($t = 2.13$, $df = 15$, $p < .05$).

Location of Children's Demonstrations of Literate Behaviors. Data collection procedures permitted the determination of where the children engaged in literate behaviors. The means and standard deviations for the percent of time spent in literate behaviors by each group of children in each area of the classroom (dramatic play setting and other—rug and table) in each condition (baseline and literacy-enriched) are presented in Table 10.2.

The analysis of variance indicated that, during the baseline condition, there was a significant group by area of the classroom difference, $F(2, 34)$ 17.59 $p < .000$. Subsequent univariate analyses of variance revealed no significant difference in the time spent in literate

Table 10.2

Means (and Standard Deviations) for Percent of Time Spent in Literate
Behaviors in Dramatic Play and Other Areas

Groups by Conditions	Dramatic Play	Other
Baseline		
Morning Children	.15 (.60)	36.44 (24.41)
Afternoon Children	.17 (.79)	4.71 (4.50)
Literacy-enriched		
Morning Children	5.70 (3.04)	19.67 (11.34)
Afternoon Children	3.18 (1.51)	10.15 (7.56)

behaviors in the dramatic play area in the baseline condition across the two groups, $F(1, 35)$ .008. There was, however, a significant difference across the two groups in the percent of time spent engaged in literate behaviors in the other areas of the classroom, $F(1, 35)$ 34.80 $p < .000$. Examination of the means indicated that the children in the morning session engaged in literate behaviors for a significantly greater percent of time in the other areas of the classroom than did the children in the afternoon session.

Similarly, analysis of the children's literate behaviors during the literacy-enriched condition revealed a significant group by area of the classroom difference, $F(2, 35)$ 7.22 $p < .002$. A univariate analysis revealed that, like the groups' behavior during the baseline condition, the morning children spent a significantly greater percent of time engaged in literate behaviors in the other areas of the classroom during this condition than did the afternoon children, $F(1, 36)$ 7.30 $p < .01$. However, the morning children also spent a significantly greater percent of time engaged in literate behaviors in the dramatic play center during this condition than did the afternoon children, $F(1, 36)$ 10.81 $p < .002$.

Adult Modeling and Literate Behavior

The second set of analyses examined the effect of adult modeling on the children's time spent in literate behaviors during the literacy-enriched condition. The mean percent of time spent in literate behaviors by the children in each group across the two literacy-enriched dramatic play settings and within each dramatic play setting before, during, and after adult modeling is presented in Figure 10.1.

Figure 10.1

Dramatic Play Literate Behavior

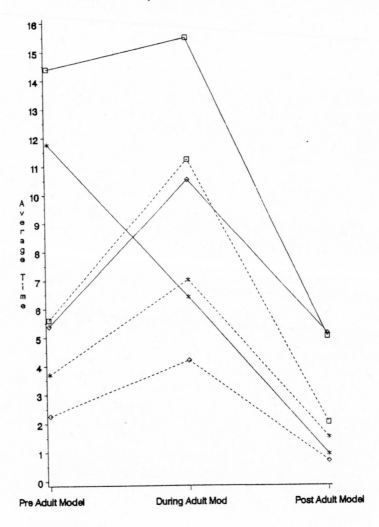

Settings
□ — Combined Dramatic (AM)
□ - - - Combined Dramatic (PM)
◇ — Bank (AM)
◇ - - - Bank (PM)
* — Flower Shop (AM)
* - - - Flower Shop (PM)

Examination of the information presented in Figure 10.1 indicates a pattern common to both groups across the two dramatic play settings and within each dramatic play setting: The percent of time both groups of children spent engaged in literate behaviors decreased in the after-adult-modeling condition to nearly the same level or lower than the level it had been before adult modeling. The information in Figure 10.1 suggests, and the analyses of variance confirms, a significant group-by-condition interaction across the two literacy-enriched dramatic play settings , $F(35, 72)$ 14.29 $p < .000$; within the bank dramatic play setting, $F(30, 62)$ 6.72 $p < .00$; and within the flower shop dramatic play setting, $F(28, 58)$ 6.83 $p < .002$. Post hoc analyses identified where within each group within each setting the differences occurred.

Morning Children. The analysis of variance for each literacy-enriched dramatic play setting revealed significant differences among the mean percent of time spent in literate behaviors before, during, and after adult modeling in the bank setting, $F(11, 24)$ 3.71 $p < .04$, and in the flower shop setting, $F(11, 24)$ 7.17 $p < .004$. Adult modeling within each setting affected the children's time spent in literate behavior differently.

Post hoc analyses revealed that, in the bank dramatic play setting, there was only one significant difference in the percent of time spent in literate behaviors: These children spent a significantly greater percent of time in literate behaviors during adult modeling than before adult modeling ($t = 2.15$, $df = 12$, $p < .05$). Similar analyses of the children's literate behaviors during the flower shop dramatic play setting revealed significant differences between the precentages of time spent in literate behaviors in two of the three conditions: The children spent significantly more time in literate behaviors during adult modeling than after adult modeling ($t = 2.91$, $df = 12$, $p < .01$) and before adult modeling than after adult modeling ($t = 4.81$, $df = 11$, $p < .001$).

Afternoon Children. Similar analyses revealed the following findings for the afternoon group. The analysis of variance for each literacy-enriched dramatic play setting revealed that the condition (before, during, and after adult modeling) affected the children's engagement in literate behaviors in each dramatic play setting— $F(18, 38)$ 3.55 $p < .04$ in the banking setting, and $F(16, 34)$ 3.27 $p < .05$ in the flower shop setting.

In the bank setting, the afternoon children spent more time (although not significantly more) engaged in literate behaviors during adult modeling than before adult modeling ($t = 1.49$, $df = 20$); significantly more time engaged in literate behaviors during adult modeling than after modeling ($t = 2.35$, $df = 18$, $p < .03$); and more time (although not significantly more) in literate behaviors before adult modeling than after adult modeling (t = 1.97, df = 18). In the flower shop setting, the afternoon children spent the greatest percent of time engaged in literate behaviors in the adult modeling condition. The difference between the mean percent of time engaged in literate behaviors was significant between the before and during adult modeling conditions (t = 2.20, df = 18, $p < .04$) and between the during and after adult modeling conditions (t = 2.32, df = 17, $p < .03$).

Discussion

Previous research (Jacob, 1984; Neuman and Roskos, 1988; Roskos, 1987) suggested that, with the materials provided in the classroom, the two groups of children in this study should engage in literate behaviors during their classroom free play. They did, although the amount of time spent in literate behaviors in the classroom dramatic play (symbolic play) area was minimal, with very few children in either group spending time engaged in literate behaviors in the housekeeping play setting. The belief driving this study was that, if the children engaged in literate behaviors when relatively few literacy materials were available, then enriching their classroom with literacy materials— and adults to model the literate behaviors appropriate to those materials—might result in an increase in the amount of time these children spent in literate behaviors. The data indicated that the enrichment of the classroom, specifically of the dramatic play area, was effective in increasing only one group of children's percent of free-play time spent in literate behaviors.

What might account for the differential effect of the inclusion of the literacy-enriched settings on the two groups' time spent in literate behaviors? Before the literacy enrichment of the classroom, the two groups' percent of time spent in literate behaviors during free-play was very different. For example, in 60 minutes of free-play time before the literacy enrichment of the classroom, the morning group would have spent an average of nearly 22 minutes in literate behaviors. The afternoon group, on the other hand, would have spent an average of only about 3 minutes. During the pre-enrichment aspect of the project (the baseline condition), a favorite activity of the morning children was to gather on the rug to play a lotto board game. This literacy activity continued during the literacy-enrichment phase. One possible reason that their percent of time spent in the literate behaviors decreased during the literacy-enrichment phase could be that they were moving from a literacy-intense activity (the lotto board game) to a dramatic play setting that included many activities—only some of which were literacy-based. Yet, even in the literacy-enrichment phase, their percent of time spent in literate behaviors remained higher than that of the afternoon group. Again, using 60 minutes for illustrative purposes, the morning group would have spent a little more than 15 minutes engaged in literate behaviors, whereas the afternoon group would have spent only about 8 minutes. Hence, the data suggest that the literate behaviors of children who—in non-literacy-enriched environments—spend *little* time engaged in literate behaviors can be increased by enriching the environment with literacy materials and modeling adults in thematic dramatic play settings. Simultaneously, the data raise questions about the effect of such enrichment on the literate behavior of groups of children who spend a relatively high percentage of their time engaged in literate behaviors prior to the modification of their play environment.

Literate Behavior in Dramatic Play and Other Areas

In addition to considering the amount of time spent in literate behaviors during free play, researchers and teachers might wish to consider *where* children engage in literate behaviors during classroom free play. Different areas of the classroom support the development of different aspects of literate behavior. As suggested by Neuman and Roskos (1988), in the dramatic play area, young children have the opportunity to develop hypotheses about the purposes of reading and writing. In addition, they might develop understandings about the various forms of print used in different occupations—e.g., checks in the bank or seed packets in the flower shop. Certainly, within these contexts, children can also acquire information about the conventions of print. Literacy materials (e.g., lotto board game) available to children in nondramatic play areas of the classroom seem to provide children with opportunities to develop or apply knowledge of specific conventions of print (e.g., the names of the letters and the order of the letters of the alphabet).

Clearly, in the pre-enrichment (baseline) condition, the children in both groups spent more time in literate behaviors in the other areas of the classroom than they did in the dramatic play area. There appear to be two possible reasons for this finding. First, in the post-project data-reporting interview, the classroom teacher indicated that, prior to this project, the classroom's dramatic play area had been a house-keeping setting for several months. Perhaps the children's interest in the housekeeping setting had dissipated. This might suggest that, in order to maintain children's interest in the dramatic play area, teachers should change the setting periodically. Another explanation for both groups of children's increased time in literate behaviors in the bank and flower shop symbolic play settings is the greater number of literacy materials and the systematic inclusion of adults made available in these settings than in the housekeeping setting. The data from this study suggest that enriching the dramatic play settings does result in children spending more time in this area engaged in literate behaviors. This could be important in children's development of understandings of the functions and forms of literacy. Subsequent research might investigate how experiences in literacy-enriched dramatic play settings impact children's knowledge of the forms and functions of written language.

There is an additional point supporting the morning children's renewed interest in dramatic play (symbolic play). The author's original intent was to return to the classroom to observe the children's engagement in literate behaviors the week after removal of the flower shop. Presumably, because responsibility for the dramatic play area was returned to the teacher, the area would revert back to a housekeeping setting. The researcher arrived to discover that the dramatic play area had been converted to a library play setting. When the classroom teacher had announced that the flower shop would be removed, the morning children questioned what the next week's setting would be. The teacher replied that she would not have time to prepare a new setting, and that the research assistants would no longer be coming to the classroom. The children proposed that the area become a library, suggested that they would design the setting, and did. Their setting included such literacy materials as a labeled check-out table, books sorted by categories with labels, a poster telling the children how to check out books, a "Quiet" sign, library cards placed in each book, and a sign above some stuffed animals that read, "Animals to read to." Perhaps young children should be involved in the redesigning of their own play environments.

Adult Modeling and Literate Behaviors

Because of previous researchers' and educators' (Heath, 1980; Holdaway, 1979; Morrow, 1989; Schickedanz, 1986; Taylor, 1983; Teale, 1986, 1987) suggestions, it was hypothesized that adult modeling of the appropriate behavior associated with the included literacy materials would have a positive impact on children's time spent in literate behavior in the dramatic settings. While this study's findings provide *some* support for these suggestions, the results are inconsistent. Adult modeling significantly impacted on the morning session children's literate behavior in the bank setting and the afternoon children's literate behavior in the flower shop setting. While the anecdotal notes made by the assistants and the author suggest no reason for the afternoon children's behavior, these notes highlight the morning children's unfamiliarity with the materials used in the bank setting. One child's question—"What the heck is this for?"—as he held a deposit slip is typical of the queries recorded. Another child indicated that he was never allowed in a bank: "I always have to stay in the car." Several children nodded or said, "Me too." Clearly, the type of adult modeling used in this study did not have the same effect on the two groups of children's literate behavior in the two dramatic play settings.

Neither the afternoon nor the morning session children's behavior supports Holdaway's (1979) view that, after adult modeling of the appropriate behavior, children will be able to engage in the behavior independently. Perhaps the two days of modeling were not sufficient for the children to develop enough knowledge of the literacy forms included in the settings to engage in the behaviors independently. Of course, it is possible that the children *could* have but *chose* not to engage in the literate behaviors in the settings. Rather than the decrease being due to the lack of proficiency, it could be due to the lack of continued interest in the settings. This might suggest that a week is sufficiently long for the inclusion of a particular dramatic play setting in a classroom (a point of interest to this researcher because she began the project thinking a week might not be long enough to observe changes in the children's behavior). Subsequent research might observe changes in children's time spent in literate behaviors in settings in place for more than one week. Or the sudden siginificant decrease in the time spent in literate behaviors might be a warning to teachers about the need for their *regular and continued* participation in the classroom dramatic play settings.

This study used time spent, a quantitative measure, as the means to assess the impact of modeling on the children's behavior. In a subsequent study, it might be appropriate to use a qualitative measure to assess modeling impact. Particularly in the banking setting, the collection of writing produced suggests that many of these children initially seemed to write with wavy lines (scribbles) on the face of their checks—perhaps because of their lack of understanding of this purpose for writing. While adult modeling might not have increased the quantity of time these children spent engaged in literate behaviors, it might have changed their writing.

The intent of this study was to determine if the amount of time young children spent in literate behaviors during classroom free-play periods could be increased by including theme-appropriate literacy materials in the dramatic play area and through adult modeling of the appropriate use of the included literacy materials. The results provide empirical support for the value of the literacy enrichment of the classroom dramatic play environment for young children who, before enrichment, spend little time engaged in literate behaviors. Furthermore, through enriching the dramatic play area with materials and adult modeling, it is possible to increase young children's time engaged in literate behaviors in the dramatic play (symbolic play) area—thus expanding the forms or purposes of writing children experience in the classroom.

Notes

*This research was supported by the University of Delaware's General University Research Program. I would like to extend my gratitude to the individuals who assisted with this project—Karen, the classroom teacher; Janice, the graduate assistant; the new Dr. Pat Bent, the statistical assistant; and the many undergraduate student assistants.

References

Bruner, J. (1985). On teaching thinking: An afterthought. In: J. W. Segal, M. Chipman, and R. Glaser (Eds.), *Thinking and learning skills, Vols. 1 & 2* (pp. 597-608). Hillsdale, NJ: Lawrence Erlbaum.

Cook-Gumperz, J., and W. Corsaro (1977). Socio-ecological constraints on children's communicative strategies. *Sociology, II,* 411–434.

French, L., et al. (1985). The influence of discourse content and context on preschoolers' use of language. In: L. Galda and A. Pellegrini (Eds.), *Play, language, & stories: The development of children's literate behavior.* Norwood, NJ: Ablex Publishing Corporation.

Heath, S. (1980). The functions and uses of literacy. *Journal of Communication, 30,* 123–133.

———— (1982). What no bedtime story means: Narrative skills at home and school. *Language Society, II,* 49–76.

Holdaway, D. (1979). *Foundations of literacy.* New York: Ashton Scholastic.

Jacob, E. (1984). Learning literacy through play: Puerto Rican kindergarten children. In: H. Goelman, A. Oberg, and F. Smith (Eds.), *Awakening to literacy,* (pp. 73–86). Exeter, NH: Heinemann Educational Books.

Miller, P. , and C. Garvey (1984). Mother-baby role play: Its origins in social support. In: I. Bretherton (Ed.), *Symbolic play: The development of social understanding.* New York: Academic Press.

Morrow, L. (1989). *The development in the early years: Helping children read and write.* Englewood Cliffs, NJ: Prentice-Hall.

Nelson, K. and S. Seidman (1984). Playing with scripts. In: I Bretherton (Ed.), *Symbolic play: The development of social understanding.* New York: Academic Press.

Neuman, S. and K. Roskos (1988). *Preschoolers' conceptions of literacy as reflected in spontaneous play.* Paper presented at National Reading Conference, Tucson, AZ (December).

Olson, D. (1977). The language of instruction: The literate bias of schooling. In: R. Anderson, R. Spiro, and W. Montague (Eds.), *Schooling and the acquisition of knowledge.* New York: Wiley.

Pellegrini, A. (1980). The relationship between kindergartens' play and achievement in prereading, language, and writing. *Psychology in the Schools, 51,* 144–155.

———— (1982). The construction of cohesive text by preschoolers in two play contexts. *Discourse Processes, 5* 101–108.

———— (1985). The relations between symbolic play and literate behavior: A review and critique of the empirical literature. *Review of Educational Research, 55,* 107–121.

Roskos, K. (1987). *The nature of literacy behavior in the pretend play episodes of four- and five-year-old children.* Unpublished doctoral dissertation, Kent State University.

Sachs, J., Goldman, J., and Chaille, C. (1982, April). *Planning in pretend play: Using language to coordinate narrative development.* Paper presented at the American Educational Research Association, New York.

Saltz, E., D. Dixon, and J. Johnson (1977). Training disadvantaged preschoolers on various fantasy activities: Effects on cognitive functioning and impulse control. *Child Development, 48,* 367–380.

Saltz, E., and J. Johnson (1974). Training for thematic-fantasy play in culturally disadvantaged children: Preliminary results. *Journal of Educational Psychology, 66,* 623–630.

Schickedanz, J. (1986). *More than ABC's: The early stages of reading and writing.* Washington, DC: National Association for the Education of Young Children.

Scribner, S., and M. Cole (1978). Literacy without schooling: Testing for intellectual effects. *Harvard Educational Review, 48,* 448–461.

Silvern, S., et al. (1986). Young children's story recall as a product of play, story familiarity, and adult intervention. *Merrill-Palmer Quarterly, 32,* 73–86.

Snow, C., et al. (1986). Learning to play doctor: Effects of sex, age, and experience in hospital. *Discourse Processes, 9,* 461-473.

Taylor, D. (1983). *Family Literacy.* Exeter, NH: Heinemann Educational Books.

Teale, W. (1987). Language arts for the 21st century. In: J. Jensen (Ed.), *Stories to grow on.* Portsmouth, NH: Heinemann Educational Books.

———— (1986.) The beginning of reading and writing: Written language development during the preschool and kindergarten years. In: H. Goelman, A. Oberg, and F. Smith (Eds.), *Awakening to literacy.* Portsmouth, NH: Heinemann Educational Books.

Vygotsky, L. S. (1978). *Mind in society.* Cambridge, MA: Harvard University Press.

11

Play and Early Literacy Development: Summary and Discussion

James F. Christie

This book contains two types of research on play and early literacy. The first is basic research on play's role in early reading and writing development. These investigations have explored relationships between play and literacy through the use of correlational, experimental, and case study methodology. The second type is applied research which has investigated the educational implications of play/literacy connections. Specifically, the applied studies have focused on how teachers can encourage literacy-related forms of play by: (a) providing appropriate types of experiences with children's literature, (b) placing literacy materials in play centers, and (c) giving guidance during play episodes.

This chapter begins with a summary of these two strands of research. Next, limitations of current studies are discussed, and suggestions are made for future research in each area. The final section presents recommendations for educational practice.

Research Summary

The reader may have noticed that there is considerable overlap between the basic and applied research sections of this book. Several of the chapters in Part II, Play's Role in Early Literacy Development, deal with instructional strategies and other applied issues. Conversely, two chapters in Part III, Educational Applications, report findings on the functional uses of literacy during play, a basic research topic. The results of the studies in both sections are summarized below, and instances of overlap are noted.

Basic Research

The investigations reported in Chapter 3 (Pellegrini and Galda) are the most sophisticated descriptive studies of play/literacy relationships conducted to date. Unlike earlier research, these investigations featured longitudinal designs, state-of-the-art assessments of emergent reading and writing behavior, and a measure (the Peabody Picture Vocabulary Test) to control for the effects of the subjects' intellectual ability.

This latter feature—controls for intelligence—is extremely important in this type of research. Without such controls, any relationship found between play and literacy may be due to variations in the subjects' intellectual ability. For example, an earlier descriptive study by Pellegrini (1980) found significant correlations between the frequency with which kindergartners engaged in dramatic play and their scores on the Metropolitan Readiness Test, a test of phonics knowledge, and a writing fluency measure. Because intelligence was not controlled, the possibility exists that children who scored high on the literacy measures and who engaged in frequent dramatic play also had above average IQs. In other words, high intelligence may have been responsible for both the frequent occurrence of dramatic play and high performance on the literacy measures.

Results of Pellegrini and Galda's current studies reveal that, with the variance due to intelligence removed, play was significantly related to only one literacy measure—emergent writing—and then only for the older subjects. Neither the children's emergent reading nor their scores on the Concepts About Print test were significantly correlated with the play measure. As Pellegrini and Galda point out, these findings may indicate that early writing is a representational activity that has its origins in the make-believe transformations that occur in dramatic play, whereas early reading may be an activity that develops independently from play.

The possibility also exists that Pellegrini and Galda's choice of measures may have been responsible for these puzzling results. Play was measured in terms the number of make-believe transformations—a procedure not commonly used in developmentally-oriented play investigations. A different pattern of relationships may have been found if play had been coded by conventional cognitive categories (e. g. , functional, constructive, dramatic, and games with rules). The choice of literacy measures may also have affected the results. Although Sulzby's (1985a, 1985b) emergent reading and writing scales do reflect the current state-of-the-art in assessing early literacy development, both scales are quite recent. Little is known about their reliability and validity, and there is considerable controversy as to whether or not the writing categories are hierarchical in nature.

The results of the series of studies reported in Chapter 4 are much easier to interpret. Williamson and Silvern found that thematic-fantasy play—teacher-guided story re-enactments—increased children's comprehension of stories. Not only was recall of specific stories enhanced, but comprehension of stories in general also improved. This latter finding is of considerable applied significance, suggesting that guided story re-enactments can be used as a strategy in school language arts programs to enhance children's story schemata or sense of story.

Williamson and Silvern found that two subject variables—age and ability—interacted with the thematic-fantasy play treatment. Results of their first study indicated that thematic-fantasy play was only effective with children less than 6.7 years old. It was hypothesized that older children already had well-developed concepts about the nature of narrative stories and had little to gain from the story re-enactments. The second study, however, suggests that children's ability also interacts with the effectiveness of thematic-fantasy play experiences. Results showed that the training enhanced the story recall of older children who were below average in story comprehension. Taken together, these findings suggest that the thematic-fantasy strategy is effective for use with kindergartners and beginning first graders in general, as well as with some older below-average readers.

Williamson and Silvern's third study is commendable for its focus on causal components. Play experiences are multifaceted, and it is of considerable theoretical and practical importance to determine which aspects of these experiences are responsible for the ensuing benefits. The results of the third study indicate that the language children use during play and instances of metaplay—where children step out of role and communicate about the ongoing play episode—appear to be primarily responsible for thematic-fantasy play's positive impact on story comprehension. This finding lends support to Rubin's (1980) theory that peer interaction may be responsible for much of dramatic play's impact on cognitive development. It also has practical implications, suggesting that teachers should try to encourage peer interaction, particularly of the metaplay variety, during thematic-fantasy play sessions.

Branscombe's case study in Chapter 5 of De and Tutti's home and school literacy experiences illustrates the value of qualitative, case-study methodology. Only through detailed, extended observation of individual children can we learn about the multiplicity of factors that can affect literacy development. This particular case study illustrates that, when children perceive literacy experiences as self-selected play activities, those experiences become meaningful and have a positive impact on development. On the other hand, when literacy experiences are perceived as adult-imposed tasks, the activities may become unreal and meaningless to children. These findings argue strongly for child-centered language arts programs in which children have considerable input and control over their literacy activities.

Applied Research

The research reported in Part III, Educational Applications, deals with three topics. The first concerns how literature activities and materials can enrich children's play experiences. The second involves interventions to infuse literacy behaviors into dramatic play. Finally, several chapters also report on investigations of children's functional uses of written language during play, a topic that overlaps with basic research on play's role in literacy development.

Literature. Chapter 6 (by Martinez, Cheyney, and Teale) reports a case study of the literature activities in two kindergarten classrooms, focusing on factors that encouraged children to engage in spontaneous re-enactments of stories during free-play periods. The availability of predictable books, repeated readings of favorite stories, and opportunities to engage in many different types of response activities were all found to be associated with frequent story re-enactments. The study clearly indicates that activities in academic parts of the curriculum can influence and enrich children's play experiences. It also shows that many children may not need adult-structured thematic fantasy-play training (described by Williamson and Silvern in Chapter 4) in order to re-enact stories. Repeated teacher read-alouds of interesting children's books and access to predictable books for independent reading are all that is needed to get some children to engage in story re-enactments.

In the last part of Chapter 7, Morrow and Rand describe a study of factors that can increase children's use library corners during free-play periods. Children were found to be more likely to use library corners that: (a) contained a wide variety of good children's books, (b) were partially partitioned off from the rest of the classroom, and

(c) had enough space for seven children. Other positive features included accessible bookshelves, comfortable seating, and literature manipulatives such as flannel boards, puppets, and roll movies. These findings indicate that, by providing well-designed and equipped library areas, teachers can promote children's independent interactions with books during free-play periods.

Intervention Studies. The intervention study reported by Morrow and Rand in Chapter 7 featured a sophisticated design with three different experimental treatments and a nontreatment control condition. The three play interventions were: Unthemed Materials Plus Guidance, Themed Materials Plus Guidance, and Themed Materials Only. Results showed that significantly more literacy behavior during play occurred in the three experimental treatments than in the control condition.

Differences were also found among the interventions. The Unthemed Materials Plus Guidance and Themed Materials Plus Guidance conditions resulted in more literacy-related play than Themed Materials Only—a finding that suggests teacher guidance can be an important factor in helping children integrate literacy into their play. Apparently, some teacher scaffolding was needed to get literacy play started.

The types of reading and writing materials added to play settings were also found to influence literacy play. The general types of literacy materials (e.g., pencils, markers, pens, paper, blank books) in the Unthemed Materials Plus Guidance condition resulted in more writing behavior that was not linked to dramatic play episodes. This writing typically involved practice and experimentation with the form and structure of print, such as practicing writing letter characters and words. Themed literacy materials, on the other hand, resulted in more reading and writing behavior that was related to ongoing dramatic play episodes. This literacy play focused on the functional uses of print rather than on its form and structure. For example, children acting in the doctor role wrote make-believe prescriptions, jotted down notes on patients' charts, and filled out appointment cards for future checkups. These findings suggest that it is valuable to include both unthemed and themed literacy materials in dramatic play areas so that children can play with both the structural features and functional uses of written language.

In Chapter 8, Neuman and Roskos' intervention study had a simpler design, with just one treatment condition: the addition of theme centers and theme-related literacy props. However, their study also featured qualitative play observations and Clay's (1972) Concepts

About Print test, the only pre- and post-treatment assessment of children's literacy development used in any of the intervention studies in this book. Results showed that theme centers and literacy materials brought about statistically significant increases, both in the number of literacy demonstrations observed in the children's play and in their scores on the Concepts About Print test. Qualitative observations revealed that children's literacy-related play behaviors became more role-defined, situationally based, sustained, and socially interactive after the theme centers and literacy props had been added.

Vukelich's intervention study in Chapter 10 used a rather complex repeated measures design featuring the following cycle:

(a) Days 1—3—Baseline observations were made as children played in their normal classroom play centers, including a housekeeping corner with few literacy materials;

(b) Day 4—The housekeeping corner was converted to a theme center with an abundance of literacy materials;

(c) Day 5—Observations were made while children played in the enriched play setting;

(d) Day 6—Adult modeling was introduced to the theme center;

(e) Day 7—Observations were made while the children played in the enriched play setting with adult modeling;

(f) Day 8—Observations were made as the children played in the enriched play setting without any adult modeling.

This cycle was repeated twice using different theme centers—a bank and a flower shop.

The subjects were students from one teacher's morning and afternoon kindergarten classes. Vukelich analyzed the data from the two classes separately and found some interesting differences between them. The morning class exhibited much more literacy behavior during the baseline period than did the afternoon class, with most of this literacy activity being connected with nonfantasy types of play (e.g., playing lotto games). When the literacy materials were added to the theme centers, the morning children did increase their amount of literacy activities during dramatic play, but their *total amount* of literacy play decreased. The afternoon class, on the other hand, showed significant increases in both literacy-related dramatic play and total literacy play when the materials were added. This finding suggests that treatment-by-subject interactions may occur when literacy materials are added to dramatic play areas. Such environmental manipulations may be most effective with children who initially exhibit little reading or writing behavior during free-play periods. The same literacy props may be less beneficial for children who initially engage in large amounts of nonfantasy literacy play, causing them to abandon these activities in favor of dramatic play.

Several interesting findings were also reported concerning adult modeling. Vukelich analyzed the amount of literacy behaviors occurring before (Day 5), during (Day 7), and after (Day 8) the modeling was administered. Literacy-related play increased during adult modeling but fell sharply after modeling was discontinued. The other finding was that modeling appeared to interact with two groups of children and the two play themes. It facilitated the morning class's play in the bank setting and the afternoon class's play in the flower shop. Vukelich commented that theme familiarity appeared to be partially responsible for this interaction. The morning class, for example, appeared to be less familiar with bank activities than the afternoon class, perhaps explaining why the modeling helped the morning class more in that theme setting.

It should be noted that the adult guidance procedure used by Vukelich was considerably different from that used by Morrow. In Morrow's study, the teacher remained outside children's play episodes and made suggestions aimed at enriching and extending children's ongoing play activities. In Vukelich's procedure, an undergraduate research assistant entered the theme center, adopted a theme-appropriate role, played with the children, and modeled how to use one literacy material during dramatic play.

The second study reported by Schrader in Chapter 9 sheds additional light on the adult involvement issue. Schrader used naturalistic observation procedures to study the play interaction patterns of four preschool teachers. Two styles of play interaction emerged: (a) extending, in which the teacher took cues for children's ongoing play activities and supplied new ideas and suggestions which helped enrich the play, and (b) redirecting, in which the teacher ignored the children's current play and redirected their attention to a new, unrelated activity. Schrader's observations indicated that the extending style was much more effective in getting children to incorporate literacy into their play. By contrast, the redirecting style tended to disrupt the "play frame" and caused some children to withdraw from playing. Morrow's adult guidance strategy appears to have been "extending" in nature, with the teacher supplying suggestions as to how literacy could be incorporated into ongoing play activities. Vukelich's adult guidance was more "redirective" because the research assistant had already decided in advance which literacy activity to model. This may help explain why Morrow's strategy was the more successful of the two.

Functional Uses of Literacy During Play. Two chapters in Part III contain sections describing research on how literacy is used by children during dramatic play. Neuman and Roskos (Chapter 8) first obtained written protocols of preschoolers' free-play behavior and then examined these protocols to establish five "functional domains" of literacy play: exploratory, interactional, personal, authenticating, and transactional (see Table 8.1). Schrader (Chapter 9) obtained similar findings using different naturalistic observation techniques. She first collected triangulated data on preschoolers' free play via videotape, field notes, and interviews, then analyzed this data using an adaption of Halliday's (1973) categories of the functions of oral language. Results showed that children used literacy for instrumental, regulatory, interactional, personal, and informational purposes during play. Both studies are actually basic research, providing evidence that dramatic play is a context in which children can express and develop concepts about the everyday uses of written language, an important aspect of literacy development.

Future Directions

There is a definite need for further basic research on the relationship between play and early literacy development. Additional descriptive studies, using validated measures of emergent reading and writing, are needed to test Pellegrini and Galda's suggestions that: (a) dramatic play's primary link with literacy is with the representational aspects of emergent writing, and (b) reading develops independently of children's play experiences.

It is important that basic research on play and literacy take subject variables such as age and ability into account. Some play experiences may be effective in promoting literacy at certain ages but not at others, and within a given age, play may only be facilitative for certain children (e.g., those whose representational skills or knowledge of narrative structure are below average). If age and ability are not used as independent variables in research designs, then "masking" is always possible (see the discussion connected with Williamson and Silvern's Study 2 on page 79).

The issue of equifinality also needs to be addressed. Pellegrini and Galda found only one significant relationship between play and literacy, and this relationship was quite modest in magnitude. This suggests that play may be just one of several means through which children can develop literacy skills. While some children may advance their conceptions of the forms and functions of written language through play activities, others may acquire this same knowledge via other means—observing literacy being used by adults, watching educational television programs such as *Sesame Street*, being read lots of stories, or receiving formal reading and writing lessons, for example.

It is with regard to the equifinality issue that ethnographic methodology such as that used by Branscombe holds great promise. By studying individual children's literacy and play behaviors in great detail, in both home and school settings, ethnographers may discover the different routes that children follow during the acquisition of literacy—routes that may be overlooked in quantitative studies. Such research may reveal that play has different roles in individual children's literacy development, being a primary means of growth for some and a pleasant diversion for others.

Several issues also remain unresolved with regard to the literacy-materials/adult-involvement interventions reported in Part III. These issues include the effectiveness of different types of adult involvement, the possibility of treatment-by-subject interactions, and the impact of play interventions on children's literacy development.

Morrow found that subtle adult guidance, in which teachers suggested ways that literacy props could be incorporated into children's ongoing play activities, greatly increased the amount of literacy activity during play. Vukelich, on the other hand, found that a more directive type of adult involvement, in which a research assistant initiated a play episode and modeled a predetermined literacy behavior, had only transitory effects. Literacy-related play increased on the day the modeling occurred but dropped sharply to below pre-modeling levels the day after modeling ceased. Limitations in Vukelich's design (such as the fact that the modeling only lasted 5 minutes and occurred on just two occasions) did not give this strategy a fair test. Further research is needed in which "extending" forms of adult guidance, such as those used by Morrow, are compared with more structured modeling procedures.

The possibility that adult guidance interacts with the familiarity of dramatic play themes deserves further investigation. Vukelich found that her adult modeling treatment varied in effectiveness for different groups of children, depending on the play theme being enacted. She hyphothesized that theme familiarity may have been responsible for this interaction, with adult modeling being most effective with themes that were unfamiliar to a particular group of children. The results of

Williamson and Silvern's story comprehension research support this hypothesis. They found that a nondirective, facilitative form of adult involvement was more effective in helping children re-enact familiar stories, whereas directive play training worked better with unfamiliar stories. Research is needed to determine whether a similar interaction exists between the familiarity of play themes and the effectiveness of different types of adult involvement in promoting literacy-related dramatic play.

The possibility of treatment-by-subject interactions also needs to be addressed. Vukelich found that the addition of theme-related literacy props appeared to have differential results, depending on the children's pre-treatment levels of literacy play. Her environmental manipulation was more effective with children who initially engaged in little literacy play than with those who frequently played literacy-related games such as lotto during free-play periods. The addition of the literacy props actually decreased the total amount of time that the latter group spent engaging in literacy behavior.

As pointed out in an earlier review (Christie and Johnsen, 1985), the effectiveness of play interventions may vary according to subject characteristics such as age, gender, and social class. Future studies need to investigate whether these variables and children's initial play predispositions mediate the impact of adding literacy materials to dramatic play areas.

Intervention studies also have the potential to establish causal connections between play and literacy development (thus becoming basic research). If it can be established that the addition of literacy materials and/or adult guidance results in increased amounts of literacy play and in gains on measures of literacy development, then one can attribute the literacy gains to the increase in literacy play. This assumes, of course, that rigorous experimental controls are used to ensure that all other aspects of the subjects' school literacy experiences are equivalent.

With the exception of the Neuman and Roskos study, no attempt has been made to determine the effects of play interventions on children's literacy development. Neuman and Roskos did use pre- and post-measures of the subjects' concepts of print. Significant gains on this measure were reported, but the single-group design of the study prevented any causal connections being made.

Future play/literacy intervention studies need to address this issue by including pre- and post-treatment measures of children's early literacy development and by using full experimental controls. Possible measures include letter recognition tests, Clay's (1972) Concepts About

Print instrument, and assessments of children's level of emergent reading and writing development. These studies should have lengthy treatment durations, preferably nine months or longer, in order that literacy play will have a chance to have an observable impact on children's written language development.

It is important that future intervention studies also closely monitor what occurs during the treatment sessions and determine the extent to which each subject uses the enriched play areas. Play-intervention studies are usually conducted during free-play periods in which children are able to choose the activities in which they engage. Research has shown that young children have distinctly different play predispositions, with some preferring dramatic play and others preferring constructive or functional forms of play (Wolf and Grollman, 1982). The possibility arises that, when literacy materials are added to dramatic play areas of a classroom, some children may rarely, if ever, choose to play in these areas. Thus, large differences might exist in individuals' exposure to the play interventions. Comparing the literacy growth of children who regularly engage in literacy-related play with that of children who choose to engage in other types of play activities could shed additional light on play's role in written language development and on the equifinality issue.

Recommendations for Educational Practice

The most obvious instructional implication emerging from the research reported in this book is that preschool and kindergarten dramatic play areas should be well-stocked with reading and writing materials. Both *general* and *theme-related* literacy materials should be included so that children can play with both the structural features and the functional uses of print (see Table 8.2). Neuman and Roskos's three criteria—appropriateness, authenticity, and utility—should be useful to teachers in selecting these materials.

Children may initially need some assistance in using both types of literacy materials in their play. Teachers can provide this assistance by using an extending style of guidance, first observing children while they play and then suggesting ways in which literacy activities can be incorporated into ongoing play episodes. For example, if several children playing in the housekeeping area are planning a trip to a nearby store center, the teacher might suggest writing a shopping list and leaving a note to tell other family members where they have gone. This type of intervention should be used sparingly and sensitively. If teachers intervene too often or use a redirective style, the play frame may become disrupted, and children will lose interest in the activity.

Story re-enactments are a form of dramatic play particularly well-suited to kindergarten and the early primary grades. The research by Williamson and Silvern indicates that such re-enactments can enhance comprehension of stories by building children's knowledge of narrative structure. Story re-enactments can be indirectly fostered by providing the types of literature experiences that Martinez, Cheyney, and Teale observed in Ms. Garrett's classroom. Predictable books and activities which increase children's familiarity with stories (e.g., repeated read-alouds and opportunities to respond to stories in a variety of ways) were both found to foster spontaneous story re-enactments. If these types of literature experiences are not sufficient to prompt children to re-enact stories, teachers may want to use the thematic-fantasy play strategies described by Williamson and Silvern. These strategies may be particularly valuable for primary grade children who are experiencing difficulties in comprehending the stories they read.

Attention should also be given to physical environments in classrooms. Research reported in Part III of this book has shown that literacy play can be encouraged by providing children with well-designed and well-equipped play areas. If possible, classrooms should contain both a housekeeping area and a changeable theme center so that children can explore a variety of everyday uses of literacy. Classrooms should also have a spacious, comfortable, well-stocked library corner so that children will be encouraged to interact with books during free-play periods (see the design features listed in Chapter 7).

Time is another essential ingredient for the types of rich, sustained dramatic play episodes described in this book. Children need time to organize, plan, and act out their dramatizations. Research by this author has indicated that children were much more likely to engage in dramatic play during 30-minute periods than during 15-minute periods (Christie, Johnsen, and Peckover, 1988). At the preschool and kindergarten levels, a half-hour per day seems to be the minimum amount of time that should be allocated for indoor play activity. In the primary grades, curriculum pressures may prohibit setting aside large amounts of time exclusively for play. However, play experiences can be integrated into the normal language arts program. For example, story dramatization can be made an option during times in which children engage in literature response activities. If teachers use learning centers, the addition of a drama center is another way to provide older children with classroom play experiences.

The final implication is that teachers should not expect play to have a substantial impact on every child's literacy development. As mentioned earlier, research has shown that young children have distinctly different play predispositions, with some liking to engage in dramatic play and others preferring other forms of play (Wolf and Grollman, 1982). Thus, it is likely that some children will rarely choose to engage in the types of literacy-related dramatic play described in this book. Literacy play is just *one* component of a well-balanced early literacy program and should be accompanied by functional literacy activities (using reading and writing for real-life purposes), story reading, shared book experiences, and language experience story dictation (see Morrow, 1989; Noyce and Christie, 1989). In accordance with the concept of equifinality, this type of well-rounded program will allow children to traverse a variety of routes to the same destination—proficiency in reading and writing.

Opportunities for children to engage in literacy-related dramatic play and in story re-enactments should be considered an essential component of early childhood language arts programs. By providing literate play centers, ample time for play, rich literature experiences, and appropriate types of adult involvement, teachers can give children opportunities to have authentic, meaningful engagements with reading and writing. While these activities may not promote every child's literacy development, ample evidence exists that they will provide many children with rich opportunities to demonstrate and practice their growing conceptions about the forms and functions of written language and to learn about the structure of narrative stories. These types of meaningful, contextualized literacy experiences are needed to balance the abstract, isolated skill exercises featured in many early reading programs. Literacy play has the additional advantage of being enjoyable and free from the risk of failure. What better way could there be to get children started in school literacy programs?

References

Christie, J. F., and E. P. Johnsen (1985). Questioning the results of play training research. *Educational Psychologist, 20,* 7–11.

Christie, J. F., E. P. Johnsen, and R. B. Peckover (1988). The effects of play period duration on children's play patterns. *Journal of Research in Childhood Education, 3,* 123–131.

Clay, M. M. (1972). *The early detection of reading difficulties: A diagnostic survey.* Auckland, New Zealand: Heinemann Educational Books.

Halliday, M. A. K. (1973). *Learning how to mean: Explorations in the development of language.* New York: Elsevier North-Holland.

Morrow, L. M. (1989).*Literacy development in the early years.* Englewood Cliffs, NJ: Prentice-Hall.

Noyce, R. M., and J. F. Christie (1989). *Integrating reading and writing instruction in grades K–8.* Boston: Allyn and Bacon.

Pellegrini, A. D. (1980). The relationship between kindergartners' play and achievement in prereading, language, and writing. *Psychology in the Schools, 17,* 530–535.

Rubin, K. H. (1980). Fantasy play: Its role in the development of social skills and social cognition. In: K. H. Rubin (Ed.), *Children's play* (pp. 69–84). San Francisco: Jossey-Bass.

Wolf, D., and S. H. Grollman, (1982). Ways of playing: Individual differences in imaginative style. In: D. J. Pepler and K. H. Rubin, (Eds.), *The play of children: Current theory and research* (pp. 46–63). Basel, Switzerland: Karger.

Index